Dear T.L., A Love Story of the American Revolution

THE BOSTON MASSACRE

The bloody massacre perpetrated in King Street Boston on March 5th, 1770, by a party of the 29th Regt., Revere, Paul, 1735 to1818, engraver

TERRY R. SATER

Liberty Song Publishing

Published by Liberty Song Publishing

First edition: April 2026

Front cover design by Terry R. Sater
Copyedit by Brooks Becker

ISBN: Assignments
Ebook: 979-8-9952060-0-2
Paperback V. 1: 979-8-9952060-1-9
Paperback V. 2: 979-8-9952060-5-7
Paperback V. 3: 979-8-9952060-4-0
Hardcover: 979-8-9952060-2-6
Audio: 979-8-9952060-3-3

www.terrysater.com

Amazon.com version printed in the United States of America

Contents

For Denise
You helped me live again

Prologue

LOVE – FAITH – LIBERTY!

That's why patriots sacrificed everything to fight America's Revolutionary War. Two of those patriots were Samuel Benjamin and Tabitha Livermore. This is the true story of their love, faith, and fight for liberty.

Samuel and Tabitha had to pick a side based on their love of each other, their faith in God, their families, and the liberty they could only dream about. They were just like you and me.

As we celebrate the 250th anniversary of our great nation, we must understand that the patriots declared their independence in 1776. But they weren't truly free of the tyranny of the British Crown and its redcoats until September of 1783.

Samuel and Tabitha, and their communities, were on the frontlines of the sacrifice for liberty. The fight included the struggle for religious liberty and freedom from the Church of England with the King as the head of the church and colonists forced to tithe by the government.

The Continental Congress opened in prayer on its second day of meeting on September 6, 1774, months before Lexington and Concord.[1] It called for national days of thanksgiving and of "humiliation, fasting, and prayer" at least twice a year throughout the war.[2] So it was that faith guided Samuel and Tabitha.

---

[1] First Prayer of the Continental Congress, Office of the Chaplain, United States House of Representatives, https://www.supremecourt.gov/opinions/URLs_Cited/OT2013/12-696/12-696-2.PDF

[2] Religion and the Founding of the American Republic, The Library of Congress, https://www.loc.gov/exhibits/religion/rel04.html#:~:text=Congress%20also%20proclaimed%20days%20of%20thanksgiving%20and,agreement%20with%20a%20nation%20and%20its%20people.

They aren't the famous names many of us know from American history. But it was tens of thousands of Christians like Samuel and Tabitha who fought and won the Revolutionary War. Samuel picked up a musket, a bayonet, and a sword as a man of Christian faith. He wrote more than four dozen Bible verses in the back of one of his war diaries. He was in the Corps of Light Infantry, which historian Michael Sheehan calls "the Navy Seals of the day."[3]

I am eternally thankful to Lieutenant Benjamin and his sweetheart, Tabitha Livermore, who are my fourth-great-grandparents, as well as their compatriots and their families. Samuel's younger brothers, Jonathan and John, also served as soldiers. They represent the sacrifice made by tens of thousands of common people for the ideal of liberty—freedom from the rule of a King. Twenty-five thousand souls made the ultimate sacrifice. Their blood was spilled over thirteen years, including the Boston Massacre. Amazingly, Lieutenant Benjamin survived serving for more than seven of those years during multiple battles, disease, and other hardships to help found the United States.

His service began at the Battle of Lexington in 1775 as a Minuteman from Watertown, Massachusetts. It ended with the Continental Army's decisive victory at Yorktown, which proved to be the turning point in the war against the British monarchy.

Because of the sacrifices of Samuel, Tabitha, and their fellow patriots, our nation remains a shining light to the world. The great American experiment began with imperfection, and much work is left to be done as we continue to strive to form "a more perfect union."

What drives someone to leave home, family, and the incredible woman he loves, and plunge himself into danger time and time again—not over a matter of months, but over a matter of years? Why would the woman on the other side of the equation put up with it? How did she endure the torture of loving someone who

---

[3] Levine, David, How George Washington Won the Battle of Stony Point, Hudson Valley Magazine, Life & Style, July 21 2021, https://hvmag.com/life-style/battle-stony-point/

submitted himself to the possibility of death repeatedly for an ideal? And yet, that's what brave Tabitha did.

You will also read about other incredible women who served the army as camp followers, as well as the first women to engage in combat. But like most women of the Revolutionary War, Tabitha helped her mother and father work the home front taking care of younger siblings and the family farm. She joined the Daughters of Liberty and came from a town that made its abolitionists' views official.

To share a sense of that commitment to the cause of liberty, I have included verbatim portions of Benjamin's diary [1], and images of pages from that same diary, into this work of historical nonfiction. His letters to Tabitha, and from her, are my own creation based on his diary entries, his family history, and the work of many historians.

I am thankful for the passion and diligence of scholars of

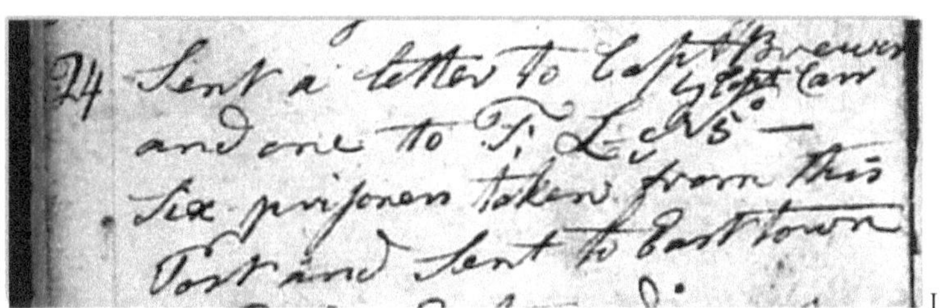
24 Sent a letter to Capt Brewer
and one to T. L.
Six prisoners taken from this
Post and sent to Easttown

Image from Lieutenant Samuel Benjamin's war diary, Yale University Archives

American history. The characters in this book were real people. I refer to indigenous people as Indians, and people of color as negroes, because it was the vernacular of their time. Misspellings in Samuel's letters are intentional in keeping with his habit of misspelling words in his diaries. As far as the battles, I have sought to be as accurate as possible. But I've also taken a little creative license to serve the story. A list of references follows at the end of this labor of love for, and devotion to, our great United States of America.

The love shared by Samuel Benjamin and Tabitha Livermore of colonial Massachusetts was battle tested. He referred to Tabitha in his war diary as T.L. Did he use only her initials to protect her from the enemy should his diary fall into enemy hands? We'll never know. But an image from his diary is seen above: "Sent a letter to Capt. Brewer and one to T.L." You'll learn about Captain Brewer in the pages ahead.

After the war, Samuel and Tabitha married and settled in Livermore, Massachusetts, which in 1820 changed from being a Massachusetts district to the separate state of Maine. Samuel and Tabitha parented six sons and four daughters. I descended from one of those daughters, Betsey Benjamin. Now, let's get on with a love story that helped create a nation.

An 1829 portrait of Samuel Benjamin, Jr., who bore a strong likeness to his father.

Chapter 1
For Love Of Liberty

The red-coated soldier screamed in agony as Lieutenant Samuel Benjamin drove his bayonet into his belly. Life quickly slipped from the man's eyes as he dropped to his knees. The flickering light from a nearby fire would be the British soldier's final glimpse of this world as he breathed his last. Samuel had little time to yank his bayonet from his victim's stubborn flesh and bones before the bayonet of a regular running toward him nearly returned the favor. The soldier's war cry woke Samuel from his nightmare.

He found himself soaked in sweat even with the cool of night pouring over him. It was not the first time the same dream had haunted Samuel. If only it were just a dream and not a memory of yet another battle he had survived. Hoping he'd find sleep again, Samuel prayed a silent prayer.

"Lord, please help me to find peace and rest even as we face a battle ahead. You have brought me this far. I ask for your grace and mercy, and to deliver me home to Tabitha, and my family when this war is done. In your precious name I pray. Amen."

Samuel reached in the dark to find the letter he had written to Tabitha just before he fell asleep, exhausted from digging trenches. This night, members of the Light Infantry slept at the base of a fascine, a protective bank of dirt and logs, not two hundred yards from the enemy. A mound of dirt at the rise in the trench served as a pillow.

Samuel had this nagging sensation that it could be the last time he'd be able to write to the woman he hoped to marry when the war was finally over for him. Maybe God would spare him one more time after more than seven years of dodging death. The weaker part of his faith made him wonder if maybe luck would also play a role. He knew sleep wouldn't come for the rest of this night. So, he dug into his breeches for his steel striker, flint, char cloth, and a candle. It took a few strikes before the cloth glowed and the wick caught fire. He wanted a last look at his letter to Tabitha before sending it with the courier who was headed back up the coast at daybreak.

October 13, 1781,
Yorktown
My Dearest Tabitha,
I long more than ever to be in your arms again. Know I love you more than life itself. I place my life in our Lord's hands and trust he'll deliver me to your arms. I am more than ever commited to this cause of Liberty. And I sense the end of our great struggle against the King is near. As I told you when I signed on again, I fight so that you and I, our famlies, and our neighbors might be free of the tyranny of the Crown and the burdens of a king who does not care about our wellbeing. I hope this letter is not my last. I have so far survived where many others have not including the leader of our regiment. We learned a few days ago that Colonel Scammell has died from wounds sufered while on patrol. I wish I had been there to protect him. I pray God's providence in the fight ahead. Hence, I often think about the hunt for deer and other game when at home. I did not hesitate to point my musket at a buck and pull the trigger. It's a much different feeling aiming my firelock at another man and ending his life or looking into his eyes and running him through with my bayonet or saber. God commands us to pray for our enemies in Matthew. I am eager for this killing to end and to return home for good. I think often of the joy I feel looking into your eyes, my arms around you.

Thoughts of you bring me peace even amidst the roar of battle. I dream of life with you and of our future children. As for the army's situation, we are finally in Yorktown having disembarked the Glasgow on the James River. I sailed with some fine men. My favorite is Dr. Thatcher. He is the surgeon for our regiment and was hand-picked by Col. Scammell for our regiment of light infantry. He is a kind soul who truly cares about those of us who must face the enemy in battle. After we reached the shore, we marched toward the enemy. All is quiet now after we spent the night digging trenches about 150 yards from Lord Cornwallis' troops. This is my first chance to write in a while and I hope my words find their way to you. I treasure your letters which I keep in my haversack. I continue to escape the enemy's grasp. There has been cannonading. "There was a cannon shot which struck within twenty yards of our battalion, and hopped over it within about twenty feet of the ground."[4] By God's grace none of us were harmed. It was another of those moments when I wondered if I would ever get to hold your hand again. Please give your parents my best. Tell your mother I miss the smell of her venison stew. When I think of those wonderful aromas, I also think of you and I, laughing in your family's parlor at some silly thing or another. Also, give my best to your father. We trust his Excellency General Washington will lead us well hunting the redcoats in the fighting ahead. There is talk Lt. Col. Hamilton and Lt. Col. Laurens will have us charging the enemy's works with bayonets only, our firelocks unloaded, as we did at Stony Point. By the time my letter reaches you, our fate will have already been decided. Pray for my safe return to your arms. I cannot tell you enough how much I love you and hunger

---

[4] Excerpt from Benjamin's Diary

for your embrace. I dream of laying my head on your sweet bosom again dear Tabitha. Forever yours,

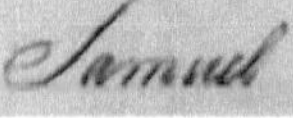

(Samuel Benjamin's signature from historical documents)

"Thump, thump, thump!"

Samuel heard pounding on the front door of the Watertown home as he finished up his breakfast. The pounding was more than a gentle knock, and it sounded like trouble. Samuel hurried to answer.

"Leonard. Jonas," Samuel said in surprise.

"The redcoats attacked at Lexington and killed some of the militia!" Leonard said in a panicked voice.

"How do you know?" asked Samuel.

"The alarm came from Abraham Whitney and also from Joseph Palmer, who is on the Committee of Safety and was staying in town with family. We're all to head to the meeting house!" said Leonard.

"Who is it, Samuel?" said his younger brother Jonathan.

"We will grab our muskets and cartridge boxes and meet you there," Samuel told the brothers.

And with that, the Bond brothers turned and raced off.

"Was that the Bond brothers?" asked Jonathan.

"Yes. They said the redcoats attacked at Lexington and the militia are gathering to respond. Grab your musket. We must get moving," replied Samuel.

"I'll grab extra cartridges," replied Jonathan.

Samuel had just turned twenty-two in his small village just west of Boston. Jonathan was two years younger. Little did they know they had just been told of a shot that would be heard around the world. That shot rang out roughly seven miles north of the Benjamin brothers' hometown. [2]

It's not surprising that they felt so strongly about preparing for a fight against the British Crown. Their father, Abel, died serving in the King's militia during the French and Indian War when Samuel was just six years old. The brothers didn't know much about how their father died. Only that the father they barely remembered disappeared from their lives just a few days after the Battle of Quebec.

Abel Benjamin served in a regiment of foot raised by Massachusetts Bay as the British fought the French in Canada. Samuel and Jonathan's mother found it too painful to talk about. And the brothers believed their family had sacrificed enough for a King an Ocean away. The bitter taste of not having their father was on their tongues each day. And now King George II's grandson wanted the Benjamin family, and their neighbors, to sacrifice even more of their hard-earned wages without giving them a voice.

Their mother often complained about not being able to afford to pay the government's church tithe. She thought congregants should want to give freely as they were able. So, this time, if Samuel and Jonathan were to fight, it would be against the selfish king who cared not about the struggles of the colonists.

Samuel and his family were far from alone in their distaste for the ravenous desires of the Crown. The Sons of Liberty in nearby Boston set the stage for rebellion. That's why Samuel thought about all of that, and the life he hoped to live with his beloved Tabitha Livermore. It's also why he signed up for the Watertown militia and Jonathan joined him.

Samuel was no stranger to government service. He had just turned eighteen years old when the Watertown Selectmen chose Samuel to be a warden.[5] He'd returned to the family farm the year before. And town leaders took notice of his maturity and devotion to his faith. Both Samuel and his brother were eventually selected to be Minutemen. The town selectmen agreed to pay those who signed up for military service, and the brothers used the wages to help fund the Benjamin farm on the north side of the Charles River. [3]

---

[5] Watertown Records, Comprising the Fifth Book of Town Proceedings (1745/6 – 1769), and the Sixth Book of Town Proceedings (1769 – 1792). Prepared for publication under the direction of the Town Clerk in 1928. Transcribed by Miss Helen Hadley of the Office of the Secretary of the Commonwealth, p. 36

On the night of April 18, 1775, the alarm went out that the King's regulars were on the hunt for rebels Samuel Adams and John Hancock, along with their arms and gun powder. But the Watertown militia wasn't aware until early the next morning when Palmer, who was staying with family in town, got word from an alarm rider after the redcoats opened fire at Lexington.

Regimental Commander Colonel Thomas Gardner sounded the alarm and the Watertown Minutemen gathered along with others at the Watertown Meeting House. Michael Jackson's Newton Company then arrived and reported that the regulars had killed militia men at Lexington Green. Jackson said the time for fighting back had come and all were to take the shortest route to get a shot at the King's soldiers.

Captain Samuel Barnard ordered the Watertown Minutemen to hasten toward Lexington. In an instant, Samuel and Jonathan found themselves marching with their friends and neighbors to a confrontation with the regulars who sought to crush their rebel voices at the end of a musket, bayonet, or cannon. [4]

Samuel didn't understand why the alarm rider had bypassed Watertown the night before. [5] Captain Barnard mustered more than a hundred ready souls, including Samuel and Jonathan. They had been training more intensely in recent months and took great pride in their marksmanship and readiness to defend their rights against the King's red-coated thugs.

Samuel marched alongside Jonathan and their good friends Elisha Brewer and Thomas Hunt as well as the Bond brothers. Leonard and Jonas were born not even two years apart, just like Samuel and Jonathan. Jonas was eighteen, and Leonard, twenty. Leonard had taken some boards from the tea crates of the Boston Tea Party as souvenirs and made a doll crib. That made Samuel laugh.

He knew their younger brother, John, would have wanted to be in on the action too. But he was exactly five years younger than Samuel. Samuel and John shared a birthday. They were born on the same day, February 5. John was still living with their mother in Needham, where they all moved after the boys' father had died and their mother remarried Nehemiah Mills. John was also apprenticing a ship joiner with a family friend in Needham. [6]

Samuel and his stepfather often clashed. And wherever Samuel went, Jonathan followed. So, when Samuel returned home to the farm where they'd lived until their father died, Jonathan said he would go with him to help till the soil. The brothers knew danger lurked everywhere in Watertown. It was a hot spot of rebellion, and Samuel suspected a few neighbors were still loyal to the Crown. [7]

He often wondered whether Dr. Benjamin Church, who had visited friends in Watertown, was secretly a Tory. Samuel had met him briefly and his gut told him there was something not quite right with Church. Even though he was a member of the Sons of Liberty. There were those who didn't believe in the rebel cause. They'd grown comfortable or prosperous with the way things were.

There were also rumors that two suspicious men, possibly spies, had passed through Watertown a few weeks back asking questions about the roads and countryside. [8] If it was true. Certainly, they had the help of a few loyalists. [9] That meant the Watertown Minutemen could be rushing into an ambush. But after word spread that the regulars had killed several townspeople in Lexington, everyone's blood was boiling.

The Watertown troops marched the seven miles to Lexington and quickly found themselves under fire from the King's cannons. Brigadier-General Hugh Percy and a thousand regulars had rushed in to cover the retreat of the regulars who had earlier killed the provincials at Lexington and Concord. The Watertown Minutemen reorganized once the regulars' cannonading stopped, and they gave chase.

Earlier, they had received orders from Brigadier-General William Heath to march ahead and block the bridge at Cambridge. One sergeant and two dozen men carried out the order. Perhaps they could trap the redcoats on this side of the Charles River. Suddenly they heard gunshots and yelling. And just as quickly, Samuel's heart was pounding.

He could see militia from other towns darting in and out of the woods firing their muskets along Concord Road. Somehow Samuel had to steady himself against a fear that rose up from deep within and stuck in his throat. It was a cold and sunny day and easy to see the red uniforms of the enemy. He also spotted Joseph Coolidge, a man he knew from Watertown who hadn't marched with them but was somehow in the fight nonetheless. Joseph's younger brother Simon was a Watertown Minuteman. And in a flash Samuel's fellow soldiers joined the fight.

Samuel and Jonathan had practiced over and over trying to load their firelocks faster. Both had learned to get off roughly three shots a minute. But Samuel's hands were shaking. Thankfully the rain that fell the day before had stopped, and Samuel and his fellow Minutemen didn't have to struggle to keep their powder dry. [10] The roads though were muddy and tough to navigate.

Before Samuel and Jonathan could fire, they heard a pfft, the distinctive sound of black powder igniting five yards away. They saw Elisha lower his musket and reload. Then Samuel heard the crack of a more distant Brown Bess firing, and the sound of a musket ball whizzing by his left ear. Out of the corner of his eye, he saw Thomas Hunt and some of his other compatriots ducking down. And then he saw Joseph Coolidge lying on the ground, blood spewing from a wound in his chest.

Joseph's brother, Simon, kneeled on the ground pleading for Joseph to hold on and trying to stop his brother's life from oozing away. But it was clear to Samuel that Watertown had just suffered its first death in the fight against the regulars. And now it hit Samuel hard. He or Jonathan could be next. The fight for liberty was no longer just words. Black smoke from musket after musket firing back and forth spilled across Concord Road. His nose filled with the acrid odor of burning Sulphur. Mixed with cannon fire, the sound of the muskets was deafening. Samuel's instincts kicked in and he ran toward the danger of the red-coated enemies who would often turn to fire. But something he could not explain compelled him to keep moving forward. Eventually he took cover behind the trunk of a large tree. Then he saw his first target, took aim, and squeezed off a shot, watching an enemy soldier fall into the mud. Samuel had just killed a man for the first time. But there wasn't time to think about it. He lowered his musket, half-cocked the hammer, and grabbed another paper cartridge from the cartridge box, the strap straddling his shoulder. He held the cartridge with his thumb and two fingers and then placed it between his teeth. With a quick jerk he tore open the cartridge, exposing the black powder. Spitting out the paper top, he placed the open cartridge next to the metal pan of his firelock and filled the shallow bowl. Then he pinched the cartridge shut and snapped the frizzen closed. Samuel tipped the barrel back toward the sky while lowering the musket, then moved the cartridge with the lead ball and remaining gunpowder to the top of the barrel. He poured the gunpowder down the barrel, dropped the ball in, stuffed the paper into the top, and pulled the ramrod out from the thimble along the barrel. As smoothly as possible, he used the ramrod to push the paper, powder, and lead ball to the bottom of the barrel. He slammed the ramrod back and forth twice, pulled it out, and returned it to its home; pulled back the hammer; raised his musket; and looked for a new target. At the end of his barrel, he tracked a redcoat who had turned to fire on a group of Newton Minutemen. Samuel squeezed the trigger, sparks flew from the powder igniting in the musket pan, and the enemy soldier fell. A hint of black powder now stained the side of Samuel's face as he, Elisha, Thomas, and others from Watertown chased the regulars toward Menotomy. [11] Bodies now littered Concord Road. Samuel saw a couple of negro militia also firing at the redcoats. [12] They must be free men, thought Samuel.

The deadly hunt continued for about four miles as the regulars retreated toward Boston. [13] Gunshots came from behind Samuel. The redcoats had flanked the militia, and he ran for cover. [14] There was a commotion coming from a house along the road in Menotomy. Samuel saw what appeared to be militia men running into the home and redcoats racing after them from behind the house. [15] At least a half dozen patriots were brutally cut down by gunfire in the front yard. One limping man fell on the doorstep after being shot and redcoats brutally finished him off with bayonets. [16] Those British soldiers now stormed the house. Samuel heard more yelling and gunshots as well as screams of agony. [17]

Moments later redcoats fled the home, blood dripping from their bayonets, and Samuel and other Minutemen fired at them as the regulars retreated along the road. [18] Hundreds of militia from surrounding towns had answered the call, and now they continually overwhelmed the redcoats as they escaped toward Boston. [19] As they reached the bridge at Cambridge, the regulars realized the planks had been pulled and their commander, Lord Percy, quickly turned his column upriver and toward the Bay Road to Charlestown. [20] The moving battle continued as an incredibly bloody affair. Militia tried to trap the British troops shooting from behind rock walls and houses while flanking parties of redcoats spied out snipers and inflicted damage to anyone in their way. [21] Homes were burned or ransacked, and lives sacrificed. Mothers forced out by redcoats ran with children in their arms shrieking in horror. [22] Samuel spotted a little girl who was alone screaming for her mother. He scooped her up and frantically looked around. He spotted a woman who had just taken cover with a baby behind a rock wall. He ran toward her, and the woman screamed, "Elizabeth!"

As Samuel drew close, she gave him a knowing glance that, yes, the little girl was her daughter. He handed off the tiny brunette and ran on. He could see some regulars fifty yards ahead dragging their wounded through the mud while others returned fire at Minutemen now lining both sides of the road. [23] More citizen soldiers continued to pour in and engage the regulars as they marched closer to the Charles River. Samuel had lost count of how many times he had loaded and fired. But his cartridge pouch was now nearly empty. He loaded his musket again, found a target, and fired. He missed. But he heard another musket fire ten yards ahead, and the regular fell. More militia now poured into the road ahead of him. [24] Samuel was winded. It was clear to him that it was time to regroup with his fellow Minutemen from Watertown. [25] A few weeks ago, Samuel had taken the Bond brothers under his wing. Even though there was a difference in age, they had become fast friends. Samuel was relieved to see Jonas and Leonard walking toward him.

"Jonas! Leonard!" Samuel shouted.

"Samuel, I'm glad to see you unharmed," replied Jonas.

"A musket ball or two came too close. But we sent those regulars running back to Boston," said Samuel. "Sadly, poor Joseph Coolidge was struck down."

"I saw his brother with him," said Leonard.

Samuel saw Elisha and Thomas walking toward them through the woods and yelled to him.

"Are you unharmed?"

"Not even a scratch," said Thomas.

"Did you see Mr. Coolidge fall?" asked Elisha.

"We did," replied Samuel.

Silence overcame them all as they thought about the loss of one of their own as well as the lives they'd each taken that day. Overall, the Watertown Minutemen had survived well. A couple suffered minor wounds, having been grazed by musket balls. In one Watertown home the mood would be much darker. The Coolidge family was devastated. In the morning Mr. Coolidge had been working his fields and a few hours later, he was dead.

By nightfall word of Joseph's demise descended on Watertown like a grievous fog. That made Samuel more thankful than ever that his sweetheart's home was miles from Concord Road and the violence of the day. Tabitha's family's farm was three miles from his home near Trapelo and Pond End, near Sudbury Road in Waltham. Samuel and his fellow Minutemen kept marching after the regulars, and they could hear musket and cannon fire ahead. As the sun began to set, thousands of militia and Minutemen from surrounding towns Roxbury, Brookline, Dorchester, and others trailed the British soldiers to Bunker Hill. It was the end of fighting for the day. [26] The Watertown Minutemen would sleep on the ground tonight. Samuel, Elisha, and Thomas spent the next three days camped in Cambridge on guard for additional fighting. After three days, their commander

Captain Samuel Barnard finally sent them home to regroup and re-supply. When Samuel reached his farm in Watertown, he headed straight for the barn, and took Samson from his stall. Samson was Samuel's horse. A Narragansett Pacer he bought the year before for eighty shillings after selling corn and three deer skins.

He saddled up and rode off to Tabitha, eager to let her know he was okay. Samuel stopped briefly in a field to pick some mayflowers that had just started to bloom near Tabitha's home. He wanted to give her something to make her smile and hoped to find her waiting with open arms. Thanks to Samson, Samuel arrived at the Livermore farm in a quarter of an hour, quickly dismounted, and ran to Tabitha's front door. He pounded his fist a few times and heard quick footsteps. The door flung open, and Samuel discovered Tabitha in tears at the sight of him. He threw his arms around her, and moments later they pressed their lips together. Neither wanted to talk about what Samuel had suffered through hours earlier. It was simply enough that he was alive and his body next to hers. What neither could have known in this moment is that many more battles would keep them apart for more than seven years.

"Oh Samuel! I spent the day on my knees praying for your safe return," Tabitha sobbed. "I thank God my prayers are answered."

Tabitha wore her lapis blue Sunday dress and white linen cap. She wanted to look her best for Samuel. Her dress was covered by a long apron of white linen.

"I am happy to be with you again. I picked these along the way," said Samuel as he handed her the wildflowers. "The war has begun. And I am home for just a little while. I, and the others from Watertown, must gather more ammunition and return to Boston. I'm sure you heard about Joseph Coolidge?" Tabitha nodded her head without speaking.

Samuel continued, "Thank God Thomas is okay. I know not what lies ahead. But perhaps our leaders can convince the King for fairer treatment and an end to this bloodshed."

Tabitha hoped Samuel was right. But her intuition whispered something else deep in her thoughts.

"I hope you are right, my dear. Can't you just wait here and see what happens next?" Tabitha asked. Samuel had already made his decision. Just hours earlier he witnessed the monstrous behavior of the retreating regulars and knew he must return to the fight. There could not be a greater divide between the violence he'd taken part in earlier and the calm he experienced right now looking into her eyes. Whenever he met her gaze, Samuel felt a peace he did not understand and could not describe. It simply was.

She often caught him just staring at her. And she would ask, "What?" As if somehow, she did not understand why he would look at her so intently. Tabitha looked so beautiful. He smelled her hair, and the faint scent of rose water. He felt his hand in hers. Samuel wished this moment would never end. Oh God, he just wanted to stay. But liberty's pull was strong right now.

"I love you above all else, Tabitha. And dream of a life together with you. But I must return with my fellow militia to continue what we have now shed bled for," exhorted Samuel. "Now I must head home and prepare."

Tabitha knew that to say more, to try to convince Samuel to stay, would be fruitless. They exchanged a long embrace. Samuel turned and left her. He tried not to think about when the next time would come to hold her. Tabitha walked Samuel to the door and watched him walk to Samson, untie the horse, mount, and gallop away. She felt so alone. Her mother, Martha, came in from tending the family's garden and found her daughter crying at the kitchen table. Martha had seen Samuel ride up and decided to give her daughter some moments alone with the man she loved. But she worried about the grief that would overwhelm her dear Tabitha should Samuel be killed. Tabitha felt her mother's arms around her. And for a few moments a mother's love filled her with hope. Tabitha was proud of her Samuel for signing up for the militia and being chosen as a Minuteman. He was deeply devoted to the cause of the patriots. But she worried endlessly about the price he might pay. And now that Joseph Coolidge had been killed, the sacrifice had a name that would forever live in Samuel's heart.

Samuel Benjamin Jr
Appears with rank of Private on
Lexington Alarm Roll
of Capt. Samuel Barnard's Co.,
Col. Thomas Gardner's Regt.,
which marched on the alarm of April 19, 1775,
from Watertown
to
Town to which soldier belonged,
Watertown
Length of service, 3 days.
Remarks:—
Not given
Lexington Alarms; Vol. 11, page 214

Jonathan Benjamin
Appears with rank of Private on
Lexington Alarm Roll
of Capt. Samuel Barnard's Co.,
Col. Thomas Gardner's Regt.,
which marched on the alarm of April 19, 1775,
from Watertown
to
Town to which soldier belonged,
Watertown
Length of service, 3 days.
Remarks:—
Not given
Lexington Alarms; Vol. 11, page 214

US, Revolutionary War Service Records, 1775–1783
Samuel Benjamin's Record of Service as a Minuteman, April 19, 1775

Chapter 2
Bunker Hill

Samson knew to walk to the barn without leading. He removed the saddle, watered, and fed his friend oats. He'd already spotted his mother's horse-drawn chaise tied up and wondered how she knew he'd be home. He brought her horse water and some oats. When he got inside, he found his mother sitting at the dining table with Jonathan, a concerned look on her face. Samuel leaned his musket against a wall and gave his mother a hug.

Elizabeth spoke softly.

"I knew you were both okay when I returned from the neighbor's farm. One of the Needham boys was back home from chasing the redcoats and said the Watertown militia had also returned with their only loss being Joseph Coolidge."

"I hope you understand, I raced to see Tabitha and let her know I was safe?" said Samuel.

"I imagined so. She is a lovely girl and worthy of your attention. It's so terrible about Mr. Coolidge being shot and killed," replied his mother.

"Yes. Thankfully Watertown's only loss. Other towns suffered much worse," said Samuel. "Jonathan served bravely today, Mother. You should be proud."

She nodded in agreement. Elizabeth was thankful her sons came home only dirty, not bloody. She didn't ask for any details. The memory of the boys' father dying in uniform sent shivers through her body. Now she could also lose her sons.

"I brought you and Jonathan some bread, Samuel. Now I must get back to Needham. But I needed to lay eyes on the both of you.

Please, sons, promise me you won't be too brave and foolish," said Elizabeth.

"We understand, dear Mother," they both said almost in unison.

"We wouldn't be much company anyway," said Samuel. "We have a lot to do before those of us in the militia return to Roxbury. Please send our greetings to John, Josiah, and the others," said Jonathan.

"I watered and fed your horse," said Samuel.

His mother replied with a thank-you and hugs, then walked outside to make the roughly ten-mile journey south to Needham. Samuel and Jonathan watched as their mother's chaise carried her away. Then Samuel started a fire in the stove and began to boil some water. The brothers needed to clean their guns. Samuel's flintlock was a .69 caliber Tulle-made French 1728 Infantry Musket. Jonathan had a .77 caliber 1730 King's Pattern musket with a double-bridled lock and a wooden ramrod. The different calibers meant they couldn't share musket balls. Each had to make their own ammunition. The guns had served them faithfully in the past to hunt animals for food. Now their muskets had been used to kill men in their hunger for liberty.

Samuel and Jonathan had purchased their muskets secondhand; they didn't know the histories of their guns. Both weapons had likely taken lives during the French and Indian War. Samuel's musket was probably seized from a captured French soldier or abandoned by a dead one. Jonathan's probably had a similar past. Here's what they did know: The muskets had helped keep them and their fight against tyranny alive.

Once the water was bubbling, Samuel slipped on his wool coat and his tricorne hat, and grabbed the pot and musket. He headed outside with some cleaning tools under his arm. Jonathan followed.

Samuel used a very small wooden peg to plug the touch hole near the breech of the barrel. Then he set the butt plate on the ground and leaned the musket against the front door bench. He slowly poured the hot water down the barrel, plugged it, and let it soak for a couple minutes. Jonathan did the same thing with his musket.

Samuel grabbed his gloves to hold the hot barrel with his left hand, and with his right, held on to the wooden barrel plug. He shook the water back and forth, then removed the plug and poured the black, smokey water out. He repeated the process with the remaining hot water. This time the water came out much clearer. Samuel grabbed the cleaning rod and threaded the screw-like metal worm on to the end.

The worm looked like a small corkscrew you'd use to open a bottle of wine. He attached a piece of rough, dry cloth to the worm and slowly inserted the assembly down the barrel, turning it around several times while he pulled the rod up and down the barrel. When he was satisfied the barrel was clean, he grabbed a small flask with whale oil.

He used a new piece of cloth to dip in the oil and attached it to the worm and coated the inside of the barrel. Then he used a slender wire pick to clean the touch hole, and a small iron brush to clean the pan and the mostly flat frizzen. The steal frizzen needed to be kept clean so that when the flint on the hammer struck it, there would be enough spark to ignite the gun powder. The bottom of the frizzen also served to cover the pan and keep the gun powder from spilling out before you fired.

He knew more strongly than ever that a musket that failed to fire in battle could cost you your life. He made sure the flint was still solid and screwed down tight and then wiped down the outside of the barrel. Jonathan had mirrored every action.

Satisfied that his musket was returned to good order, Samuel moved on to the business of preparing more cartridges. The brothers benefited from a community that supported the militia. Not just with words, but also with money. In the fall, the Watertown selectmen voted to supply the Minutemen with arms and ammunition. In addition, town leaders paid for carriages to mount two cannons in defense of their "rights, liberties, and privileges." Samuel was suddenly overcome with exhaustion as the excitement of the day wore off and the sun was setting.

"I'm whipped. How about you?" Samuel asked Jonathan.

"Same," replied Jonathan.

"I'm heading to bed," said Samuel. He walked back inside the house while Jonathan finished cleaning up outside.

Samuel lay down on his bed, closed his eyes, and prayed.

"Father in heaven, I pray for Joseph Coolidge's family. Please comfort them in their great loss. This is difficult for me, Lord, because there's a part of me that hates my enemies. But I also pray for those who oppose our cause for liberty. I pray that you would give comfort to the families of those who died. And I thank you, Lord, for keeping Jonathan and me safe. I fear, God, that this may be the beginning of a long, dark struggle against the King. I pray it is not. Guide our leaders, Father, that peace might be restored. In your name I pray, Amen."

When he was thirteen years old, Samuel had come to faith in Christ after his heart was moved and he prayed for salvation. The verse that stuck in his mind was First John 3: 3: "Jesus answered and said unto him, verily, verily, I say unto thee, Except a man be born again, he cannot see the kingdom of God."

Samuel accepted Jesus into his heart and felt his relationship with God had truly changed. He continued to find great comfort in his faith. But as he closed his eyes to sleep, he was greatly troubled that he had killed men who not long ago might have been called fellow soldiers or neighbors. Now they were his enemies, and he had been called to love his enemies. Still, he was at war with them. For the first time, he truly understood the dilemma faced by the Quakers. And yet, Samuel had heard a sermon based on St. Augustine's theory of a "just war" as well as what Genesis 9:6 had to say: "Whoso sheddeth man's blood, by man shall his blood be shed: for in the image of God made he man."

The colonists had pleaded with the king for fair treatment and in response, his neighbors had been attacked and killed. The patriots had no other choice. They had to fight back against the evils of a repressive King. Eventually he fell asleep. He awoke to the sun shining in his eyes. It was time to get up and get moving.

"Jonathan, you up?" he shouted.

"I am now," Jonathan replied in an unhappy tone.

After breakfast, Samuel grabbed his powder horn next to his musket and headed back to his room. There, he stored the precious pulp paper for cartridges in the desk along with musket balls he'd made weeks earlier with molten lead poured into a mold. He made a cartridge template for hunting long ago out of tin. It was shaped like a trapezium, one side longer than the other.

He cut the paper with a very sharp knife. And a wooden dowel was used to roll the paper around to form a tube. Samuel pinched one end shut, then dropped in a lead ball and tied it off with a piece of string. The next step was to use a brass powder measure to get the proper mixture of gun powder to drop in the rest of the tube. Then fold over the paper top and seal it with wax so that no powder leaked. It was a tedious process, and he'd spend a few hours making four dozen cartridges. God forbid he'd need more.

It was a cool morning, so Samuel would need his wool cocked hat and coat before heading out. Samuel saddled up Samson. Jonathan saddled up his horse. And they began the trek to Thomas' house to see if he had decided to return to the fight. The brothers got an answer when they found Thomas throwing a saddle onto his horse in front of his family's home. They road together to Coolidge Tavern, where the Minutemen had agreed to meet after their return to Watertown yesterday. Samuel tied up Samson out front next to Jonathan and Thomas's horses.

The tavern's front door needed a little extra muscle to push open after the winter. It scraped on the bottom as Samuel forced it open. They found Captain Barnard and Lieutenant Stratton sitting at a table in the back of the dining room with Sergeants Grant and Capen, and John Remington. Corporal Stone was also there. At the next table sat Spencer Gooding, Thomas Learnard, and Zechariah Sheed. No doubt others would soon arrive.

Samuel felt certain Simon Coolidge would not be there after losing his brother the day before. Samuel, Jonathan, and Thomas greeted all and took chairs at an adjacent table. There were no smiles. Only passion. Their faces now bore the scars of men who'd taken lives and watched one of their own fall. They got word that eight had died in Lexington with nearly a dozen more wounded. And Samuel learned that several men from Danvers as well as others had lost their lives at the home where he witnessed a limping man die.

After a few minutes of conversation, Samuel and his fellow patriots committed to returning to Boston, where a siege to encircle the British Army was underway. Thousands of militia had now descended on the city. No one knew what would come next. But there was talk that the Provincial Congress would meet in Watertown on the weekend along with the Committee of Safety.

Samuel and Jonathan decided if they were going to commit to the cause for more than a few weeks, they'd forgo planting their land this year. Since no one was dependent on them to provide, they'd be free to sow freedom and liberty for their family's future.

Within days the Provincial Congress had voted to raise a force of thousands and Samuel, Jonathan, Elisha, and Thomas enlisted in the New England Army.

The rebels cut off the British from the countryside by controlling Boston Neck. Militia from around Massachusetts now manned siege lines and were eventually joined by troops from New Hampshire, Rhode Island, and Connecticut. The colonists had now surrounded Boston on three sides from Chelsea, around the peninsulas of Boston and Charlestown, to Roxbury. In June, the Continental Army was established. And because of the leadership, heroism, and Minuteman training that Samuel and Thomas showed on the day of the Lexington Alarm, they were both promoted as sergeants. Jonathan enlisted as a private.

The three were assigned to Colonel Thomas Gardner's regiment in a Watertown company under the command of Captain Abner Craft, 37th Regiment of Foot. [27] Elisha had joined with the Watertown Minutemen because of his apprenticeship there. And Samuel knew because he'd fallen in love with Tabitha's older sister Martha, who was named after their mother. That was partially the result of scheming by Tabitha and Samuel, who thought they might get along. It turned out Tabitha and Samuel were right.

But when it came to joining the new Continental Army, Elisha decided to be loyal to Captain Aaron Hayes, who was from Elisha's hometown of Sudbury. Elisha was quickly commissioned a lieutenant. Meantime, Sergeants Samuel and Thomas, because of their experience drilling as Minutemen, spent hours leading newer soldiers in practicing loading, aiming, and firing their weapons. Sometimes they would practice loading without gunpowder because of a shortage of ammunition.

As a sergeant, Samuel was issued a spontoon, or half-pike. A spontoon was a pole about the same height as the man who carried it, with a blade on the end. Soldiers could look for the spontoon in the heat of battle as a rallying point, and Samuel also used it to indicate when troops should halt or march forward.

Beyond preparing for battle, Samuel, Thomas, and others were often tasked with trying to find supplies wherever they could. Feeding the troops was an immediate and enduring challenge for the new army. Food was gathered from around Cambridge and surrounding communities. They often ate beef, pork, and bread, or anything left behind by the King's forces.

The standoff in Boston grew from days to weeks. Samuel and Thomas had pitched their small tents side by side. And the smell of hundreds of men without proper privies became overwhelming not just to Samuel, but to every soldier in camp. Samuel thought better organization was sorely needed. He and Thomas had talked about better ways to run the camp. But the boring days of training and waiting were about to end.

In late May, patriots exchanged fire with the enemy while scouring Chelsea for food and supplies. Royal commanders ordered the British schooner Diana closer to shore to support the royal soldiers, and she got stuck in shallow water. Colonial troops attacked, looted the ship of her cannons, and burned the vessel after the crew escaped. (28) Samuel could see the smoke rising from the harbor.

Within a day, British commanders began to plan a major attack. Colonial commanders intercepted word of the plan and on the sixteenth of June, Samuel learned some of the colonial troops would begin building a makeshift earthen fort on Breed's Hill. They carried out construction overnight so the regulars could not see.

By morning, Samuel and Thomas awoke to the sound of boom after boom. At first light the royals had discovered what the colonists had done, and the British Navy began firing their cannons at the colonial redoubt, which was a small makeshift fort.

Within seconds, Samuel heard a drummer and fifer calling formation. He always slept in his long linen undershirt. Samuel pulled his wool socks over his knees and buckled leather garters around each leg to hold his socks in place. Then he slipped on his breeches before pulling his hunting frock over his head. His leather boots were still wet from stepping in a mud puddle the day before, and he struggled to get his feet to slide in. His wool bounty coat and tricorn might prove too warm for the battle ahead.

He crawled out of his tent with his musket and grabbed his spontoon. Thomas was right there also ready for action. They quickly learned their regiment had received word that royal forces were moving in for a ground invasion. Captain Abner Craft gathered his officers and told them they'd been ordered to march to Patterson's Station on the road to Lechmere Point to await further orders.

Samuel heard the drummers beating the "March"[6] and bowed his head, quietly praying for God's protection as the enemy cannons continued to pound Breed's Hill. He could hear continual musket fire across the water, and after a little while they received orders to march to Breed's Hill.

British cannons then bombarded Charlestown and set home after home on fire. Soon the whole town seemed ablaze. The main royal force had moved ashore, led by General William Howe, and had

---

[6] Camus, Raoul F., Military Music of the American Revolution, The University of North Carolina Press, Chapel Hill., 1976, p.88, Camus, Raoul F., Military Music of the American Revolution, The University of North Carolina Press, Chapel Hill., 1976, p. 87

charged up the hill to attack the colonists' earthen fort and trenches. The patriots waited until the royal forces were nearly upon them before opening fire and hundreds of regulars died in close combat.

A second charge by the Brits was met with a similar fate. Bodies clothed in red began to pile up. But the colonial troops in and around their fortifications were running out of ammunition and strength. A number defended themselves with the butts of their muskets or rocks.

Samuel and the other soldiers reached the base of Breed's Hill and charged up the slope to reinforce their fellow rebels with Colonel Gardner in the lead. Samuel could hear screams of pain as the regulars overran his compatriots and began stabbing the colonists with their bayonets. Samuel, Thomas, and the officers tried to maintain order amid a rush covered by thick smoke from musket and cannon fire. The smell of spent gunpowder made it hard to breathe and filled Samuel's nostrils with a choking odor.

The fifer and drummer signaled new orders. Suddenly Gardner shouted in pain. He was shot, mortally wounded, with a musket ball. Samuel saw Gardner's son from another unit come upon his father. He tried to carry his father from the field. But the Colonel courageously urged his son to stay in the fight for the glorious cause. (30)

Captain Abner Craft then signaled the drummer to beat out "Retreat" and led Samuel's regiment in reverse to a rail fence that ran to the shore of the Mystic River. Colonial forces had barricaded the beach up to the rail fence on the north side of Bunker Hill trying to stop the regulars from flanking them. But colonial forces faced overwhelming musket fire from the regulars.

For a time, thick smoke caused Samuel to lose sight of Thomas and the men he was leading. Samuel again and again loaded and raised his musket to shoot at the scarlet-clothed soldiers. He heard groans of agonizing pain as the wounded lay all around on both sides. Some had been hit by cannon fire and had lost limbs.

Samuel was running low on cartridges as the grisly scene seemed to go on and on. He caught a glimpse of Jonathan through the smoke and was relieved he was safe. Gardner's Regiment, Samuel and

Jonathan among them, was the last to give up the fight and move out of harm's way. A colonial cannon covered their retreat. (31)

Once again, he, Jonathan, and Thomas had survived unharmed. However, the losses on both sides were severe and heartbreaking. Word quickly spread among the troops that the heroic doctor and President of the Provincial Congress, Joseph Warren, had stayed in the rebels' earthen fort until the last. His bravery was repaid with an enemy musket ball right between his eyes. (29)

The cries of widows blanketed the ears of all in Charlestown. Many of the wounded bled out before doctors could treat them at the makeshift hospitals set up in nearby homes. The cause of liberty was now bathed in the blood of her sons. More than a hundred patriots died with more than three hundred wounded.

As for the regulars, the cost was even greater. More than two hundred died for King George with more than eight hundred wounded.

Samuel Benjamin
Appears among signatures to an
Order for Bounty Coat
or its equivalent in money, due for the Eight Months Service in 1775, in
Capt. Abner Crafts Co.,
Col. Wm Bond's (late Col. Gardner's) Regt.,
dated Cambridge November 13, 1775
Payable to Capt. Craft.
Remarks:—
Coat Rolls: Eight Months Service. Orders.
Vol. 57, page File 26

Samuel Benjamin
Appears on ~~An Order~~ a Receipt
dated Watertown July 5, 1775.
for 2 days rations for Capt. Crafts Co.
signed by himself, given to Commissary Jonathan Brown
Rank – Sergeant
Mass. Muster and Pay Rolls.
Vol. 70, page 280.

U.S. Revolutionary War Service Records, 1775–1783

Samuel learned Jonas Barnard was struck down. Barnard was a fellow Watertown Minuteman. Samuel thought of Tabitha again. How devastated would she be if he had been killed this day. And again, he thanked almighty God he had been spared. He also wondered why Tabitha's prayers had been answered for him while others' prayers had not. He thought of the fellow soldiers he watched die today. Surely the prayers of their loved ones were just as earnest—just as pure. The thought of it enraged Samuel and strengthened his resolve to fight for the patriot cause. But as night fell, his regiment pulled back to Bunker Hill, where they would attempt to sleep on their arms.

Samuel couldn't get the explosions, smells, and screams out of his mind and it led to a restless night's sleep.

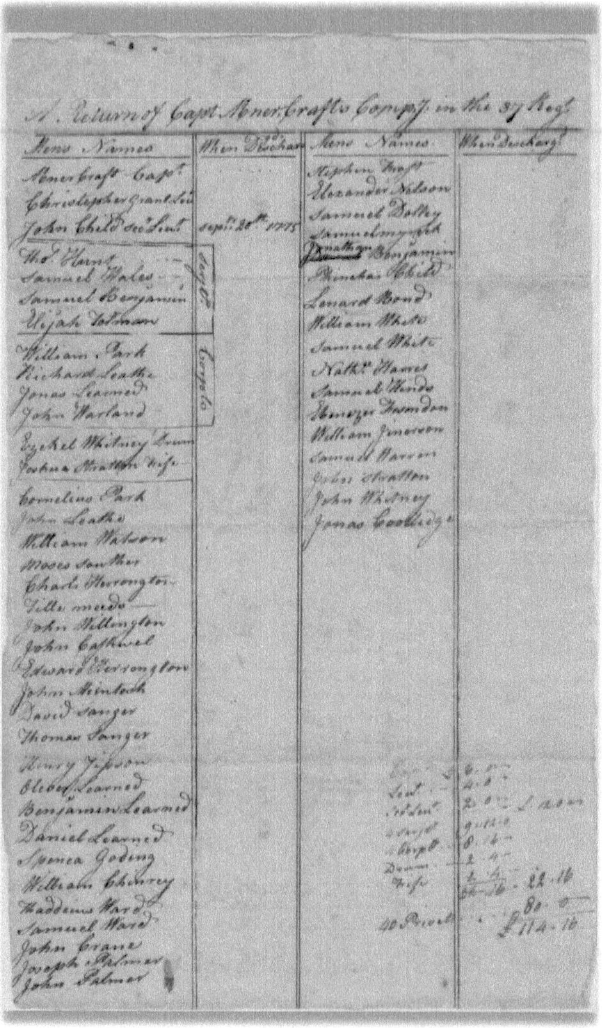

A Return of Capt. Abner Crafts Compy. in the 37 Regt.

Mens Names | When Discharged

Abner Craft Captn.
Christopher Grant Lieut.
John Child Sec. Lieut. — Septr. 20th 1775
Thos. Harris
Samuel Wales
Samuel Benjamin
Elijah Tolman
William Park
Richard Leathe
Jonas Learned
John Warland
Ezekel Whitney Drum
Joshua Stratton Fife
Cornelius Park
John Leathe
William Watson
Moses Sawther
Charls Herrington
Tille meads
John Wellington
John Cathwel
Edward Herrington
John Mcintosh
David Sanger
Thomas Sanger
Henry Tipson
Oliver Learned
Benjamin Learned
Daniel Learned
Spencer Goding
William Cheney
Thaddeus Ward
Samuel Ward
John Crane
Joseph Palmer
John Palmer

Mens Names | When Discharged

Stephen Craft
Alexander Nelson
Samuel Dolley
Samuel Wright
Jonathan Benjamin
Phinehas Child
Lenard Bond
William White
Samuel White
Nathl. Hames
Samuel Hinds
Ebenezer Herndon
William Jimerson
Samuel Warren
John Stratton
John Whitney
Jonas Coolidge

William Bond Papers, 1768 to 1795, MSS.0080, Box 1, Folder 19

Chapter 3
George Washington Takes Command

"Thomas," Samuel said as he spotted his friend awakening from what seemed to be a nightmare. His eyes half open.

Thomas then slowly spotted Samuel nearby.

"Morning, Samuel," replied Thomas.

"Morning. We survived, brother," said Samuel.

"Yeah, I think I was dreaming I had been shot," said Thomas.

"You're safe, friend. We're safe," replied Samuel.

"Sergeants!" shouted Captain Craft.

Samuel and Thomas were quickly alerted.

"Yes sir," both said, almost in unison.

"I need you men to get our troops assembled and return order and discipline. We're going to establish camp where we were before the battle at Breed's Hill," said the captain.

"Yes sir," said Samuel and then Thomas.

The soldiers were all stunned by Colonel Gardner being wounded so quickly in battle. Samuel and Thomas filled their days by focusing on the mundane tasks of returning their men to training and camp duties, digging privies and such, finding food, and resupplying ammunition.

The days of June ended, and July 3 arrived with word that Colonel Gardner had died in the hospital from the wound suffered on Breed's Hill. It was bitter news. Samuel didn't know when he'd be able to return to Tabitha, so he decided to write her a letter.

July 5, 1775
Roxbury
Dear Tabitha, I learnd a courier would be heading to Watertown and quickly devoted my hand to writing you this note. I am well and unharmed after the latest fighting. Jonathan, Elisha, and Thomas are also in good form. I miss you more than you know and think of you with a full heart. Happy belated birthday my love. I am sorry I could not be with you on your special day. I pray you are in good health and not too full of worry about me. Greet your family with my best wishes. I trust Samson is finding his new home on your farm to be pleasing. He is a good horse, and I hope of service to your father. I'm sure you heard of the ghastly loss of life suffered in Charlestown little more than two weeks ago. You may have seen the smoke rising from the burning homes. I trust you also heard nearly all of us from Watertown survived unharmed, except for poor Jonas Barnard. He was in Colonel Jonathan Brewer's Regiment. The Brewers are a Waltham family you know. Jonas was wounded near Breed's Hill and died a few days later. I will remember Jonas fondly as my fellow minute man. We trained together and he was a good soul. You may have also heard that our commander Colonel Gardner, your family also knows him from Waltham, was shot through on Breed's Hill. It was a horrid loss for us during the fight. But it sparked us to rally in his stead and we fought with honor. Day before yesterday we learned the Colonel's fate was sealed by the redcoat's musket ball and he has died. It's a brutal blow. His Excellency General Washington ordered our regiment to attend his funeral yesterday at Cambridge Cemetery and we were given leave from our duty on Prospect Hill to pay our respects. I pray our Lord will give comfort to his family and that of Jonas. I am also happy to report that His Excellency in those same orders implored us to attend Sunday worship to ask our Lord for help in our safety and defense. Our Watertown neighbor, Lt. Col. William Bond, had already been promoted to lead

us. As I'm sure you know, we are now the Continental Army. His Excellency has since taken command of the whole of us at the will of the Provincial Congress meeting in Watertown. He's made it clear some behaviors I have witnessed are no longer tolerated to which I find great pleasure. There has been too much drunkenness. He encourages all of us to set aside our allegiances to our colonies and fight as one united army against the Crown.[7] We are already showing better discipline. Officers above me in rank appear to be pleased with my leadership. The courier is leaving soon so I must end my writing for now. My truest devotion and love to you my darling,

Samuel

Samuel folded the letter onto itself, sealed the edges with wax, and wrote Tabitha's address on the outside. He didn't have much time to get the letter to the rider. So, he hurried to find the courier and handed him the letter. He was less achy this morning after so many nights sleeping on straw inside his tent. But with the advent of summer came more bugs. Some provided pain and itching. Others were just a nuisance. And the camp smells could at times make you retch depending on the wind direction.

Tabitha opened Samuel's letter with some fear in her heart. She did not know whether he'd been wounded. When she saw the letter was dated after the battle on Breed's Hill, she was immediately relieved. At least she knew Samuel had survived well enough to write her. Her father, Nathaniel, had business in Cambridge and had harnessed Samson to the shay and journeyed there. He retrieved the letter from the home of Jonathan Hastings. He'd taken over post duties for James Winthrop, who had been wounded on Breed's Hill and had recently resigned. She didn't even know if there would be

[7] Washington, George. George Washington Papers, Series 3, Varick Transcripts, 1775–1785, Subseries 3G, General Orders, 1775–1783, Letterbook 1: July 3,1775–Sept. 30, 1776, https://www.loc.gov/item/mgw3g.001/.

a letter. But Samuel had promised to write her. Tabitha continued to read the letter with joy when it was clear her Samuel was unharmed. Yes, she had heard about poor Jonas as well as Colonel Gardner. She had prayed for Mr. Gardner's widow and children in their incredible loss. The cost of this cruel struggle was mounting. Tabitha read the letter no fewer than three times in a matter of minutes and wished Samuel had written more. She clung to each word.

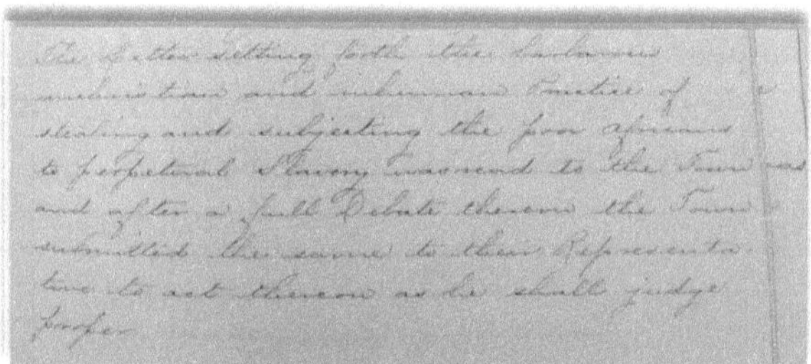
The Letter setting forth the barbarous
unchristian and inhuman Practice of
stealing and subjecting the poor africans
to perpetual Slavery was read to the Town
and after a full Debate thereon the Town
submitted the same to their Representative to act thereon as he shall judge
proper

Town of Waltham official meeting notes, May 10, 1773, Waltham Historical Society

News of General Washington's arrival nearby had spread quickly, as did that of him staying in the mansion that had been abandoned by slaveholder John Vassall on the road to Watertown. Tabitha was glad to see the Vassall family gone. They were loyalists who had fled to Boston for protection by the Crown, and she was fiercely opposed to their practice of owning slaves to enrich themselves.

The cruelty of slaveholding did not square with Tabitha's faith. Her views were shared by many others during a vote by the Town of Waltham, which made opposition to slavery official. It was written into the record during a town meeting in May of 1773. The Selectmen chose Jonas Dix as their representative to officially speak against slavery in Boston, referring to the "barbarous unchristian and inhuman practice of stealing and subjecting the poor Africans to perpetual slavery."

Tabitha's faith made her think of how she and Samuel had first noticed each other at First Parish Church in Waltham. She'd already been dreaming about Reverend Jacob Cushing performing the vows. As she turned eighteen last month, she thought about it a lot.

How long would she have to wait to marry her beloved Samuel? He had certainly hinted that he would ask some day. Would the musket ball of some redcoat take him from her before they could even be joined in marriage? She knew she should stop thinking of such things as it made her too sad and that wouldn't serve her well as she prepared to pen a letter to Samuel.

Her father had already agreed to return to Cambridge to send the letter for her. It was so strange that Samuel was only a few miles away and yet she felt a vast chasm kept them apart. She needed to stay cheerful when writing to Samuel lest her melancholy thoughts seep through to her quill.

She took out a small knife to sharpen the point of the goose quill she would use to write. She'd already stripped the feathers. She used the linen paper on her father's desk. And took out his ceramic ink well. What should she say first? How could she express how she ached for Samuel's touch? She missed his voice and the way he looked at her. Then her heart spoke clearly.

> Waltham
> July 15, 1775
> My Dearest Samuel, my hands long to be held in yours. My eyes wish to meet yours. You are my all, the very breath I breathe in each moment of the day. I love you beyond all measure and I eagerly await your return to my arms. I miss your touch and the sound of your voice in our home. My heart leapt with joy reading that you had endured the fighting without harm. I have been praying for the families of Jonas and Colonel Gardner as I thank God, he has spared you. My darling I am so proud of you and your passion for the patriot cause of which we all feel so strongly. I pray the King will end his cruelties upon the colonies and move for a swift end to this conflict. It is difficult to know who of our neighbors might be aiding the Crown after what happened in Lexington and Concord. In

the past I have wondered if the tavern keeper enjoyed too comfortable a relationship with the regulars who would frequent his establishment. What price could any of us be forced to pay if there's a spy amongst us? But do not worry. Know that my father is careful as am I about what we say of your whereabouts and duties in the army. My mother and I have been tending the garden which is already showing promise. We miss having you for our family meals and wish we would be able to share the fruits of our labor in the soil. I have dirt under my fingernails from toiling in the garden today. I must scrub when I am done writing you. But I could not wait to share my thoughts on paper. It was a beautiful morning here after yesterday's rain. There is always promise in the sunshine. I imagine you are wondering about Samson. He seems happy here. Although sometimes I look into his eyes and wonder if he is searching for you—wondering where you are. Father rode him to Cambridge on business and to retrieve your letter which I was overjoyed you had sent. Papa has promised me he will deliver this letter to Cambridge and hopefully it will find its way to you. We have heard there are other families also trying to send letters to their loved ones in the army through the new mail route. I will seal my scribblings with a kiss. Hopefully you will be home soon my dear. All my love, I am truly yours,

Tabitha

Deliver to Sgt. Samuel Benjamin, Late Col. Gardner's Regiment, Craft's Company, 37th Regiment of Foot, Roxbury

Tabitha dripped a little rose water onto the paper, folded the letter upon itself, and addressed the back. She sealed the edges with wax and laid a kiss upon it and for a moment held it to her breast.

She said a quick prayer for Samuel and his fellow soldiers and hoped God was listening. Tabitha laid the letter on her father's desk where he would easily find it for his return trip to Cambridge.

She grabbed a water pail from the kitchen and headed outside to let her father know the letter was on his desk. It was a beautiful day with the bluest of skies and a breeze that carried the scent of wild-flowers from a nearby prairie. Tabitha wondered how long it would be until she could share a summer day like this with Samuel. She did not linger long on the thought of it. There was too much yet to do. Tabitha found her father in the barn sharpening a scythe to cut hay.

"Hi, Daddy. I knew I'd find you here. I've written a letter to Samuel and left it on your desk," said Tabitha.

"I knew writing Samuel would come before the rest of your chores," said her father.

"Don't worry, Father. I brought out a bucket to pump water so I could help Mother with the laundry," replied Tabitha. She gave her father a quick hug and headed back outside toward the well.

Pumping water in July was a much easier task than during the winter, when ice would often form and need to be chopped away before the warmer water underground would flow. She would need to pump at least three buckets full before heating the water on the stove. She'd clean the garden dirt from her nails when she scrubbed the clothes with lye soap that she'd helped her mother make a few days ago.

Boredom now filled Samuel's days as he and those in his regi-ment waited for the next action. It was clear they were in a stalemate with the regulars. The patriots learned they had killed the respected Major John Pitcairn of the British Marines. Word also spread through the ranks that not only had the regulars been commanded by revered General Howe, but also Generals John Burgoyne and Henry Clinton.

Considering who they were up against, Samuel and those around him considered they had fared well. It also meant the days ahead would not be easy. The King was obviously not going to give in to the colonists' demands for fairer treatment and representation.

The colonial troops had lost all but one cannon in their retreat and Samuel knew they were outgunned. Still, they had the royal troops and loyalists trapped. But the colonial troops needed more firepower. And, unfortunately, the Royal Navy still controlled the harbor. So, the patriots formed a makeshift navy made of whaleboats to harass the King's ships. (33) (34)

Samuel and Thomas were growing exceedingly bored with day-to-day camp life and duty. They wished they could join one of the whaleboat raids they were hearing about for the regulars' cattle and pigs on Noddle's Island and Hog Island. Samuel checked with the mail courier day after day, and then Tabitha's letter arrived.

Ducking into his tent, he smiled before he even opened the letter. When he unfolded the paper, he caught a hint of the smell of rose water. He held the paper to his face and then pulled it away and began to read, poring over the letter twice and carefully placing it in his haversack for safekeeping.

How could he be falling deeper in love with Tabitha when he wasn't even able to be with her? And yet, that's what he knew to be true. When he thought of his growing love for her, he questioned why he had chosen to be here on the front lines of this fight for liberty, when he could have chosen to remain home near Tabitha. But he also knew he was here because deep inside he could not live with himself if he didn't commit to this sacrifice. He was building their future here.

When Samuel crawled out of his tent, he heard one of his fellow soldiers telling a story. On July 18, Major Joseph Vose of Heath's Regiment had led about four hundred soldiers from the Milton militia onto whaleboats and sailed to Nantasket peninsula. They seized barley and hay for the Continental Army. Then, on the twentieth, they rowed to Light House Island, surprised the enemy guards, and set the lighthouse on fire. The Royal Navy alerted when they saw the flames and launched a few barges to attack the retreating whaleboats. But their guns and broadside attempts mostly failed and only a couple of patriots were wounded. The regulars, though, were quickly repairing the damage to the lighthouse. So General Washington had ordered another attack.

This would be the chance Samuel and Thomas were looking for. Major Benjamin Tupper of Colonel John Fellows's Massachusetts Regiment was to carry out the next assault on the lighthouse. But several of his men had become ill with smallpox and he sought volunteers from the late Gardner's regiment. When Samuel and Thomas learned of it, they were quick to sign on. By now it was the end of July and Samuel and Thomas, and a few others, made their way down to Dorchester to meet Tupper's troops and the whaleboats that would transport them. The plan had some other troops and boats leaving from Squantum.

Whaleboats were generally about twenty-four feet long and were essentially double-ended rowboats. They were good for navigating shallow bays and rivers and could land on either end. With a dozen men at the oars, they could also row much faster than the wind could carry big ships of the British fleet, which bullied the harbor. (35) (36)

On Sunday, July 30, Samuel and Thomas were among three hundred soldiers in roughly three dozen boats rowing in the dark toward Beacon Island and the lighthouse. By the time the colonial fleet arrived, it was early Monday morning, and this time the regulars were prepared for another attack.

Samuel and Thomas had their muskets at the ready when their boat neared the shore. A familiar feeling rushed from Samuel's belly to his throat as his heart pounded. He heard the British marines yelling an alarm as the whaleboat slipped onto the beach. Several dozen redcoats began firing. Despite the flutter in his chest, Samuel's hands were steady.

He stepped on shore, quickly took aim, and gunned down a marine. The whaleboats landed all around, on different parts of the island, and the redcoats were quickly overwhelmed. The colonial troops shot and killed a half dozen guards, including a lieutenant.

The rebels again set the lighthouse on fire and took some two dozen marines and a dozen loyalists prisoner, including some who were badly wounded. Major Tupper lost one soldier and two were wounded in the raid. The rest returned safely to shore, including Samuel and Thomas.

Samuel was happy to step onto solid ground, thankful he wasn't shot or drowned. He wondered if it was courage or foolishness that lured him toward danger. His heart was calm now and he could finally smell the salty air of the harbor. There was a peacefulness that came with listening to the waves lapping against the shore. And sometimes he wished he'd grown up a fisherman instead of a farmer. He, Thomas, and a few others now had to make their way back to their regimental camps while Tupper's regiment returned to theirs.

Samuel settled back into daily duty, training, and gathering supplies. General Washington had ordered trenches be dug and defenses fortified from Roxbury to Chelsea and wherever it was deemed the regulars might strike. He shared a meal with Jonathan from time to time. The summer dragged on with occasional firing back and forth between the colonists and the King's soldiers with little effect. The royal forces brought in more cannons to Boston, which the colonial forces couldn't help but notice.

In August it seemed as if the regulars fired at the Continental forces almost daily. And during one barrage two patriot soldiers were killed in Roxbury. Samuel wondered where the standoff would lead. Both sides would fire cannons at each other. The King's forces had no access to the mainland and could only resupply by ship. Surely the regulars and loyalists had to be running short of food and supplies.

Summer turned to fall, the changing of the leaves. Soon Samuel awoke to frost on his tent, and it was only late September.[8]

---

[8] McCurtin, Daniel, Journal of the Times at the Siege of Boston, printed for the Seventy-Six Society, T.K. and P.G. Collins Printers, Papers Relating Chiefly to the Maryland Line During the Revolution, edited by Thomas Balch, 1857

As expected, October nights were often even colder and the wind cut to the bone. Heavy rains occasionally added to the misery of the camp.

By mid-November Samuel was as cold as he'd ever been. A half foot of snow fell on the seventeenth and made guard duty difficult for a soul to endure.

By December, some regulars deserted to the Continental lines. The redcoats told stories of firewood growing scarce. Regulars were cutting down every tree in town and dismantling buildings. Even some houses of worship fell victim to the effort to stay warm. Christmas was only two weeks away, and Samuel grew more sentimental knowing he and Tabitha would be apart.

Even colder weather settled in, making the loneliness seem starker. Both sides continued to fire at each other from time to time. The British cannons thundered. But mostly did little damage.

Christmas Day arrived and Tabitha awoke praying for Samuel, for his health and safety. She looked out on a sunny, clear blue sky with a great deal of snow having fallen in previous days. She wondered how Samuel would spend the day. Was he too cold? What would he eat? She missed him terribly.

Yesterday, Reverend Cushing asked those at First Parish to pray for Samuel and the other soldiers before delivering his sermon. They were Congregationalists and hadn't begun to celebrate Christmas until recent years, and then only quietly. Most Congregational pastors still frowned on the tradition practiced by the King's Church of England. But she and Samuel both liked singing Isaac Watts's "The Nativity of Christ," and celebrating Jesus' birth softened the cold of winter. (37)

Tabitha's mother watched her daughter staring out the window, and without saying a word, she and Tabitha shared a knowing glance. Each knew Samuel and Elisha were on their minds. Tabitha's mother knew if Samuel or Elisha died by musket or disease, her daughters would be filled with grief beyond words. A mother can only protect her children so much from the cruelties of life. But that wasn't her only worry.

At twenty-two, Eunice was her oldest daughter. And just two weeks before the Lexington alarm, Eunice married Waltham Minuteman Josiah Mixer. Thankfully, Josiah had also returned home unharmed and for now didn't plan on enlisting. He had to help with the family's farm.

Tabitha thought about all of that as she continued helping Martha make the plum porridge. Father had hunted for fowl with two of her younger brothers and they were also preparing roast beef from the cow Daddy slaughtered earlier in the month. They would also enjoy mince-pie and pudding. Without Samuel nothing would taste the same to Tabitha despite the wonderful smells that now filled their home. But thankfully she was distracted by caring for her large family.

It was a noisy and busy household. Tabitha's youngest sibling Nathaniel turned three in September. Then there was David, who turned six the month before; Ruth, eight; Amos, ten; Lydia, twelve, who helped the most with the younger brother and sister; John, fourteen; and Moses, sixteen. Tabitha worried that if the war continued, Moses would be next to enlist and that made her think of Samuel again.

Samuel was also thinking about her. He was thankful for a clear day with no rain or snow. It would make camp duty easier. He smiled picturing Tabitha and her family celebrating the birth of Christ today. But soon those thoughts were replaced by concerns about some of his fellow soldiers leaving soon.

Many colonists had only signed up to serve until the end of the year and talked of leaving after Christmas. That included Jonathan, who told Samuel he would be leaving the army to head home and prepare their farm for winter. Samuel thought it a good idea. That way Jonathan would be home for spring planting and could get the help of neighbors to tend to and harvest the crops in the new year. One growing season had already been abandoned.

Samuel and Thomas, though, decided they would stay on and welcome new recruits to camp. Training new arrivals would give Samuel continued purpose. But would there be enough new soldiers for the army to remain strong? Would their service become even more deadly? Thankfully, their regiment had received glorious news. General Washington had ordered Colonel Henry Knox to haul cannons and other arms captured from Fort Ticonderoga to Cambridge.

Not long after the Lexington Alarm, Ethan Allen and his Green Mountain Boys, along with Benedict Arnold, had captured the fort from a small group of regulars who were surprised and overrun. Samuel and Thomas talked about the enormous task of hauling the massive guns across Lake George and over the snow and ice of the Berkshire Mountains of Western Massachusetts. It was a nearly three-hundred-mile journey.

The new year rolled in and by mid-January stories reached camp that, amazingly, Knox's men had made it across the mountains. (38) They had used boats and sleighs, crossing the Hudson River several times. The caravan of cannons had been dubbed the Noble Train of Artillery and had moved through Albany and Springfield to Brookfield, on to Worcester and Shrewsbury, and into Framingham.

On January 27, Samuel and Thomas watched as Colonel Knox and his men delivered fifty-eight pieces of artillery into Cambridge. There was a massive twenty-four-pounder as well as thirteen eighteen-pounders plus ten twelve-pounders, and other smaller cannons and mortars. (39) Some of the smaller cannons were immediately used to fortify Roxbury, Lechmere's Point, and Cobble Hill. The arrival of the artillery gave Samuel and his fellow soldiers a new confidence after months of enduring the King's cannonballs reigning down on them. Now they could return the favor.

The biting cold of January was followed by the icy winds of February. Samuel and Thomas continued to help train the new soldiers in their regiment. Sometimes there wasn't much food to be had, and rationing was necessary.

Fifers and drummers often helped lead the way for Sunday worship. Samuel and the other officers were expected to follow General

Washington's orders given on the fourth of July in the prior year, soon after His Excellency assumed command of the army.[9]

Powder and arms were in short supply in some parts of the army. By the end of February, word spread through camp that a plan was in play to move the big cannons from Fort Ticonderoga to Dorchester Heights. Samuel's regiment had helped move the bigger cannons from Cambridge to Roxbury. His gut told him this could be the answer to forcing the King's soldiers out of Boston.

"Boom, boom, boom!"

Samuel was startled awake.

"Thomas, Thomas!" Samuel called out to his friend.

"I hear it, Samuel. The cannons also woke me," replied Thomas.

"Those sound like they're coming from our side. Our labor moving the big guns to the hill is taking effect," said Samuel.

"Huzzah!" yelled Thomas.

And soon the shouts of joy could be heard across the camp in Roxbury. And so it was that on March 2, the patriot guns began to fire an endless barrage of cannonballs at the regulars in Boston. The cannonading continued into the third, and by the fourth, Brigadier-General John Thomas used the distraction and muffled wagon wheels to quietly move the cannons and 2,000 troops onto Dorchester Heights. The Continental Army finally had the upper hand on the royal forces. The Continental artillery continued pounding the regulars.

Howe finally sent troops to Dorchester Heights on March 5, trying to stop the guns, but a snowstorm moved in and blocked the attack. (40) The weather continued to help the Continental Army hold off the regulars.

The Continental soldiers could see from afar that General Howe was burning what he did not want to leave behind for the rebels. It appeared Howe was preparing to leave Boston.

---

[9] "General Orders, 4 July 1775," Founders Online, National Archives, https://founders.archives.gov/documents/Washington/03-01-02-0027. [Original source: The Papers of George Washington, Revolutionary War Series, vol. 1, 16 June 1775 to 15 September 1775, ed. Philander D. Chase. Charlottesville: University Press of Virginia, 1985, pp. 54 to 58.]

Samuel's company of soldiers, as part of Bond's Regiment, received orders from General Horatio Gates on March 15 to march to Norwich, Connecticut and on to New York. The King's occupation of Boston was ending.

It would take a few days to prepare for the march south. Finally, on March 17, Samuel and his fellow soldiers witnessed an incredible scene. Boston Harbor was full of ships. Howe brought in more than a hundred vessels to evacuate the 11,000 regulars who needed to evacuate. Roughly a thousand Tories would also leave because they feared what the patriots would do to those who had sided with the King. The patriots received word not to fire on the evacuating troops, which His Excellency General Washington had agreed to in exchange for Howe leaving.

The eight-year-long occupation of Boston ended. (41) But Samuel, Thomas, and thousands of other patriots would never forget what the regulars had done on the streets of Boston six years earlier. Seven redcoats fired their muskets into a crowd of unruly, but unarmed Bostonians on King Street. Five patriots died and a half dozen others were wounded for speaking out against the King's unfair taxation.

The patriots were shot outside the Boston Custom House, where the royals collected taxes from the colonists. Escaped slave Crispus Attucks was the first to get shot.

Attucks carried only a stick and was shot twice. Samuel and Tabitha found Attucks's death to be most troubling because they held abolitionist beliefs. Attucks was of mixed African American and American Indian descent. (42) He'd already escaped one form of tyranny as a slave, and then as a sailor, was threatened by the danger of being forcibly drafted into the King's Royal Navy.

Samuel could recite the names of all those who died, two of whom bore the same first name as him: Samuel Gray, Samuel Maverick, Patrick Carr, and James Caldwell. (43)

Now that the regulars were gone, some of the Continental soldiers moved into the streets of Boston to help with the cleanup. They found cannons the regulars had spiked as well as the charred remnants of burned artillery and transport wagons. Whatever Howe could destroy before leaving, he had.

It was clear that the King's soldiers and sailors, as well as Tories, had deliberately destroyed houses and shops and dumped salt and other stores into the water. The Royal Navy also blew up the Boston Lighthouse on their way out of the harbor. (44) The senseless destruction added to the hate Samuel, Thomas, and their compatriots felt for the King.

It was suspected the British fleet would head for the safety of Canada. General Washington put General Putnam in charge of Boston. And began fortifying the town and harbor against another attack from the King's forces.

Smallpox continued to be a threat, and only after a few days was Boston reopened to everyone. Samuel figured their march to Connecticut and New York had something to do with His Excellency General Washington wanting to protect the colonies from the King's forces as well as a possible attack on New York.

The Continental forces had suffered a painful defeat during a New Year's blizzard as they tried to capture Quebec. Dozens of patriot soldiers died and the British also killed General Richard Montgomery with a cannon blast and wounded Benedict Arnold. Some others were taken prisoner. Whatever the reason for his regiment leaving Massachusetts, on March 18, Samuel's service in the army took him much farther away from Tabitha and home. (45)

Chapter 4
Farther From Home

Samuel awoke to the sound of the fifer and drummer playing Reveille. His regiment would begin the march southwest toward New York this morning. There would be long, grueling days ahead with sore feet and blisters.

Samuel had packed for the march before the sun set the night before. While he was packing, he included a copy of a new pamphlet he'd acquired that supported the patriot cause. Samuel had been told by one of his commanding officers that he should read it. He'd read only a few pages so far. But the author clearly spoke against the English monarchy and the ruling of kings. The pamphlet was titled "Common Sense" and used scripture to support its claims. It was written by a man who wished to remain anonymous. Samuel found it inspiring.[10]

Samuel quickly tore down his tent this morning only to leave it behind. It was too heavy to carry while marching. He, Thomas, and their fellow soldiers would sleep in the open now.

Each would carry roughly forty-five pounds of gear. Samuel would also carry his own sergeant's spontoon, musket and bayonet, haversack with hardtack biscuits and salt pork, knapsacks with a tin cup, bowl and spoon, a blanket, extra shirt, writing paper and a pen, steel striker, flint, char cloth, and a candle. He'd also have his canteen on a strap and a cartridge box on another across his shoulders.

They would march more than 270 miles on the Post Road—trying for about twenty miles each day—then set up camp, feed

---

[10] Walker, Malea, 250 Years Ago: Thomas Paine's Common Sense, Library of Congress Blogs, Headlines & Heroes: Newspapers, Comics & More Fine Print, https://blogs.loc.gov/headlinesandheroes/2026/01/250-years-ago-thomas-paines-common-sense/#:~:text=%2DCommon%20Sense%2C%20Thomas%20Paine,of%20responses%20to%20the%20author.

themselves, and prepare for the next day's march before heading off to sleep.

They would rotate guard duty lest the King's soldiers surprise them with an overnight attack in the dark.

Samuel's company formed up, and soon came the drummer's slow step call to march. A few minutes later the regiment was underway and then the fifer joined the drummer playing the "The Girl I Left Behind Me."

As they marched, the tune made Samuel think of Tabitha and, again, he wondered how long they would be apart. For better or worse, the soldiers would know how far they had to march to get to the next town, thanks to Benjamin Franklin's stone mile markers he'd placed decades earlier when he became Postmaster for the colonies. (46)

Some sections of the road challenged the strongest horses and wagons with steep and rocky hillsides and at times swift-moving streams. But, except for some rainy days and nights, the journey was mostly uneventful even if, as expected, exhausting.

Samuel's regiment moved through Connecticut and arrived in New York City on March 30 along with the other Massachusetts regiments led by Colonel John Paterson and Colonel John Greaton, along with the New Hampshire regiment led by Colonel Enoch Poor.

Samuel was glad he had a good pair of shoes. Some of his fellow soldiers were not so well equipped and their feet bore the brunt of the burden. Some marched with bloody bare feet and bare legs. They hadn't yet been provided shoes or uniforms. And there was little rest once they arrived.

The regiments set up camp. And were put on alert almost immediately for fear of the redcoats invading. But not for long.

On the fifteenth of April, General Washington ordered Samuel's regiment, along with three others, to be ready to move toward Canada in relief of Benedict Arnold's forces. They were to be ready to move at an hour's notice. That meant their mission changed from defending New York to preparing to move north to Albany and beyond.

"Form a line, men!" shouted Captain Craft.

"Form a line, men!" he repeated the command.

"You heard the Captain, men. Line up and maintain order!" shouted Samuel, Thomas, and their fellow sergeants.

Within a week the troops were boarding bateaux and sloops.

The bateaux were boats roughly thirty feet long, shallow with a flat bottom built to be the same on both ends. They were perfect for navigating the river's shallow spots and could be rowed. But also had a single mast and sail that could be used if the winds were blowing in the right direction. The sloops on the Hudson River measured anywhere from seventy-five to ninety feet long with low sides and a shallow draft. There was a single mast near the front of the boat, and the crew could hoist three sails. (47) (48)

Moving hundreds of soldiers up the Hudson was a massive undertaking. Each sloop or bateau could carry roughly thirty men. So, the effort required dozens of boats. The Continental forces would also have to march on land in two key places after leaving the Hudson crossing to Lake George and then to Lake Champlain before reaching Canada.

"I hope these things don't spring a leak," Samuel joked with his fellow soldiers.

"Me too. I don't know how to swim," replied one soldier in his boat.

Their sloop glided smoothly up the river. Samuel could hear the warbling of the bluebirds along the banks as well as the songs of goldfinches and the piping of bald eagles.

He loved traveling on the water, the whoosh of the wind catching the sails and the splash of the water against the shore. The sounds here were peaceful compared to the noise of thousands of soldiers huddled around Boston. For now, there were no sounds of muskets cracking or thunderous booms of cannons firing.

In this moment he could almost forget about being a soldier at war. He knew Tabitha would love the beauty of the Hudson River

Valley and suddenly he missed her more than ever. There were no guarantees he'd ever see her again or feel her in his arms. What dangers would he and the other men in his regiment face ahead?

He could see his friend Thomas in the sloop following behind. Would either one of them survive this next confrontation with the redcoats?

He hoped Tabitha would get the letter he penned just before they left New York. The King's spies tried to intercept mail sent by Continental soldiers looking for clues on troop movements.

Perhaps Samuel would have too much time to think in the roughly four days it would take to reach Albany. Thankfully winter's ice had left the river, so the troops wouldn't have to navigate that treachery and risk running aground.

Samuel was struck by the steep mountains and hilly hardwood forests which on occasion gave way to beautiful little farms and orchards. Farming was something he knew. Samuel wondered if the farmers here along the river used the same type of horse-drawn wooden plows used back home.

His thought was broken with the sound of a splash. From time to time the soldiers were startled by sturgeons jumping from the water. The flotilla of soldiers needed a calm and low shore to cast anchor for the night. They sailed a little while longer as the sun was setting, then found a favorable shoreline that was a suitable place to get some rest until morning. The soldiers would lie upon their arms on deck, which seldom led to restful sleep. (49)

Samuel awoke to the sloop sliding off the sand before daybreak as the winds were favorable and the tide had cooperated.

Fog hung over the water until the sun rose higher. Then Samuel could see high mountains on the west bank that had a blue sheen. He could feel a thud occasionally. The Hudson River bottom was filled with perils, sands and rocks that the keel struck here and there. It's why the sloops were built with cedar sides that resisted rot and harder oak for the bottom.

After four days the Continental Army flotilla reached Albany and then continued their journey north to Fort Ticonderoga and

Lake Champlain in upstate New York. Samuel's sacrifice for a budding nation reached a new stage.

Chapter 5
To Fort Ticonderoga

Samuel's regiment crossed into Canada, along with the others that had moved north to reinforce Arnold. They arrived at Chambly in Quebec on the twelfth of May.

Three days later the Continental Congress ordered May 17 to be a day of "fasting, humiliation and prayer, humbly to supplicate the mercy of Almighty God, that it would please him to pardon all our manifold sins and transgressions, and to prosper the Arms of the United Colonies, and finally, establish the peace and freedom of America, upon a solid and lasting foundation." The General commanded all officers and soldiers to pay strict obedience to the Orders of the Continental Congress, and by their "unfeigned and pious observance of their religious duties, incline the Lord, and Giver of Victory, to prosper our arms."[11]

By the end of May thousands of Continental soldiers had arrived and were in place along the St. Lawrence and Richelieu Rivers. (50) Unfortunately, the army didn't bring much food with them. All they had to eat for several weeks was salt pork and wheat meal. The local water often led to dysentery.

Adding to the challenges, smallpox remained a constant threat. So, the army began inoculations at Sorel on the St. Lawrence. But not before the disease struck hundreds of soldiers ill. (51)

Inoculations involved a crude process called variolation. A doctor used a knife to cut into a pustule on a smallpox victim. Then

[11] "General Orders, 15 May 1776," Founders Online, National Archives, https://founders.archives.gov/documents/Washington/03-04-02-0243. [Original source: The Papers of George Washington, Revolutionary War Series, vol. 4, 1 April 1776–15 June 1776, ed. Philander D. Chase. Charlottesville: University Press of Virginia, 1991, pp. 305–306.]

inserted the blade under the skin of a healthy soldier. The soldier typically developed a mild case of smallpox in about two weeks. Inoculations carried risk. In some cases, the disease would kill the soldier. If he survived, he'd be fit for fighting.

The deteriorating conditions had patriot leaders thinking it would be better to attack the Brits sooner rather than later. Brigadier-General John Sullivan was among a trio of newly arrived generals who, armed with their newly arrived forces, began planning another attack on the British in Canada at Trois-Rivieres, roughly halfway between Quebec and Montreal.

Patriot leaders received a flawed scouting report that fewer than a thousand redcoats were there. Samuel had an uneasy feeling when he heard about the plan and was glad his regiment would not be involved.

Sullivan launched the assault at three in the morning on June 8 with the supposed help of a guide who led the patriot forces astray and into a swamp. By the time the commanders realized the blunder, they were several miles off course.

Patriot soldiers lost shoes and boots in the muck. When daylight struck, their position was exposed to the enemy. A planned, surprise attack was anything but, and the British began firing cannons from their ships on the St. Lawrence River.

The Continental commanders still tried to attack. But soon they realized the number of British regulars was three times the force they had expected to battle. The patriots faced murderous fire and were forced to retreat through the swamp. Nearly four hundred Americans were killed, captured, and wounded.

Word of the disastrous outcome reached Samuel's camp and morale continued to decline. Then, about the third week of June, Samuel's brigade was camped on the Isle aux Noix on the Richelieu River.

"Sergeant Benjamin," called out Captain Craft.

"Yes sir," replied Samuel.

"I need you to form a search party. Take a dozen men with you without delay. Some soldiers from a Pennsylvania company have not returned from a scouting mission and we're being asked to help in the search for them," ordered the Captain.

"Yes sir," Samuel replied.

Samuel quickly sought out a dozen men he knew he could rely on and began a march along the shore downstream. About twenty minutes into their walk through the brush, they came upon a horrendous scene.

"Halt, men!" Samuel shouted.

"Oh Lord have mercy on their souls," said Samuel.

Samuel and his search party found the men they were looking for. On the ground before them lay the mangled and bloody bodies of some Continental soldiers.

It appeared the Pennsylvania soldiers had traveled downstream without weapons. They were near what appeared to be an abandoned house. The soldiers had apparently been attacked by Indians. One of the men wore the uniform of a captain. Another that of a lieutenant. Both officers had suffered fatal blows from a hatchette along with three privates. They'd also been scalped. (52)

It was a cautionary incident for the other soldiers about the dangers of the northern territory. Some men deserted in response to the danger and fear .

In June, Benedict Arnold and his remaining troops continued their retreat south after the failed siege of Quebec. Samuel's regiment and the others from Massachusetts ended up at Crown Point in July as the soldiers continued to move south.

The point at the southern end of Lake Champlain had been home to a French fort named Fort Saint-Frederic built in the earlier part of the century. But as the French and Indian War dragged on and the French lost ground, they destroyed Fort Saint-Frederic to prevent it from falling into the hands of the British Army.

Then the Brits built Crown Point as their own fort. Most of it accidentally burned to the ground in 1773. And only a small number of regulars guarded the remaining building and cannons. That made it easy work for the patriot Green Mountain Boys to capture in 1775. So, by the next year, it became a temporary camp for the retreating

Massachusetts regiments once they understood that trying to conquer the regulars in Canada was foolhardy.

Brigadier-General Benedict Arnold also had a sawmill built at Crown Point to help provide lumber for a makeshift fleet of war ships. The men under his command scoured the remains of Crown Point for cannons he could use to arm his new gunboats.

Arnold had been tasked by patriot General Horatio Gates with overseeing ship building some thirty miles farther south on Lake Champlain at Skenesborough. Arnold's primary mission was to stop the King's ships from sailing south on Lake Champlain and launching an attack on patriot forces.

Arnold arrived to see the completion of one of the gunboats christened as Philadelphia. One of eight newly built gundalows, Philadelphia was fifty-four feet long and armed with three cannons and eight swivel guns. There was a single mast for a sail. But oars and rowing were the primary driving force.[12]

In the meantime, smallpox and other illnesses also continued to plague the patriots. The horrible disease spread easily among the soldiers, leaving them with fevers, severe fatigue, and muscle aches as well as vomiting. Soon red spots appeared in the mouth and spread across the body. The red spots turned to pus-filled blisters and scabs that left scars if a victim survived. Samuel suffered through a bout of smallpox and recovered with a few scars. His regiment continued to lose fellow soldiers. Smallpox killed some. Others were sent home after the regimental doctor determined they were too weak to continue their service. That meant the remaining soldiers could send letters back home with the transports for the sick and wounded. Samuel could finally write Tabitha.

---

[12] The gunboat "Philadelphia" is now on exhibit in the National Museum of American History in Washington, D.C.

July 10, 1776
Crown Point
My Dearest Tabitha, I am well having survived our voyage up the Hudson and the perils of the wilderness. Indians fired arrows at us from the shore, and one came close to striking me in the chest. I have also survived being struck with smallpox although not without much sufring. The plague has killed others in our regiment. I hope this letter finds you and our families well. Some in our regiment have left to return to their farms. But I feel deep in my heart that I belong here and remain in the fight for liberty. We marched into Canada but have since retreated to New York at a place called Crown Point on Lake Champlain. In the past the French and the regulars have built forts here. Much of their works are now in ruins so we camp in the open. We've not much good to eat mostly salt pork and lousy bread. We hear we will eventualy keep moving south to Fort Ticonderoga. I long for the sound of your voice and a glimpse of your eyes. It is misery not being able to hold you and not knowing how long our struggle against the King will last. We know not when we shall face the enemy next. General Arnold's navy is preparing to fight the Royal Navy soon north of here. I fear it will be a difficult struggle for our side. ~ Your loving

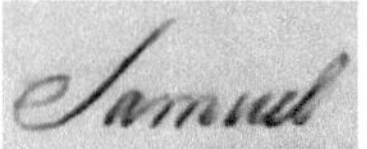

Smallpox followed the army wherever it went because many soldiers refused to be inoculated. So too, patriot commanders continued to plan for the King's forces to follow them south to Fort Ticonderoga on Lake Champlain. That's why in July Continental troops began building another fort on the opposite, or eastern, shore, where the lake narrows to just a quarter mile across.

Samuel's regiment ended up cutting down trees on a place called Rattlesnake Hill during the summer. The rocky peninsula proved a formidable place for a companion fort to stop the King's forces should they try to move against the Continental Army. Soldiers clear-cut three hundred acres of the forest on the mount to build huts and fortifications.

Samuel was used to the hard work of farming and found the work a welcome change from marching, drilling, sentry duty, and foraging for food.

A copy of the Declaration of Independence arrived by late July and was read to the troops. They responded on the twenty-eighth by naming their new fortress Mount Independence.

Samuel was amazed at what the artificers had planned for their new fort. One of his fellow soldiers from Massachusetts was the chief engineer. Lieutenant Colonel Jeduthan Baldwin also had the help of a Polish general who Samuel learned had a very long name. Andrzej Tadeusz Bonaventura Kosciuszko arrived at Fort Ticonderoga late that summer. The Continental commanders simply called him Thaddaeus.

Baldwin and Kosciuszko designed a sophisticated defensive system that had three tiers. There was a large shore battery and a horseshoe-shaped battery with a picket fort in the center of the mount.

"Elisha!" shouted Samuel.

Samuel recognized his good friend as Elisha marched to quarters on the mount. "Samuel!" replied Elisha.

The two friends had gotten separated when they were assigned to different units during the Siege of Boston.

"What are you doing here?" asked Samuel.

"Our regiment was ordered north to join others from Massachusetts," replied Elisha. "We're now assigned to Colonel Whitcomb along with your regiment."

Samuel was overjoyed to see his good friend. Elisha went on to explain that he'd also been writing to Tabitha's sister Martha because they'd been secretly seeing each other before Elisha enlisted. Now Elisha wasn't just Samuel's friend. There was a good chance he could become family.

At least for a time, they'd be serving together again, which made both feel not so far from home.

By early August, Brigadier-General Benedict Arnold's little fleet was almost ready and he'd received orders to sail from General Gates. His fleet comprised fifteen patriot war ships and sailed to Valcour Island.

Tragically, Samuel's regimental commander Colonel William Bond had taken horribly ill. It wasn't clear from what illness he suffered. At the end of August, Bond was jaundiced and he died from bilious fever at Mount Independence. Samuel had a good relationship with Bond, and his death was another setback to patriot morale.

The fight for liberty would play on without one of its most passionate leaders.

"Elisha," said Samuel, trying to get his friend's attention outside his tent.

"Good morning, Samuel. It looks like you have a secret on your tongue," replied Elisha.

"I heard some of the senior officers talking. It sounds like Arnold's fleet is going to attack the King's ships today," said Samuel.

"I hope our little navy doesn't end up on the bottom of the lake," said Elisha.

"It's going to be tough on our boys. Arnold can be reckless," said Samuel cautiously.

On the morning of October 11, Benedict Arnold's fleet lay in wait for the British fleet in a channel off Valcour Island. Arnold's navy was vastly outnumbered.

The British under the command of Sir Guy Carleton had built their own fleet including five ships, twenty gunboats, and twenty-eight longboats with the expertise and leadership of the Royal Navy.

Arnold's fleet hid behind the heavily wooded island. But were finally spotted by the King's navy around ten in the morning. The patriot ships formed an arching battle line and opened fire. Unfortunately, Arnold's biggest ship, Royal Savage, had run aground and was no longer in the fight after the crew abandoned ship.

Cannonballs flew back and forth with bloody results. Arnold was aboard Congress, which eventually took heavy fire from the King's navy. Cannonballs tore through Congress's hull, gutting some of the patriot sailors and tearing off arms and legs from others. (53)

The battle raged on until the sun dipped behind the shore and darkness descended against the flaming wreckage of patriot and British ships. A cannonball had ripped through the side of the Philadelphia, and the patriot gunboat finally sank into the depths of Lake Champlain.

Arnold wisely used the cover of night to slip away before morning. But at daybreak the Royal Navy hunted down the remaining patriot boats and began a running gun battle.

The faster Royal ships finally overtook some of the patriot gunboats, forcing the crews to scuttle their boats. The crippled Washington and crew of more than a hundred men surrendered. Arnold made his escape aboard Congress. British cannons eventually tore the sails and rigging to shreds. Arnold ordered the five patriot vessels still in the fight abandoned and torched. Four patriot boats managed to survive by escaping the battle off Valcour Island early on.

Arnold had lost. But the patriots' brave fight with the British fleet still met with some success. British General Guy Carleton delayed a planned attack farther south when his scouts discovered there were 12,000 Continental troops with cannons on both sides of Lake Champlain's narrow passage. Carleton retreated to Canada for the winter. The patriot sacrifice left eighty men dead and 120 captured.

Chapter 6
The Homefront

Tabitha woke up to the sound of her father outside chopping wood. When she breathed in, she felt the coolness of the retreating winter night on her tongue.

The home's two fireplaces struggled to keep up during the freezing darkness of December. There was plenty of firewood already available to feed the hungry fires. She knew father was chopping wood just to "get his blood flowing," as he liked to say. Still, you could never have too much wood chopped during a Massachusetts winter.

She hated to leave the warmth of the wool blankets and bed rug that covered her bed. She was blessed to have a brass bed warmer. But the embers had long since burned out. And it was time to get up and start the day's chores.

She opened the bed curtains and immediately felt the icy fingers of Old Man Winter. Her feet, covered in heavy wool stockings, slid out and reached the wood-plank floor. Tabitha slowly rose and stretched. She took off her wool nightcap and swapped it with the white linen cap on top of her dresser. Her linen shift had helped keep her warm while she slept.

It felt a little colder today. So instead of wearing a corset, she put on two petticoats before donning her homespun gown. Tabitha was excited for the hours ahead. She and Mother would take part in a spinning bee at church. Tabitha and her mother had joined the Daughters of Liberty a few years before to protest the King's Stamp Act. Now they celebrated their homespun clothing to protest taxation without representation in a different way than the Sons of Liberty.[13]

There were no imported ribbons on their dresses now. Simplicity became the new source of pride. Their group also banned foreign tea at the gatherings and chose to drink local herb concoctions or water.

A few of the ladies imbibed in homemade rum, which also avoided the King's taxes. Father would help them load their spinning wheels onto the wagon and hitch up the horses that would deliver them to the meeting hall.

They would spend several hours chatting with the other women to the music of the whirring spinning wheels. Their goal for the day was to spin dozens of skeins of linen yarn. (54)

At least the spinning bee would help keep her from worrying about Samuel. She had written him a letter in October. But had not received anything back. She still didn't know much more of his whereabouts than north to Canada. Thoughts of Samuel filled her prayers, whether it was on her knees at night or her conversations with God throughout the day, begging for the Almighty to keep him safe. For now, she consoled herself with the adage that "no news is good news." As Christmas Day approached, she was certain it would be another without the man she cherished.

---

[13] Egner, Kate, The Daughters of Liberty, American Battlefield Trust, https://www.battlefields.org/learn/articles/daughters-liberty#:~:text=The%20Daughters%20of%20Liberty%20were%20a%20group,goods**%20*%20**Nonimportation%20movements**%20*%20**Spinning%20bees**

Chapter 7
Christmas Day

"God damn you! God damn you!" yelled the uniformed man on the dark dirt road.

The man had drawn his sword and was running toward Samuel and his group of friends. Samuel was instantly confused by the man's anger. It was after ten o'clock at night on Christmas Day and Samuel and his fellow Massachusetts soldiers were returning from seeing a friend. The man had already yelled to them asking if they were friend or foe. And Samuel answered they were friends. The hostile officer's sword glistened in the moonlight as he came within a few feet of Samuel.

"God damn you!" the man yelled again. Samuel recognized the uniform as that of a Pennsylvania officer.

"Who be you?" the officer yelled again and then waved his sword at Samuel and pricked him several times. Samuel could smell liquor on the officer's breath. The officer then hit one of Samuel's friends over the head with his sword. Confused by the officer's attack, Samuel and his friends ran off toward their camp. Then two more Pennsylvania soldiers ran toward them in the dark. Samuel thought they would help. But they also confronted Samuel and his friends with angry demands.

"God damn ye! Where do you belong!" the soldiers yelled.

"We're in Colonel Whitcomb's Regiment. God damn Colonel Whitcomb!" Samuel replied.

Then one of the Pennsylvania soldiers grabbed Samuel by the collar and tried to stab him and hit him over the head. Samuel was still confused by the violent confrontation from fellow Continental soldiers and ran away with his fellow Massachusetts soldiers. They reached camp and Samuel grabbed his musket and headed to Captain Daniel Whiting's log hut. He yelled for Captain Whiting to come to the door as he saw the Pennsylvania soldiers coming toward him with their swords drawn. Samuel ordered one of the men to stand back, or he'd shoot him through, even though Samuel instantly knew he wouldn't pull the trigger, because a court martial would await for killing a fellow soldier. Captain Whiting then appeared at the door.

"What's the matter, Colonel Craig?" said Whiting.

Captain Whiting clearly recognized the Pennsylvania officer, which further confused Samuel.

Colonel Craig then grabbed the barrel of Samuel's musket. He tried to stab him several times and hit him over the head with the hilt of his sword roughly a dozen times. Samuel thought he was going to be killed by a senior officer, so he dropped his musket and made his escape. Colonel Craig tried to stab Captain Whiting, who defended the blow. Samuel then heard a man whistle and soon, roughly forty Pennsylvania soldiers gathered and demanded to know where Colonel Whitcomb's log hut was.

"God damn! I know where his tent is!" another soldier said, and the group ran off. Samuel was ordered by Captain Whiting to stand down and return to quarters. Soon Samuel heard gunfire and more yelling from the camp around Colonel Whitcomb's hut. The Pennsylvania soldiers were armed with guns, bayonets, and swords. They forced their way into the tents and huts of the Massachusetts officers. Most were dragged out naked, then wounded and robbed. (55) Amazingly, none of the Massachusetts soldiers were killed. Samuel learned the next morning that Colonel Craig had attacked Colonel Whitcomb, dragging him from his quarters and slashing his ear.

Samuel knew there had been friction between the Pennsylvania and Massachusetts troops. But couldn't comprehend what played out the night before. He discovered Colonel Craig was upset with Colonel Whitcomb because he had his sons on the muster roll as his servants. One of them, a soldier, was selling his services as a shoemaker from his father's hut and Craig thought it disgraceful. Craig smashed the shoemaker's bench in anger. The Colonel's drunken behavior got him arrested. But the good-natured Colonel Whitcomb entirely overlooked the affair, and none of the parties were punished. (56) Craig later faced a court-martial. But was acquitted. Senior officers wanted the whole affair to just go away, and for the Continental troops' focus to be on the real enemy—the King's army. Thankfully, Elisha had escaped harm from the violent business. The Pennsylvania rioters had missed his hut.

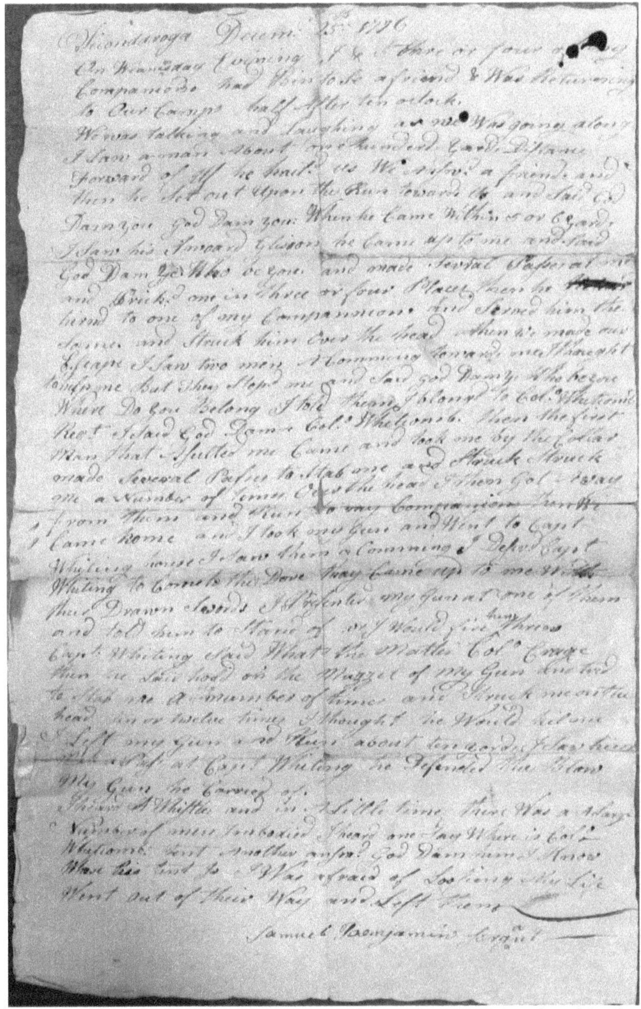

Ticonderoga Decem^r 25th 1776
On Wensday Evening I & three or four of my
Companions had been to se a friend & Was Returning
to Our Camps half After ten oclock.
We was talking and Laughing as we Was going along
I Saw a man About one hundred Yards Distance
forward of us he hail'd us We answ'd a friend and
then he Set out upon the Run towards Us and Said God
Damn you God Damn you When he Came Within 5 or 6 Yards
I Saw his [illegible] he Came up to me and Said
God Damn Ye Who be you and made Several Passes at me
and Prick'd me in three or four Places then he
turn'd to one of my Companions And Served him the
Same and Struck him Over the head then we made our
Escape I Saw two men A Comming towards me I thought
[illegible] But they Stop'd me and Said God Damn ye Who be you
Where Do you Belong I told them I belong'd to Col. Whetcomb
Reg^t I Said God Damn Col. Whetcomb then the first
Man that [illegible] me Came and took me by the Collar
made Several Passes to Stab me and Struck Struck
me a Number of times Over the head I then Got Away
from them and Run to my Companions [illegible]
Came home and I took my Gun and Went to Capt
Whiting house I Saw them a Comming I Desired Capt
Whiting to Come to the Dore they Came up to me With
their Drawn Swords I [illegible] my Gun at one of them
and told them to Stand of or I Would fire [illegible]
Capt Whiting Said What's the Matter Col. [illegible]
then he Laid hold on the Muzzel of my Gun and tried
to Stab me A number of times and Struck me on the
head ten or twelve times I thought he Would kill me
I Left my Gun and Run about ten Yards [illegible]
[illegible] at Capt Whiting he Defended the Blow
My Gun he Carried of.
[illegible] A Whistle and in A Little time there Was a Large
Number of men Embodied I heard one Say Where is Col.
Whetcomb [illegible] Another answ'd God Damn him I Know
Where he [illegible] I Was afraid of Losing My Life
Went out of their Way and Left them

Samuel Benjamin Serg^t

Photo of Samuel Benjamin's report on the Christmas Day Riot of 1776 as found in the archives of Yale University

Transcription of Samuel Benjamin's Report on the Christmas Day Riot at Fort Ticonderoga
Ticonderoga December 25th, 1776

On Wednesday Evening I and three or four of my companions had bin to se a friend & was returning to our camp half after ten o'clock. We was talking and laughing and we was going along I saw a man about one hundred yards distance forward of us he hailed us We answered a friend and then he set out upon the run towards us and said God dam you God dam you: When he came with 5 or 6 yards I saw his swoard Glisson he came up to me and said God Dam you. Who be you and made several passes at me and pricked me in three or four places when he turned to one my companions and served him the same and struck him over the head then we made our escape I saw two men a coming towards me I thought to help me. But they stopped me and said God dam ye who be you where do you belong. I told them I belong to Col. Whitcomb's Regt I said God Damn Col. Whitcomb. Then the first man that assaulted me came and took me by the collar made several passes to stab me and struck, struck me a number of times over the head. I then got away from them and run to my companions. Then we came home and I took my gun and went to Capt. Whiting house I saw them a coming I delivered Capt. Whiting to come to the door. They came up to me with their drawn swords. I presented my gun at one of them and told him to stand off or I would fire him through. Capt. Whiting said what's the matter Col. Craig then he laid hold on the muzzle of my gun and tried to stab me a number of times and struck me on the head ten or twelve times. I thought he would kill me. I left my gun and run about ten yards. I saw him make a pass at Capt. Whiting He defended the blow. My gun he carried off. I heard a whistle and in a little time there was a large number of men embodied. I heard one say where is Col. Whitcomb's tent. Another one said God Dam him I know where his tent is.

I was afraid of losing my life. Went out of their way and left them.
Samuel Benjamin Sergeant

Samuel was recovering from minor wounds on his head and chest when word reached camp that mail had arrived. Soon he was reading a letter from Tabitha that had been written two months earlier. Snow was falling outside, and dreariness had spread over the forts. But the letter soon made all that disappear.

Waltham
October 6, 1776
Dear Samuel, I'm unsure where you are and whether this letter will reach you through the turmoil of this war. We're hearing that some of our mail is being intercepted by the King's spies. We are well here. The harvest is underway and with it the work of preparing our stores for winter. Father did fall off Samuel when some critter spooked him on a ride from the tavern in Watertown. Thankfully only father's pride and left shoulder were harmed. But he has recovered well enough to take in the corn. The days and nights are growing colder and I wonder how you will stay warm with the coming of winter. What are you eating? We hear smallpox is plaguing the army and I worry as much about that for you as I do an enemy musket ball. Mother, I, and my sisters are busy drying fruit and pickling. Thankfully we have had mostly sunny weather to lay out the apples. Father harnessed Samuel to the shay last week and brought home vinegar for the pickling crocks. We've already prepared some vegetables. Reverend Cushing delivered a powerful sermon about God's harvest of souls. I wish you could have been here to listen. I have not received a letter from you for a while. But I will wait patiently knowing you're in God's hands. My prayers are for

you each morning and night my dear Samuel. Please keep me in yours. I eagerly await your return home to my arms. I am forever yours –

Tabitha

(Tabitha Livermore's signature from historical document)

Samuel held the letter in his hands and smelled the paper, hoping for some lasting remaining scent of his dear Tabitha. But the letter had taken too long to arrive. At least he had her words and knew that her hands had held the paper that he now held. He closed his eyes and saw her in his thoughts. Imagined the touch of her bosom against his own and remembered the smell of her hair as he drew her close. The hope of the future would have to do for now.

Chapter 8
Saratoga On The Horizon

The Pennsylvania attack on the Massachusetts soldiers was proof the winter at Ticonderoga and Mount Independence was challenge enough, let alone the threat from the King's forces.

In one sense, Samuel understood the anger the Pennsylvanians felt for the New England troops. He'd known for a while they considered themselves more professional than the men from Massachusetts who prided themselves on representing equality, liberty, and freedom.

Months earlier, Samuel overheard Pennsylvania General Persifor Frazer dictating a letter to his adjutant talking about the troops from New England.

> We have heard that a large number of New England Troops are to be sent here to reinforce us. There are now at this place 12 Regiments of Troops, chiefly New Englanders, besides our Battalions, and the whole amount to 3100 effective, 2600 sick, & 1300 said to be on Command somewhere, but to the General and everyone but themselves unknown. Our Battalions amount to 1600 fit for duty. The miserable appearance, and what is worse the miserable behaviour of the Yankees, is sufficient to make one sick of the service. They are by no means fit to endure hardships. Among them there is the strangest mixture of Negroes, Indians, and Whites, with old men and mere children, which together with a nasty lousy appearance make a most shocking spectacle. No man was ever more disappointed than I have been in respect to them. (57)

Frigid temperatures had combined with boredom, fear of an impending British attack, and too much alcohol to inflame the soldiers' spirits. (57) The clear-cutting of Mount Independence gave way to Mother Nature's cruelty. Officers lived in rough planked cabins.

The common soldiers tried to survive in tents and were much more exposed to the cold and wind, which swept across the mount with a furious bite. At least a half dozen soldiers froze to death each night. A third of the soldiers didn't have shoes. The crisp air of frigid nights was filled with the sound of painful coughing from pleurisy. (58)

Disappointment and despair were constant companions. Not to mention many of the soldiers were veterans of combat. They were now killers and had watched friends die from musket balls and bayonets. Bloodshed has a devilish way of sneaking into a man's soul and turning his heart cold.

The deep chill of winter dragged on mercilessly into January and February of 1777. Thankfully, March brought warmer nights and longer days. The melting snow made the camp a muddy mess. But the advent of spring lightened the soldiers' hearts. Little did they know as they continued to drill and resupply that a great battle lay ahead. Samuel learned another courier would be heading east toward Boston and it was time to write a letter to Tabitha.

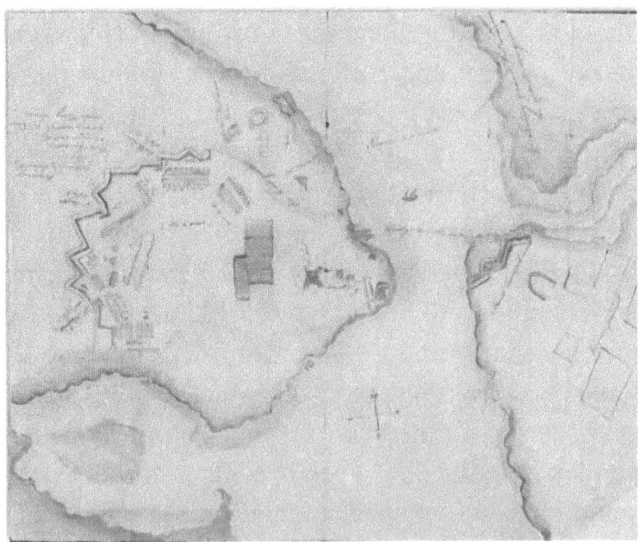

Trumbull, John. Ticonderoga,[October 1776] Map.

March 29, 1777
Fort Ticonderoga
My Dearest Tabitha, I have so much to tell you. I thank God the winter here is soon over. Everyone's spirits are improving with the coming of Spring and warmer nights. I finally receeved one of your letters and thank you for it. It is cherished as I cherish you. I hope your father has fully recovered from falling off Samson. It is unlike my four legged friend to be spooked. It has been a tough few months here. Sadly, my former commander Col. Bond died at the end of August. We are no longer under the command of Col. Whitcomb. I now serve another Massachusetts Colonel. Michael Jackson is from Newton and we are now part of his Regiment. First let me say I am okay now. But I tell you I was attacked by enemies within our own ranks. Soldiers from Pennsylvania harbored anger against those of us from Massachusetts and on Christmas Day came at us with drawn swords. In the moment I was horribly confused by their actions. I nearly shot one of them.

But thought better of it and made my escape. I was cut on my head and arm and suffered a few shallow cuts from sword tips on my belly. Nothing serious. After the attack I was promoted to Ensign in January under Col. Jackson. John Hancock signed the order. Tell your sister Martha that Elisha was not harmed in the riot. I know they are sweet on each other. It sounds as if the two of them are getting on quite well. Perhaps they will beat us to the altar. But my love for you is patient. Colonel Whitcomb asked me to write a report on the attack which will be presented at Court Martial for the Pennsylvania Colonel and his men who took part in the raid. They fired their muskets into our tents and huts and pillaged some of our quarters. Miraculously none of us were killed. Those tensions have since eased. His Excellency Gen. Washington has urged us to put our teritorial differences aside and remember who the real enemy is. We thought we would have to face the King's army in October. But snow began to fall, and they headed back to Canada for the winter. Now that the snow is melting, I know we shall have to take up arms soon. We built another fort on a rocky mount across from Fort Ticonderoga and spent many days constructing fortifications. We also built a hospital for the sick and wounded. The most curious thing our troops built was a floating bridge where the lake narrows. First, they built wooden boxes out of logs then filled them with rocks so they sank. The sunken boxes became the foundation under water. We then linked timbers and built a platform to walk on. Thankfully my regiment stayed on the Ticonderoga side for the winter where there was more protection from the cold. Even so, some nights during the winter were the coldest I have ever been and some of our lot froze to death if they were only in tents. More so across the lake on the mount. It was a bitter predicament that soured the spirits of many men. I shall try to write you again once we leave our current camp. You are always in my thoughts and prayers. And I see you in my dreams and awake with my heart full. With my deepest love,

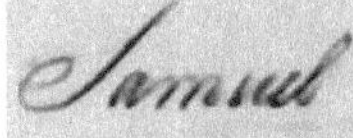

Samuel folded the letter and prepared it for the courier, hoping it would not take too long to arrive in the hands of his sweetheart. There was always the risk of a letter being intercepted or some other mishap along the route to Massachusetts. He imagined the pain of waiting for word of his well-being was just as difficult as the pain he suffered waiting for news of home. Continental soldiers continued to reinforce Mount Independence and prepare for an expected onslaught from the redcoats. The British had retreated for the winter. But Samuel and Elisha knew it would only be a matter of time before they would make another run at attacking the patriots.

Many soldiers were sent home to their farms before winter. Smallpox, pleurisy, and other perils had shrunk the patriot force to roughly 3,000 troops. April, May, and June turned into months of recovery from the violent winter that had plagued Continental soldiers.

The days were filled with drilling, target practice, and cleaning muskets as well as foraging for food. In the meantime, British General John Burgoyne assembled an army of nearly 8,000 British regulars, Hessians, American loyalists, and Native Americans.

The British general's goal was to take control of the Hudson River Valley, including forcing the rebels out of Fort Ticonderoga and Mount Independence. Burgoyne moved south from Canada to Lake Champlain in mid-June. (59)

On July 5, the dark of night was suddenly punctuated with an alarming light that greeted Samuel and his regiment. There were suddenly campfires on Sugar Loaf Hill, which stood above Mount Independence and Fort Ticonderoga. Patriot commanders had failed to guard the higher ground, thinking it not possible to haul cannons up the thickly wooded and steep incline. The redcoats proved them wrong.

The King's guns now had a clear line of attack on Fort Ticonderoga, Mount Independence, and the much smaller Continental force. Everything the Continental Army had accomplished in building Mount Independence and controlling the Hudson at Fort Ticonderoga turned to failure.

Major General Arthur St. Clair said he simply didn't have enough soldiers or supplies to fight it out with the redcoats and ordered an immediate retreat from both forts. The patriots had built a floating bridge across the lake to connect the forts. So, the soldiers left Fort Ticonderoga behind, crossed the bridge, and joined with Samuel, Elisha, and the troops at Mount Independence, escaping south.

Samuel and Elisha's regiments helped load the wounded and much-needed supplies onto bateaux to float south to Skenesborough. Soldiers well enough to march escaped south through the New Hampshire Grants (later Vermont) reaching Castleton. That's where Ethan Allen had mustered the Green Mountain Boys two years prior. On the sixth of July, Burgoyne was surprised to find both forts abandoned.

Chapter 9
The Battles of Saratoga

The King's Brigadier-General Simon Fraser learned of the rebel retreat and immediately gave chase.

"Hurry up, men. The redcoats aren't far behind," yelled Samuel.

He worried about whether Elisha's regiment got out of camp fast enough. It was a chaotic retreat away from the fort and across the floating bridge. Leading the retreat, Continental Major General Arthur St. Clair ordered the main part of his army, including Samuel's and Elisha's regiments, to continue southeast through Hubbardton, then south to Castleton and on to Fort Edwards, a journey of more than sixty miles on foot.

To protect his flank, St. Clair had Colonel Seth Warner, along with his Vermont troops, lagged behind to command a rear-guard force with the 11th Massachusetts, the Green Mountain Boys and Colonel Nathan Hale's 2nd New Hampshire regiment.

The redcoats and Hessians caught up on the morning of July 7 and attacked at Hubbardton. The patriots put up a valiant fight and slowed the British advance suffering forty-one killed, ninety-five wounded, and 234 missing or captured. Sixty redcoats died, with more than a hundred wounded.

The patriot sacrifice saved the main force to fight another day. Samuel knew some of the men who died and wondered if he too would soon pay the ultimate sacrifice for his budding United States.

Tabitha and Martha would be crushed if both he and Elisha died in battle, never to return to the arms of their sweethearts. But both knew they needed to stay focused on the here and now. Not the what-ifs. They arrived safely to Fort Edwards. But not for long.

"Good morning, Elisha," said Samuel to his likely future brother-in-law. Samuel had sought out Elisha's regiment at first light.

"How do you fare?" replied Elisha.

"I'm trying to put my best foot forward. But I'm a bit stiff from sleeping on the ground again," uttered Samuel.

"Me too," replied Elisha. "I don't think we're here for long. Word in camp is our scouts spotted the King's soldiers headed our way."

"That's why I hear General Schuyler has ordered Nixon's militia to cut down trees and destroy bridges on their likely route," said Samuel.

"I have some news to share with you," said Elisha a little quietly.

"Oh yeah. Spit it out, Elisha," said Samuel.

"You and I are going to be family if I make it through these coming battles. Martha and I are going to get married. Sooner rather than later. She's with child and her parents aren't too happy with us," said Elisha.

"Oh, I see," said Samuel.

"I was on furlough a few weeks back and...let's just say Martha and I got a little carried away...and well...she's pregnant," said Elisha sheepishly.

"Ha, ha, ha," Samuel just laughed at first. "You old dog! Serves you right. When is the baby expected?" asked Samuel.

"Before Christmas," said Elisha.

"Well then, you best not get yourself killed," said Samuel.

Both laughed. Then Samuel spoke.

"I mean it. Keep your head down. The rest of us can kill a few lobsterbacks for you," said Samuel.

"I also have news of your brother Jonathan. He signed up again for the army under Colonel Edward Wigglesworth," said Elisha.

"I knew he couldn't stay out of the fight forever," replied Samuel.

Samuel wondered what that meant for the farm. Perhaps a neighbor had agreed to plant the soil in return for a share of the harvest.

He shook hands with Elisha, and they moved on to their respective duties with their regiments.

There wouldn't be much to eat again today. Salt meat and hard biscuits. The thought of it made Samuel miss Tabitha's cooking even more. Fort Edward was along the Hudson River and at least drinking water was easily found. But there was no guarantee that it wouldn't lead to dysentery. Samuel discovered that the hard way. He was soon struck with bilious dysentery. Breakfast quickly turned to running to the privy time and time again.

Samuel, now an ensign, was supposed to muster the troops for daily drilling. In battle, Samuel's new role as a commissioned officer would be to carry the regimental colors.

Only a few minutes had passed when a new order came from Colonel Michael Jackson. Samuel's regiment was to move about three miles south to Moses Creek. But Samuel's illness became debilitating, and he would have to abandon the regiment for a doctor's care at the hospital in Albany.

The others, roughly 3,000 troops, would be marching and setting up camp without him. That included General John Nixon's and General Ebenezer Learned's Brigades of Continental soldiers along with General Abraham Ten Broeck's Militia Brigade and Colonel John Ashley's Battalion of Militia from Berkshire County, Massachusetts.

The Continental troops at Moses Creek numbered around 1,800 with the militia about 1,300, but "badly clad and Armed." (61)

Major General Benedict Arnold arrived in camp on the twenty-first of July. The General walked with a slight limp after being shot in the left leg during his attempt to capture Quebec nearly two years earlier. The soldiers thought it somewhat amazing that the General arrived unharmed.

The woods around their camp seemed to be crawling with danger including Canadians, regulars, and Indians. Members of the Mohawk, Oneida, Onondaga, Cayuga, Seneca, and Tuscarora sided with the Crown's troops and attacked the pickets daily. The day after General Arnold arrived, Indians killed and scalped five men, wounded nine others, and took one prisoner.

Two days later, Indians killed and scalped two officers who were traveling between Samuel's camp and Fort Edward. Then hundreds of the enemy attacked the advanced guard a few days later. And before they reached the safety of the main army, one lieutenant and five privates were killed and scalped.

Because of the continued danger of straying from camp, no soldiers deserted. To be caught alone in the woods seemed to be a certain, and most horrid, death that included the likelihood of being scalped.

Samuel would later learn from his fellow soldiers that they overhead General Arnold describing an even more horrific event. Wendat warriors took two women prisoner from a house near Fort Edwards and carried them to the regular troops who were paraded nearby. One of the women was shot, scalped, stripped, and, in Arnold's words, "butchered in the most shocking manner."

That woman was Jane McCrea, a Presbyterian minister's daughter who had moved to a home that belonged to her brother. McCrea apparently wanted to be close by when her beloved, to whom she was engaged to be married, returned from Canada. He was a Tory officer in Burgoyne's army. And the Indians were apparently sent by the redcoats to bring the women safely to the fort. But the women hid in the cellar when they saw the Indians coming. The warriors dragged the women out of the house by their hair. They placed Jane on a horse, but the other woman, Sara McNeil, was forced to walk because she was too big to be lifted.

There were rumors that the redcoats were paying for scalps and the Indians apparently didn't understand Jane was a loyalist. It seems that her two captors argued over who would get the reward for bringing her to camp, and that she was killed as the warriors fought. (62) (63)

Word of McCrae's death spread like wildfire and inflamed the countryside, igniting thousands of colonists to rise up against the Crown's troops. (64)

Considering the distraction of McCrea's death and ongoing threats, it was the officers' duty to make sure the men maintained discipline, and cleanliness, including digging proper privy pits.

Drilling and camp duties kept the soldiers from thinking about getting scalped. But soon after the murder of the loyalist woman, General Schuyler learned 6,000 regulars, nearly four hundred Indians, and two hundred Canadians were headed to Fort Edwards.

So, on July 29, Schuyler abandoned the fort to the redcoats and moved all the Continental troops south. Had Samuel been well enough, he would have marched mile after mile with the 8th Massachusetts regimental colors—no longer the Continental Union flag. That duty fell to another ensign in Samuel's absence.

The old flag had thirteen alternating red and white stripes with the British Union Jack in the upper left corner. But the patriots were no longer British citizens fighting with the King.

They had declared their independence. And in June, the Continental Congress had ordered a new flag with thirteen stars to replace the Union Jack. Samuel's regiment had received the new colors by special courier, and the officers were proud to show off the new flag. It also had thirteen alternating horizontal red and white stripes, but now in the upper left corner, there were twelve stars in the shape of a square with a single center star on a blue field. (65)

Whatever flag was carried, it added to fifty pounds of gear including a musket, bayonet, knapsack, haversack, ammunition, blanket, and other necessities.

The soldiers under his command asked where they were headed. All the officers knew was that General Schuyler had ordered them to cross the Hudson River at Saratoga and set up camp. Colonel Michael Jackson, now Samuel's regimental commander, wouldn't stay long.

Scouts sent word that more than a hundred miles west, British General Barry St. Leger had surrounded the Continentals at Fort Stanwix and was demanding the 3rd New York Regiment to surrender. Patriot General Colonel Peter Gansevoort refused and prepared for a prolonged battle to keep hold of the fort.

A column of eight hundred colonial militia under the command of Brigadier-General Nicholas Herkimer rushed in to help and were attacked six miles from Fort Stanwix at Oriskany Creek. The Brits killed half of the patriots and Herkimer was mortally wounded.

When the soldiers heard about the ambush, they wondered if they would be sent in to help. Soon General Arnold accepted the dangerous task of leading a relief force toward Fort Stanwix, including Samuel's regiment. But Samuel was still in the hospital in Albany.

The hospital was large, wooden, H-shaped, and sat above the Foxes Creek ravine. It was north of the fort, and was refurbished by the local committee of correspondence, safety, and protection.[14] The committee had been formed to oppose the King's intolerable acts, which included trying to get the colonists to pay for the damages from the Boston Tea Party as well as forcing colonists to house redcoats and give them supplies.

Samuel was happy he was at least a prisoner of disease in friendly confines and not a prisoner of war. By month's end his fever had broken and he was much better.

So, Samuel was sent on recruiting duty by Lieutenant Colonel Dudley Colman.[15] Samuel heard from a scout that on August 8, a force of seven hundred, including his regiment, began a march of eighty miles toward Fort Dayton to eventually rescue the Continentals at Fort Stanwix.

It had rained the next morning, slowing the march and for a time turning it into another muddy mess of an effort. Some of the soldiers' feet had developed blisters from marching with wet boots. So, when they'd reach camp for the night, they would slip off their boots, air out their feet, and apply some lint cloth to help them heal.

Four days into the march they finally reached Palentine and boarded bateaux to float up the Mohawk River. The soldiers noticed wonderful crops growing along the river bottom. Indian corn, oats,

---

[14] New York State Museum, The Albany Hospital, https://exhibitions.nysm.nysed.gov/albany/loc/hospital.html

[15] Samuel Benjamin recruiting note signed by Lieutenant Colonel Dudley Colman, July 26, 1777, Yale University Archives

rye, and wheat were plentiful, and here and there stood Indian Castles. They finally reached Fort Dayton on the fourteenth and joined the remaining militia who survived the ambush.

Shallow water eventually forced them to leave the bateaux behind and march again. By the twenty-third, they drew closer to Fort Stanwix and lay down in a field without tents for the night. They reached old Fort Schuyler, where General Arnold had a trick up his sleeve.

To the Indians supporting the British, the General exaggerated the size of Arnold's force. The Senecas and Mohawks abandoned the British siege and soon after the King's forces followed suit. The regiment arrived at Fort Stanwix having chased away the redcoats without firing a shot.

Little did Samuel's fellow soldiers know it would also help the patriot cause in the months to come at Saratoga. (66) General Arnold, learning of the British retreat from Fort Stanwix, turned his troops around and marched back toward Saratoga. The soldiers were worn out from the march of nearly a hundred miles through the New York countryside back to Stillwater.

Samuel awoke to a new day feeling confident that his recruiting was going well. He had signed up many soldiers for service. But Samuel missed his sweetheart more than ever because his duties gave him more time to think. He decided to write Tabitha first thing and hoped there would be a courier to carry the army's mail back to Cambridge. As the sun rose higher in the sky Samuel grabbed his quill, ink, and paper.

Pittsfield
August 18, 1777
Dear Tabitha, I don't want you to worry because I am feeling much better. But I was very ill with bilious dysentery. I had been under a doctor's care in the hospital in Albany. I am much stronger and have been assigned recruiting duties in New York and Western Massachusetts. My regiment is in Stillwater and I hope to return to my fellow

soldiers soon. They're in upper New York along the Hudson. We abandoned Fort Ticonderoga and Mount Independence some weeks ago. It was a dificult journey of retreat through bug riden forests and dificult roads and trails. We were want for good food most of the time. There was little but salt meat and hard bread. We were at Fort Edwards for a little while which was mostly destroyed and in need of repair. I got sick drinking the water there. My regiment then set up camp a few miles south at a place called Moses Creek. The Indians harased our men daily and killed a few of our numbers serving in pickets in the most brutal fashion. They took scalps as a final act. The worst of it involved a loyalist woman who was engaged to be married to one of the King's officers. We heard her fiancé sent Indians to the house where she and another woman were staying to bring her to the fort. The women hid and were dragged out by the Indians who then fout over who would get the reward for captring them. The soldier's fiancé ended up shot and scalped. Word of that most horrible affair has spread through the teritory and growing numbers of militia are showing up in our camp wanting to fight the Brits. If I haven't told you I've been promoted to ensign, so I now wear a braided epaulette on my left shoulder. I should think you quite proud of me. When I return to my regiment, I will carry the regimental colors as part of my duty and honor. We have a new flag of independence which I hope you have seen flying back home. I know the Continental Congress is now meeting in Philadelphia. For how long it is unclear. We are hearing the King's troops are moving closer to Philly. We have our own concerns here. General Burgoyne has been chasing us since we began our retreat a month ago. On our side, General Horatio Gates took over the Northern Department from General Schuyler earlier this week. There were rumors Congress was upset with Schuyler's retreat from Canada and Fort Ticonderoga and Mount Independence. There was a battle not far from here a couple days ago at a place called Bennington where we patriots had a store of supplies. I think Elisha's regiment marched there. But was held in the rear in case they were needed which appears they were not. My regiment was not called to engage because there was a strong showing of militia, the Green Mountain Boys, and volunteers from our beloved Massachusetts. General Burgoyne got what was comin to him. Our troops gave him a whoopin. We hear two hundred regulars died and hundreds were takn prisoner. Now it appears, with Burgoyne so close by, the place where my regiment is camped is where we will finally face off against the King's army of the north. We are set up about thirty miles north of Albany. I finally have better food here. Fresh meat and flour and a few localy grown crops. Our regimental commander is a man we are all proud to follow. Col. Jackson has his whole family with him now, five sons and his wife Ruth as a nurse. They are a family of dedicatd patriots. If you recall the Colonel took part in the Tea Party. Then he was wounded at Bunker Hill while in hand-to-hand combat with one of the King's officers. He killed the fellow. Then last September he was shot by a musket ball while leading an attack on Montresor's Island in New York but remained committed to the cause. He now walks with a limp. With the way I miss you and my mother and other family I understand why he wants his family here. But I fear his younger boys will grow up to fast. Charles is just ten years old and Amasa - twelve. Both are serving as fifers. Amasa can also drum.[16] They are under the care of our Fife Major Thomas Lawrence from Pepperell who is a grand fellow as well as grand fifer. I pray Jackson's boys don't lose their father as I lost mine. That kind of sadness changes you. Each company has its own fifer and drummer. One of the drummers from Boston,

---

[16] "Massachusetts, Town Clerk, Vital and Town Records, 1626 to 2001," FamilySearch, https://www.familysearch.org/ark:/61903/1:1:FHT7-KVF, Entry for Michael, Simon, Ebenezer, Amasa, & Charles Jackson.

Samuel Smellage, is a jolly fellow who always makes me laugh. As for Jackson's other sons, Ebenezer is 13, serving in the infantry. Simon is sixteen and is paymaster. The oldest Michael is 18 and is quartermaster. I think their mother is willing to do anything just to not let the war separate them. I hear she is a good nurse. Maybe she's hoping he won't be too brave with his whole family is in the fray. To lose any one of them would be a sorrow too deep for the rest. There are a number of camp folowers with us who help with laundry and such so they get fed. Most have husbands who are among the troops. But I would not want you so close to the danger even though my heart longs for you my dear. You fill the breaths of each moment of my day. I pray for you each morning and night. I am confident you are doing the same on the other side of the long miles which separate us. God has continued to keep me safe and has restored me from a sickness that has killed others. I hope your parents, brothers, and sisters are well. I see Elisha from time to time when I am in camp. He told me Martha is expecting and that your mother and father aren't too happy. I'm sure your sister longs to see him. And I think she soon will. Elisha told me he's applied for furlough and they're going to do the honorable thing and get married. Both of us miss everything about home and now Elisha has a much bigger reason to make it home. Please visit my mother when you can and send along my love. To say that I love you does not capture the fullness of my feelings for you that dwell in my soul. (70) Yours forever,

Samuel

Samuel folded the letter. Dipped his quill in ink once more and wrote the Livermores' address on the outside.

He grabbed his steel striker, flint, and candle. Lit the candle and dripped wax on the outside of the folder letter to seal it, hoping his words would find their way to his sweetheart.

It had been a hot night in late August, so he had slept on top of his wool blanket in his long linen shirt. He slipped on his breeches and leather boots, waistcoat, and bounty coat, which now had an epaulette on the left shoulder.

The gold-fringed ornament identified him as an ensign. Samuel was getting stronger each day and his commitment to the cause of liberty and enthusiasm had made it easier to recruit others.

By early September, summer was fading and the nights were turning cooler. Now that Samuel was back to full strength, Lieutenant Colonel Dudley released him from recruiting duty. He accompanied some of the new recruits to Stillwater and his regiment.

When he arrived and reported for duty with his regiment, Samuel discovered the patriot forces had been ordered to build a fortified line on the heights and on the river flats. Samuel knew it was a good plan because you could see both the Hudson River and the road from the bluffs.

It was a place called Bemis Heights. Patriot cannons would be able to hit regulars amassing at both places below. The British would be forced to use the road because the forest was too dense to move troops.

The Continental troops were also building a fortified wall nearby that would stretch nearly a mile when complete in a sort of "L" shape. The wall would also be defended by cannons. The daily drilling and construction continued, and the works were complete by the first week of September. The number of Continental troops had grown to roughly 7,000 men.

"Samuel!" Jonathan shouted.

"Brother. What are you doing here?" asked Samuel in surprise.

"I'm with Colonel Wigglesworth's Thirteenth and we've come to join the fight," answered Jonathan.

"It's good to see you, brother," said Samuel.

They exchanged a handshake and a quick hug.

"I knew you couldn't stay out of the cause for liberty. What of the farm?" asked Samuel.

"The Shearman family has agreed to plant and harvest while we're away. They see it as patriot effort while we're serving in the army," said Jonathan.

"I thought as much. They're kind and God-fearing souls," said Samuel.

He continued, "I must get back to my duties, Jonathan. And I'm sure you to yours."

"That's true. I don't want to be listed as a deserter on account of my brother," laughed Jonathan.

The two shook hands and parted.

As the army grew in numbers, women known as camp followers served a vital role. Camp followers were ladies who marched with the patriot force to work as seamstresses, nurses, cooks, and laundresses. Some were married to soldiers on the march and brought their children. Others were widows or had fallen on hard times, and they were allowed to eat food provided by the army in return for their service.

Those who served as nurses could be paid eight dollars a month. Women who cooked could also get paid. General Washington expressed frustration to commanding officers at the number of women who often followed the troops. But he also understood that camp followers served a crucial role in caring for the sick and injured. (67)

Samuel missed Tabitha but in no way did he wish her to be exposed to the dangers of being on the march or in battle.

Suddenly he heard the blast of a musket firing and the startled yelling of nearby troops. Samuel ran toward the sounds and discovered a red-faced soldier who apparently had forgotten he had a powder charge still in his Brown Bess. When he picked up his musket to clean it, he did so with his finger on the trigger. He nearly shot one of his fellow soldiers in the head.

"What in the world were you thinking?" asked Samuel.

"I must have forgotten to unload my musket after the march," exclaimed the embarrassed young patriot. "I was going to clean my gun and it went off when I picked it up."

"We all know what happened, soldier!" yelled Samuel. "Carelessness can be deadly. There's your lesson for the day. I should present you with lashes and report you to our Captain. But I'll spare you this time. Have you learned your lesson?" Samuel sighed.

"Yes sir!" replied the soldier.

"Let's hope you have. A mistake like that on the battlefield could cost you your life or the life of a friend. Understand?" said Samuel.

"Yes sir!" said the soldier.

"Dismissed," replied Samuel.

So that's how the day is going to start, thought Samuel. He encouraged the other soldiers to keep quiet about what happened for the protection of their friend and, quite frankly, for the protection of the company. Still, Samuel planned to tell Captain Ebenezer Cleaveland what happened. He was confident Cleaveland would approve of his handling of the matter.

Samuel told the men to get ready for drilling after they were done cleaning their muskets and eating breakfast. This is how the days ahead would repeat themselves. Without, hoped Samuel, another accidental firing.

There was always the issue of the men imbibing too much rum while in camp. But rum was part of the rations, and some soldiers were prone to drink too much. It's a story as old as time. Samuel didn't drink at all. He wanted to be sharp for every moment. A surprise attack by the enemy was always lurking in his mind.

Suddenly Samuel spotted Captain Cleaveland rushing toward him and the other officers.

"Thousands of regulars have amassed just three miles from our camp!" shouted Captain Cleaveland.

The officers had gathered after the morning gun was fired by the artillery.[17] The fifers and drums followed with Reveille. It was the seventeenth of September.

---

[17] Camus, Raoul F., Military Music of the American Revolution, The University of North Carolina Press, Chapel Hill, 1976, p. 91

"They've set up camp at the farm of loyalist Thomas Sword," said Cleaveland. "It appears our next battle is close at hand, boys."

Cleaveland's proclamation was met with a loud shout of "Huzzah!" from all those assembled.

Samuel took the news in stride. After all, this is what they had trained for. The endless hours of drilling and target shooting would finally be put to work any day now.

Battle plans and formations were passed along to the officers. Samuel's Massachusetts regiment would be on the left wing under the overall command of Major General Benedict Arnold. The brigade commander was Brigadier-General Ebenezer Learned.

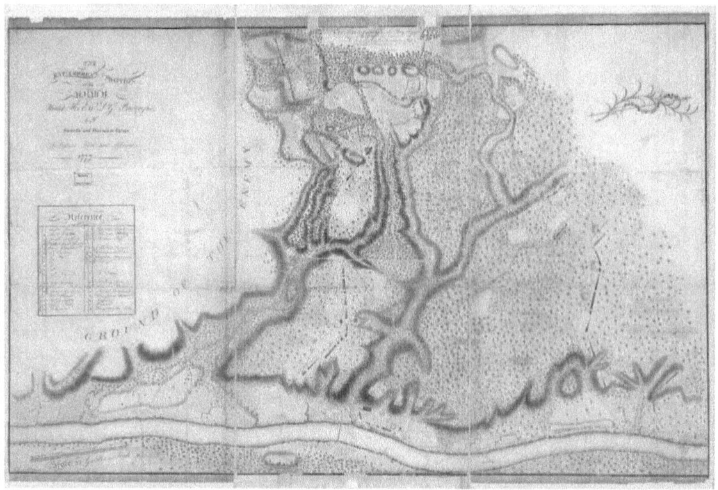

Map by Wilkinson of "the encampment & position of the army under Burgoyne at Swords's and Freeman's Farms on Hudson River near Stillwater, 1777." Library of Congress.

They'd be joined on the left side of the field by two other Massachusetts Bay regiments commanded by Colonel John Bailey and that of Colonel James Wesson as well as a regiment commanded by a Canadian who had supported the patriot cause early on, namely Colonel James Livingston. (68)

Patriot soldiers spent the next day assembling additional black powder cartridges. Samuel became highly skilled at teaching the men in his company how to pre-roll paper cartridges in the field.

One challenge the Continental Army often faced was a shortage of lead to melt down for musket balls. At times they resorted to harvesting lead from the window sashes of nearby homes or wherever they could find it.

The soldiers would build an exceptionally hot fire, then melt the lead and pour it into a ball-shaped iron mold. Once the lead cooled, most of the soldiers liked to use a jackknife to cut off the excess lead so the ball would move smoothly through the musket barrel. The next step was to take oblong pieces of tough paper that would be wrapped around a wooden dowel to form cones. A soldier twisted one end of the cone and tied it off with a piece of string, then dropped in a lead ball and tied off the paper again. That would hold the lead ball with black powder poured in the top half. The paper at the top was folded over and tucked in to keep the powder from spilling.

Each soldier carried a cartridge box that would hold roughly two dozen cartridges. There was always the chance of a battle lasting too long and a soldier running out of cartridges. (69)

When Samuel awoke on the morning of September 19, he had a feeling in his gut that today, the battle would begin. A heavy fog had descended on the Hudson River Valley. Then British troops fired a signal gun, and the patriots knew the regulars were in position to move toward the patriot defenses.

The King's forces advanced in three columns of more than 7,000 soldiers. General Gates had sentinels on post in the woods and elsewhere on the lookout for the British troops. Once it was clear an attack was imminent, Gates allowed General Arnold to move roughly seven hundred troops from Colonel Daniel Morgan's Rifle Battalion and Major Henry Dearborn's Corps of Light Infantry toward the enemy at the abandoned farm of a loyalist named John Freeman.

Samuel's regiment was ready to fight but was held in the rear. Around noon Morgan's riflemen, some hidden in the woods or behind buildings and fences, spotted the enemy and opened fire with devastating results.

Several officers died instantly because they were targeted by soldiers firing guns with rifled barrels. Those guns were more accurate at longer distances, and Morgan's men were great shots.

Samuel and his fellow soldiers could hear the sounds of the battle—the boom of cannons and multiple volleys of muskets firing.

Morgan's riflemen rushed after the retreating survivors and ran head on into a larger British force, then scattered to save themselves. Then the patriots' 1st, 2nd, and 3rd New Hampshire Regiments from General Enoch Poor's brigade joined the fight. Soon after, they were joined by the 2nd and 4th New York Regiments and two battalions of Connecticut militia.

It was some four hours into the battle before Samuel's regiment was ordered forward to join the fray along with the 10th Massachusetts Regiment, from Brigadier-General John Paterson's brigade.

The drummers and fifers signaled the march by playing "The General."[18] So, Samuel picked up the flagpole and carried the new regimental flag forward with his fellow soldiers as they all yelled, "Huzzah!"

Heavy smoke filled the farm fields and woods from thousands of muskets firing black powder as well as smoke from the cannons. At times it was tough for the soldiers rallying around the flag to see enemy targets through the smoke.

Samuel heard a scream of pain off to his left as one of his fellow patriots was shot in the belly and fell. Blood oozed through the soldier's white hunting frock. Samuel moved closer to the wounded man and recognized him. It was Nathaniel Moody from Methuen. He was in Wiley's Company. Samuel had met him just a few days before. Now life was slipping from the soldier's eyes.

Samuel had to keep moving forward with the colors. The pending death of their compatriot only fueled a greater desire to attack the King's redcoats. Samuel held the colors high to keep the rally point clear for his company. He heard the sound of a musket ball

---

[18] Camus, Raoul F., Military Music of the American Revolution, The University of North Carolina Press, Chapel Hill., 1976, p. 85

whiz past his right ear. And he felt like the good Lord had spared him one more time. He refused to duck down when he saw redcoats pointing their muskets in his direction. He felt great pride in keeping the flag easy to see despite the mortal danger in doing so.

His stomach was queasy from the excitement and fear. But if he remained brave, the men serving alongside him would be encouraged to follow his lead.

The sound of guns blasting was punctuated by the intermittent screams and groans of British soldiers cut down across the farm field. The same sounds, only louder, came from his side of the action. The battle line ebbed and flowed as one side or the other gained a temporary advantage.

Samuel heard a soldier on his right yell, "God damn!"

And when Samuel turned to look, he saw the lower part of the man's left arm had turned to a mangled mess of bleeding flesh. Another soldier rushed to the man and led him away from the front as his screams grew fainter.

The battle raged on for some three hours in a bloody back and forth tussle for dominance. It seemed to Samuel the redcoats were losing more men than the patriots. But he was impressed by the professional soldiers' discipline in launching multiple bayonet attacks against the Continental forces.

Several times, Samuel ducked the charging knives at the end of British muskets using the flagpole in one hand and his sword in the other to keep the cold steel from piercing his body. Thankfully, the men around him shot the regulars before they outmaneuvered him. But Samuel's arms were growing weary.

Another soldier toppled near Samuel's left side. Samuel scrambled over to the man to see if he was wounded. Blood was coming from the left side of his chest.

"What's your name?" asked Samuel.

"Jeremiah," replied the wounded man. "Jeremiah Dole. I'm from Varnum's Company," he said.

"Hang in there, good man," said Samuel. "I'll yell for someone to come get you and have your wound looked at. Where are you from, Jeremiah?"

"Salisbury, sir. I don't think I'm going to make it," Jeremiah's voice waivered.

"Can I pray with you?" asked Samuel.

"I'd like that," said Jeremiah.

Samuel was already kneeling. He bowed his head while continuing to hold the colors up.

"Lord, please save Jeremiah. He's a brave man. But should you choose to take him today, may he see you in heaven before this battle is over. Amen," said Samuel. Another soldier rushed up and yelled the man's name. "Jeremiah!" Life left Jeremiah's eyes. Another had died for the cause of liberty.

Samuel rose and lifted the colors high. He continued to move forward and could see what looked like the boys from Enoch Poor's New Hampshire brigade at the center of the action. They were in the thick of it at the southern end of the farm. Colonel Scammell's regiment was taking heavy losses along with Colonel Reed's.

Then, around dinner time, he heard what sounded like orders being shouted in a language he didn't understand. Samuel figured it had to be the mercenary forces of the Hessian Baron Friedrich Adolf Riedesel moving in from the east side of the battle with colors flying, and Hessian soldiers singing hymns in German.

The sound and sight of the fresh and well-organized soldiers was intimidating. The newly engaged Hessians allowed the redcoats to retreat.

The sun was setting lower in the sky and Continental soldiers fell back to the protection of their works on Bemis Heights.

On this day, the King's forces had held their own against greater numbers. But the fields were scattered with the dead as the smoke of battle began to clear.

Most of those on the ground, and not moving, wore red. Samuel was thankful he had survived another battle that nearly a hundred other patriots had not. He was saddened to hear the mournful cries of dozens of wounded soldiers. Most would survive, but some would have limbs amputated, and their lives would be forever changed.

Samuel thought it could soon happen to him. Word streamed into camp that the British had lost some four hundred souls with nearly double that number wounded and the redcoats had failed to break through the rebel lines.

Samuel wondered how either side would have the strength to fight again tomorrow if the regulars launched another attack. Samuel's face was covered in the remnants of black powder smoke that had clung to his sweaty face.

He dropped onto his bedroll exhausted and quickly fell asleep, forgetting he hadn't eaten since morning.

He awoke to the smell of something cooking on a fire and the morning sun beaming into his eyes. He was hungry. But that feeling was overwhelmed by the aching in his arms. He could also feel blisters on his hands from the hours of holding the colors in battle.

Reports of the dead and wounded patriots were coming in. Samuel's regiment lost Jedediah Adams and Nathaniel Moody from John Wiley's company. Of course, Samuel was there when Jeremiah died. A few others from Jackson's regiment were wounded. Others killed in action or wounded were mostly scattered across several other regiments. But soldiers from Scammell's New Hampshire regiment, and those of Reid and Cilley, suffered the most dead, and wounded.

As the sun rose higher in the sky, it seemed there would be no further fighting this day. Samuel had a tough time getting Jeremiah's death out of his mind as well as the images and sounds of the wounded writhing in pain.

Thankfully, he didn't have to worry about Elisha. He was back home on furlough and married by now, and soon to be a father.

As for the wounded, he was glad some of them would be cared for by Colonel Jackson's wife. She was a sweet woman with a big heart. All her sons survived unharmed.

Samuel knew he had to prepare himself and the men under his command for the next battle. The fighting could come at any moment depending on the actions of British General Burgoyne.

Questions rolled through Samuel's mind. Would more redcoat regiments show up to fight? Would more loyalist troops do the same? And there was always the nagging concern of whether God's providence would guide him safely through another battle. He, like any other soldier, was one musket ball, cannon shot, or bayonet charge away from death.

Would his luck finally run out? There was also the scourge of disease to battle. Samuel had seen and known men who died from smallpox or other maladies. He pushed those concerns to the back of his mind and prepared to organize his day.

When he saw Captain Cleaveland headed his way he knew all of it would soon be clear. Samuel removed his hat in salute.

"Good morning, Ensign Benjamin," said Cleaveland.

"Good morning, Captain," replied Samuel.

"You carried out your duties bravely, Samuel. I witnessed it myself. Several of the soldiers also told me your leadership during the battle spurred them on to stay in the fight. I'm going to recommend you receive a lieutenant's commission," said Cleaveland.

"Sir, thank you, sir!" answered Samuel.

"If Colonel Jackson agrees, it'll take a few days," replied Cleaveland.

The Captain also passed along orders, telling Samuel to ask each soldier how much gunpowder and lead they had left, and what they would need to prepare for another day of fighting.

The regiment was running short of lead. There was a possibility they would need to remove the lead window sashes from nearby homes again to make more musket balls.

Samuel needed to make sure the men in his company thoroughly cleaned and oiled their muskets. He didn't understand why some men needed to be reminded their lives depended on a musket that would fire in battle.

Minor wounds also needed to be treated so they didn't become a bigger issue.

Samuel assigned a few soldiers to gather laundry so the camp followers could do their duty. And he was constantly on the lookout to make sure those prone to drink too much were not abusing their ration of rum. That was especially true after a day of hellish battle. Getting drunk was just the way some soldiers responded to the horrors of war. Samuel didn't know why drinking too much didn't plague him. He was just glad it didn't. He chose to go to God with his pain.

"Samuel!" Jonathan greeted his brother. Samuel sought out Wigglesworth's regiment when he had a moment from his duties.

"Jonathan, I'm glad to see you suffered no injury," replied Samuel.

"I was lucky. Our brigade has three hundred killed or wounded. We exchanged fire with the bloody backs for six hours. I lost a couple of friends," said Jonathan sadly.

"I heard about Glover's brigade. That's why I came looking to see if you were okay. I'm relieved to see you brother," said Samuel.

"I'm relieved to be alive," said Jonathan.

The two shook hands and chatted for a few moments. When they parted, both wondered if the other would survive the next battle.

The next day came and still there was no movement from the redcoats. Although patriot scouts reported the British were strengthening their two redoubts. (71)

One day turned to another of restocking ammunition and supplies and drilling. Nearly three weeks passed. It appeared the regulars were waiting for reinforcements. And British deserters told of supplies running short as well as a shortage of regulars able to fight.

Patriot forces had swelled to some 13,000 men. Samuel and his commanders talked openly of the possibility that they could rout the regulars.

On the afternoon of October 3, Samuel spotted Colonel Jackson headed his way, along with Captain Cleaveland.

Samuel removed his hat and bowed his head as the Colonel and Captain drew closer.

"Ensign Benjamin," said Jackson.

"Yes sir," replied Samuel.

"I'm going to consider you for a lieutenant's commission. But you'll have to be patient. You showed leadership and bravery during battle last month," said Jackson in praise.

"Thank you, sir. I just did my duty sir," said Samuel.

"Captain Cleaveland put in a good word for you. Keep up the good work, Ensign," ordered the Colonel.

"Yes sir. It is my honor, sir," replied Samuel.

"Sir, if I may, I am glad your sons were all unharmed," said Samuel.

"Thank you, Ensign. I am proud of them," replied Jackson.

"Cleaveland tells me you can write. Can you write reports and complete muster rolls?" asked Jackson.

"Yes sir," said Samuel.

"That will weigh in your favor. Carry on, Ensign."

"Thank you, sir," said Samuel.

Samuel returned his hat to his head as the Colonel walked away. (72) (73)

Samuel held his excitement in check. But inside he was bursting with pride. As he drifted off to sleep that night, he felt confident in his future. But Samuel's gut was telling him there was trouble in the air.

On the morning of October 7, Samuel awoke to the sound of a cannon shot and a drummer again beating out Reveille. The artillery fire meant they needed to be prepared to fight again.

Then, around noon, patriot pickets spotted a British force amassing on a wheat field below the Continental positions. Commanders, knowing another battle was likely to happen, promoted Francis Tufts of Captain Wiley's company to ensign.

Tufts would now help carry the colors, along with Samuel and the other ensigns. Samuel's regiment was ordered to ready their muskets and cartridge boxes and fall in. Samuel readied his own musket and cartridge box as well as his sword, which he had kept battle sharp.

The drummers played "The Assembly." Once again, Samuel's gut had not betrayed him. Samuel readied himself and urged the soldiers in the company to stay alert.

Word spread through the officer corps that the King's Brigadier-General Simon Fraser was advancing with three columns and ten cannons toward the patriots' left. General Gates responded by ordering Colonel Daniel Morgan to launch a flanking movement against the Light Infantry on the British right farthest from the river.

General Enoch Poor's New Hampshire troops moved against the Grenadiers on the British left. And that meant Samuel's regiment, the 8th Massachusetts, as well as the 2nd and 9th, would be joined by the First Canadian Regiment and two New Hampshire militia regiments, all under the command of General Ebenezer Learned at the center. The scouts said the middle appeared to be where the Braunschweiger mercenaries would attack.

Shortly after two in the afternoon, Samuel heard the first shots fired, including the booms of cannons. It sounded like it came from the left, where the first of the King's forces were gathered. They must have spotted the New Hampshire troops below them and opened fire with cannons and muskets. Then he could hear musket fire coming from another part of the battlefield. That would be Morgan and Major Dearborn's men.

Then the captains in Jackson's regiment ordered the drummers to signal "To Arms," and Samuel and the other officers moved forward with the first line of soldiers with the colors in front. Samuel thought it odd that General Arnold had not been given a command for this battle. But his job was not to question orders, only to follow them.

Commanders ordered the drummers and fifers to signal a musket volley. The shrill of a half-dozen fifers rang out while drumsticks rolled across the deerskin drumheads.

Samuel spotted enemy soldiers lined up for battle across the field. Then Captain Cleaveland ordered the line to halt. And ordered Samuel to command the first volley of musket fire.

"Prime and load, men!" shouted Samuel. Samuel watched the soldiers around him each grab a cartridge from the box slung on their shoulder, tear off the top of the cartridge with their teeth, and pour black powder into the pans of their muskets. The soldiers then poured the rest of the powder and a musket ball down their barrels and stuck the empty paper at the mouth. Next, they pulled out their ramrods and shoved the empty paper cartridges to the bottom of the barrels on top of the powder and ball, removed the ramrods, and slipped them back into their musket thimbles. Samuel raised the colors and shouted, "Make Ready! Aim! Fire!"

The rippling sound of dozens of muskets firing at once rumbled in Samuel's ears. Smoke drifted across the firing line. And with that, Samuel's regiment was engaged in the battle.

He saw a couple of enemy soldiers fall. Then suddenly Samuel heard the pounding of a horse's hooves and yelling. It was amazing!

There was General Arnold on horseback urging the soldiers forward toward what appeared to be Braunschweiger troops. The men all shouted, "Huzzah!" and cheered on Arnold.

The patriot soldiers roared forward, formed a new line, and fired again. The field was filling with smoke. Enemy cannons blasted away and tore through the patriot lines wounding a couple of soldiers.

Samuel spotted some of Captain Varnum's soldiers moving toward the front, including a negro soldier from Amesbury he had spoken with during drilling a few days prior. (74)

Private Joseph Demus moved bravely toward the action. Then Samuel spotted Lieutenant Aldrich Wiley in front of him yelling commands. Samuel moved forward with Captain Cleaveland, making sure the soldiers held the line and continued the attack.

Then a massive volley of musket fire erupted from the Braunschweiger line. Samuel heard a loud groan in front of him and Lieutenant Wiley dropped to his knees.

Oh no, thought Samuel. He rushed forward. Wiley had a bloody hole on the left side of his chest. Wiley looked at Samuel and dropped to his side, still cradling his musket in his right arm.

"Hang in there, friend," said Samuel.

"It stings, Samuel," replied Aldrich.

"You are wounded, my friend. You were brave to be in front, and perhaps you have also spared my life. I'll have some of our men carry you to safety," said Samuel.

"If I shall not survive this grievous wound, let my wife, Marcy, know of my great love for her. I am assured through God's grace we shall meet in heaven," the Lieutenant replied in a faltering voice.

Then, in an instant, Lieutenant Wiley stopped breathing and slumped over. It again hit Samuel that the musket ball that had just killed Wiley could have easily killed him. The shot was likely an attempt to take down the regiment's colors. But Samuel hadn't long to think on it.

General Arnold was trying to rally the patriots who had fallen back after the Braunschweigers fired. The Continental soldiers rallied. Samuel now stood alongside the colors and in front of Captain Cleaveland, and the soldiers all moved forward into firing position. This time Samuel heard the Captain issue the commands.

"Prime and load, men!" yelled Cleaveland.

Samuel held the colors at his side and readied his musket.

"Make ready!" shouted Cleaveland. "Aim!"

Samuel spotted an enemy soldier through the smoke and aimed for him.

"Fire!" shouted Cleaveland.

The soldier Samuel sighted at the end of his musket fell to the ground. Samuel's was not the only successful shot.

The roar of dozens of firing patriot muskets ripped across the field and cut down several Brunswick soldiers at once.

The wheat field continued to fill with smoke as musket volleys from the patriots and the enemy led to a back-and-forth fight for territory.

Captain Cleaveland again shouted the commands for another patriot volley.

"Make ready! Aim! Fire!"

This time, more Braunschweiger soldiers dropped in bloody heaps to the ground sending the survivors into retreat. The Continental force moved forward, and Samuel could see redcoats and bluecoats running back toward their two fortifications and a couple of cabins on Freeman's farm.

Arnold rode off toward the larger redoubt. Samuel's regiment and the others in Learned's brigade marched toward the other small British fort. (75)

Samuel stepped over the bodies of enemy soldiers as he drew closer to the makeshift fort. The enemy troops made a brave stand to keep control of the cabins. But Patriot muskets and bayonets quickly overwhelmed the Canadian militia.

Samuel moved forward to the left of the redoubt alongside the colors, glancing back to make sure Captain Cleaveland was still unharmed. Samuel and dozens of Continental soldiers, now in closer range, opened fire again on the Braunschweigers.

Samuel heard the whizzing of a musket ball past his head. Then another. He saw a tug on the flag that wasn't the wind. Sure enough, a hole in the colors. Ensign Taft had good luck. He wasn't hit. Undaunted, Samuel yelled for the soldiers around him to keep firing.

As the battle raged on, some of the patriot soldiers swept through the gap left by the retreating Canadian militia. Soon they surrounded the enemy soldiers in the redoubt and fired from behind. Patriot soldiers found themselves in hand-to-hand fights to the death.

A Brunswick soldier rushed toward Samuel uttering something in a foreign language. In an instant, Samuel dropped his musket, drew his sword, and dodged the man's bayonet with the flagpole, stabbing the soldier in the belly as Samuel stepped to his left.

Some of the men in his company failed to do the same and were run through. Still, the patriots outnumbered the enemy in the makeshift fort and the end appeared near.

General Arnold again appeared on Samuel's left—still on his horse. Arnold rode into the back of the fortification yelling for a continued attack, and then Samuel heard another musket boom from the enemy ranks.

At nearly the same time, he heard Arnold cry out in pain and his horse whimper. Samuel's eyes followed the noise. Arnold had been shot in the left leg. The undersized black steed Arnold rode crumpled underneath him and appeared to be mortally wounded, lying in a heap.

Arnold was pinned under the horse, and patriot soldiers rushed to help free him. But the General's leg appeared to be broken.

Soon the Braunschweigers in the redoubt were overrun and falling or retreating. Samuel ran into the redoubt and yelled, "Huzzah!" Soon other patriot soldiers joined in. The remaining Braunschweigers quickly dropped their muskets and surrendered.

Samuel saw what appeared to be a Brunswick senior officer face up on the ground with a wound to his chest, his eyes eerily still open but lifeless. He held a bloody saber in his hand.

The officer had two gold epaulettes, a red waist sash, and a red cockade on his hat. Samuel thought he was likely a colonel. As he surveyed the scene around the officer, he was confused. There were four Brunswick soldiers with stab wounds in their blue coats. Those wounds clearly hadn't come from the swords of patriot officers since Samuel was one of the first officers inside the fortification.

One of the enemy soldiers seemed to be explaining in broken English that he had shot his commanding officer after the senior soldier started killing the men around him. They were apparently trying to retreat. "Breymann!" the man shouted.

Captain Cleaveland heard the commotion and rushed over. "I think he's trying to tell us the dead officer is Lieutenant Colonel Heinrich von Breymann," said Cleaveland. "The scouts said this redoubt is named after him." (76) (77) Samuel thought the officer got what was coming to him. There was no shame in retreating from an overwhelming force.

And this day, finally, the overwhelming force was the Continental Army and militia. Most of Burgoyne's forces had already retreated and the October sun was setting at half past five. The battle was quickly winding down as darkness approached.

Samuel had kept his captain from harm. Now he and other patriot soldiers faced the grim task of gathering the bodies of their fallen compatriots as they returned to their own fortifications.

Samuel and two others found Aldrich and carried him to where commanders wanted to bury the dead. Samuel struggled to walk away from Aldrich's lifeless body. The morning would bring the solemn duty of digging shallow graves that Samuel feared would not keep wolves or other animals from eventually digging up the remains.

It was just another horrible result of war. That the dead, in their noble sacrifice, would not be given a noble burial. Life, so quickly snuffed out by a musket ball, bayonet, or sword, now gone. And what remained of a person who once had a soul, family, and friends, would now be covered with a few inches of dirt and grass in an unmarked grave far from home.

No one who loved the soldier would ever know exactly where they lay. And yet, they died for liberty. Those patriots fought for a future someone else would live. They all knew the danger when they picked up their muskets and entered the deadly fray.

As for the slain Brunswick soldiers, Samuel looked at their bodies in the fading light and thought that they died on foreign soil, not even for their own country or cause, their blood spilled by the selfish hands of some Brunswick royal who loaned them out to King George for a price. Those soldiers would never see their homeland again. Their families would never know exactly how they died or where. They would simply never return, existing only in memories, and the hope that they would be reunited with the people they love in heaven.

The walk across the bloodied wheat field revealed an awful truth about the King's forces. Four times as many died for him as died for the new thirteen United States of America.

The casualty counts started to come in. Roughly a hundred dead on the patriot side with more than two hundred wounded. Samuel searched for Captain Cleaveland once they were back in camp. He spotted the captain on his knees praying next to a campfire and put a hand on his shoulder. The captain lifted his head.

"I fear I will lose one of my best after today, Samuel," said Cleaveland.

"Samuel Durant from Milton is gravely wounded. And our regiment lost one of our corporals, Nathan Hale of Great Barrington as well as Samuel Todd of Kittery, also dead. And Able Getchell of Berwick. He died as we moved on the Brunswick redoubt. One of the other men who was with him said he was killed by cannon grapeshot. The shot ripped off his head and it fell between his feet.[19] I don't know how Getchell's wife and children will manage their farm now. (78) It's awful tough, Samuel, and I've made it my purpose to know and remember their names."

"Their names should not be forgotten," Samuel agreed.

"Lieutenant Wiley died right in front of me. He likely saved my life, blocking a musket ball that could have found me," said Samuel solemnly.

"I've already written down other names of the dead from our regiment. Abraham Ames, Joshua Eaton, from Reading. Another lieutenant, Ezekiel Goodridge, of Amesbury. Matthew Pease of Norwich. And George Lord of Hartford is barely alive," said Samuel. (79)

"I hear the New Hampshire boys were in the worst of it again. Scammell's regiment along with Cilley's, Alden's, and Reid's lost the most," responded Cleaveland. "A few from New York also died. The troops from Connecticut fared better." (80)

"At least most of us will live to fight another day. I must report to Colonel Jackson now. Take care, Captain," said Samuel.

"You too, Ensign," replied Cleaveland.

---

[19] Grapeshot was a particularly brutal weapon made of lead or iron balls packed in a canvas bag or tied around a rod that ripped apart flesh at short range.

Samuel walked back to his camp thinking about what he'd seen and heard today—the booms of artillery fire echoed in his mind.

He silently thanked God that more of his fellow soldiers hadn't died. It seemed odd to think it. Because the loved ones of those who perished would have no thanks or solace in knowing others lived on.

Samuel reached his tent and dropped onto his bedroll. He closed his eyes but struggled to fall asleep. He kept thinking about Aldrich, the blood, and the eyes of the Brunswick officer. What madness would cause a leader to turn on his own men who were just trying to survive?

He turned his thoughts to Tabitha. Perhaps he could find peace and rest in thinking about her eyes, her voice, the way she blushed when he told her how beautiful she was.

Samuel awoke in the dark. The cool of the October night had descended on the camp, and he felt it on his face. A nightmare had interrupted his sleep. He was stepping over the bodies, and one of the fallen soldiers called his name. Tabitha, he had to think about Tabitha. Thoughts of her had helped him fall asleep. He needed her to save him again from the awful thoughts. I miss you so, Tabitha, the sound of your sweet voice, the rosewater fragrance when I hold you close…

Morning light. Samuel heard the voices of two men talking. He wasn't the only one who had struggled to rest. It was still early and it was raining.

Soon company drummer Samuel Wiley would beat Reveille. The drummer was no relation to Aldrich. Wiley was just a common last name in Massachusetts. But thinking of the surname made him think about Aldrich again. Samuel knew Aldrich was married. So, the King's fight against the rebels had created yet another grieving widow. Somewhat selfishly, Samuel hoped his Tabitha would avoid the pain and sorrow now felt by so many other patriot lovers. He'd have to write Tabitha soon to let her know he had survived this latest battle unharmed. Word of another encounter with the redcoats would soon reach Massachusetts along with an account of more killed from their colony.

But first he, the captain, and other officers would have to assign some soldiers the dismal task of laying their dead to rest. If it kept raining, some of the burials would have to wait. Samuel informed Captain Cleaveland that he would personally write to Aldrich's family. His first task of the day would be to find a dry place to craft a letter of condolence to Aldrich's widow.

> October 8, 1777,
> Stillwater, New York
> Dear Mrs. Wiley,
> This is the most solemn of notes as I lay my pen to paper. It is with great regret that I inform you of your brave husband's death in battle. I fear my words will fall woefully short in providing consolation for your untimely loss and the great grief which you are now undoubtedly suffering upon hearing of Lieutenant Wiley's death. I only hope you will find some comfort in knowing he died while leading his men in the cause of liberty in which I know he so greatly believed. I was with him when he fell, and his last words expressed great love for you. I only hoped I would not have to deliver them. But alas his wound from a musket ball was too severe. He also told me he was confident, by God's grace, he would see you in heaven. I hope the Lord will ease your pain. The book of Matthew tells us "Blessed are those who mourn, for they shall be comforted." I pray those words will find themselves true for you and all who held Aldrich dear.
> My deepest sympathies, Ensign Samuel Benjamin, 8th Massachusetts

Samuel felt great remorse and guilt in writing the letter. But he knew it was the right thing to do as he was the last to speak with

Aldrich. He had a hard time escaping the sound of Aldrich's groan and the look in his eyes as life was slipping away.

Samuel soon learned he would spend the day organizing and overseeing some of the burial parties, and confirming the names of the fallen. He would make sure the first to be buried would be his fellow officer.

He couldn't help but wonder if someday the burden of burying his own body would fall on his fellow soldiers. Samuel decided he wanted to help dig the grave for Lieutenant Wiley. He rounded up a handful of men and shovels, and in the rain, they headed to where the bodies of the soldiers were laid. (81)

Lieutenant Wiley rested in a long line of the fallen. A few of the bodies bore the signs of being hit by cannonballs. It was a gory display of liberty's price. Limbs missing. One man's body nearly cut in half. Samuel tried to stay on task and not let his emotions take hold.

He ordered three of his men to lift Wiley's remains and carry the officer about fifty feet, where they would begin digging a hole. Samuel held his shovel in both hands, and with a downward thrust pierced the top layer of grass and soil, now softened a bit by the drizzle. The grim duty was underway. The other soldiers silently joined in digging.

With each shovel full of dirt and stones, Samuel thought of Wiley's last words. The embrace of a wife he would never feel again, the coos of babies he would never hear or hold, the sunrises and sunsets he would never see.

War is a demon that tries to steal the souls of both the living and the dead.

Samuel and the five others made quick work of digging the rectangular hole. They carefully lowered the uniformed soldier's body into the dark ground along with his sword and tricorn hat. Each man began to shovel dirt back on top of the Lieutenant. Soon only a mound of dirt marked the grave of a brave soldier. Samuel tried to remember the words he had heard Reverend Jacob Cushing speak at a funeral back in Waltham. Then Samuel spoke.

"Men, let's remove our hats and pray for our fallen friend. Lord, we commit Lieutenant Aldrich Wiley to the ground, ashes to ashes, dust to dust." And then Samuel allowed the twenty-third Psalm to roll across his tongue.

> The LORD is my shepherd. I shall not want. He maketh me to lie down in green pastures. He leadeth me beside still waters. He restoreth my soul. He leadeth me in the paths of righteousness for his name's sake. Yea, though I walk through the valley of the shadow of death, I will fear no evil, for thou art with me. Thy rod and thy staff they comfort me…"

That was all he could recall.

"Heavenly Father, may Lieutenant Wiley spend eternity with you. Amen," Samuel ended his prayer, lifted his head, and opened his eyes.

He ordered the burial party back to return to the row of bodies and continue with burying their fellow soldiers. The patriot burial parties would also help bury the British soldiers.

Samuel felt tired in a way he hadn't experienced before. It was not so much physical as it was a gnawing feeling that seemed to drag him down.

He could see Joseph Coolidge on the ground bleeding at Lexington. And during that same battle Samuel, for the first time, lifted his musket, and ended a redcoat's life. He pictured a dying Jeremiah Dole at Freeman's farm, not far from where they buried Lieutenant Wiley. The bodies, the blood. He had to stop it. He had to stop thinking about it.

"Ensign Benjamin!" Captain Cleaveland called.

"Yes sir," Samuel replied.

"I need you to round up a few more men to help bury our dead," said Cleaveland.

"I'll see to it, Captain," replied Samuel.

Their uniforms were quickly drenched. The only saving grace was that their woolen coats stayed relatively warm even when wet.

It took hours and hours to dig the holes and bury the fallen. The work lasted until dusk and there would be more digging to do the next day.

Amid the digging, scouts reported that the King's soldiers apparently wanted no more of the Continental Army's musket balls. The redcoats had already retreated several miles and appeared to be trying to escape north to Saratoga to avoid the much larger patriot force.

A cold, hard rain was slowing Burgoyne's battered forces, who were short on supplies and morale. The rain kept pounding on October 9. General Gates kept his Continental Army troops dry, giving him time to organize a chase after the King's forces.

The rain stopped on the tenth and the pursuit was underway. Following the British path of retreat, Gates discovered Burgoyne had left behind some four hundred wounded at a makeshift hospital. Burgoyne also left behind a letter he gave the doctor-in-charge asking Gates to take care of his wounded.

Samuel's regiment continued their burial duties while Gates sent an advance artillery unit ahead to begin blasting the British camp.

On the morning of October 11, Gates ordered Nixon's and Glover's Brigades to attack the British defenses from the south and east. The King's forces were surrounded. But not without a fight.

The patriot forces faced continued musket fire from Burgoyne's troops. The struggle to avoid surrender would last until the fourteenth. Word spread through the patriot officer corps that Burgoyne had sent an officer to begin negotiations. Gates demanded immediate surrender. Then the competing commanders agreed on an armistice. Burgoyne finally signed terms on the sixteenth and the next day rode to Gates's headquarters to surrender his sword.

Burgoyne surrendered nearly 6,000 redcoats. (82) Samuel's regiment shouted, "Huzzah!" over and over when hearing news of the surrender.

Colonel Jackson's regiment was ordered to march to Albany and set up camp while awaiting orders. Samuel helped ready the troops for the march. Some of the patriot wounded could not be moved and died over the next few days.

Glover's troops would serve as guards to march Burgoyne and his troops to Cambridge.

The October weather began to hint of winter 'round the corner. A snowstorm blanketed the camp on the twenty-first. (83) The cold made Samuel wish he could hold Tabitha and they could enjoy each other's warmth.

By the end of the month, word spread through the officer corps that General Washington had written to Gates and requested twenty regiments be sent to support Washington at Philadelphia. His Excellency's army had suffered defeat at Brandywine Creek trying to keep British General Sir William Howe's army of 15,000 from invading the patriot capital of Philadelphia. Thankfully, the patriots managed a successful retreat without a devastating loss. And so, the march to support Washington would soon begin. (84)

Samuel thought it a good idea to write Tabitha again because word of the battles at Stillwater would certainly reach Boston and the surrounding countryside. If he didn't get a letter into the hands of a courier now, who knew when he'd have another chance.

October 21, 1777,
Albany
Dear Tabitha,
As you are reading this, you'll know the most important truth of which we can both celebrate. I am still alive. I trust word has reached Waltham of our great victories at Saratoga. You have likely also heard some in our regiment died. Thankfully, my brother Jonathan was unharmed and has since been promoted from corporal to sergeant in the 13th Regiment. I am proud of him. One of those men we did lose was a Lieutenant—Aldrich Wiley. He fell to a musket ball not ten paces in front of me. I know not why he was taken, and I was spared. I suffer a guilt from it. He was no lesser man than me. He was a brave and honorable fellow with a wife who is now set to grieving. I had the great honor of praying with him before he passed from this life to the next. I shared as much in the grim letter I wrote to his widow informing her of the terrible loss. It could have been you in her place and I dread the thought of it. I tell you my sweetheart we must give thanks to God every day we have each other. Our greatest enemy is still sickness. Smallpox and dysentery continue to strike many of my fellow soldiers harder than any redcoat has. There is someone dying every day. We received orders from his Excellency to join the main army near Philadelphia. We do not know if General Washington is planning a greater engagement with the enemy. The nights are turning colder and we know not where we shall spend the winter. I hear the drummer beating out a call for assembly so this is all I can write for now my love. You are the joy of my heart and the source of my deepest longings. I'm glad to know you are keeping me in your prayers as I keep you in mine.

You are always on my mind and forever in my heart. –

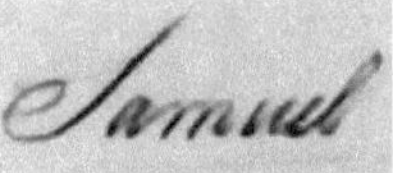

Chapter 10
The Wedding

Tabitha was beside herself when Papa returned from Cambridge with the mail. She heard the door slam, ran to the kitchen, and could tell by the look in her father's eyes that there was a letter from Samuel. He simply handed it to her with a smile and said nothing. He knew she'd disappear into the parlor to read it alone.

Tabitha sat in the chair by the window, carefully broke the wax seal, and unfolded the pages. The first thing she saw was "October 21."

Thank God it was dated after the battles near Saratoga. And when she read Samuel's first words, her eyes filled with tears. "I am still alive."

Those words were the happiest she'd read in a long time. She pulled the handkerchief out of her dress pocket and dabbed at the streams of joy now flowing down both cheeks. Yes, they had all heard of the victory at Saratoga and the British surrender. But until she received Samuel's letter, she wouldn't allow herself the peace of knowing he had survived the battle unharmed.

Her joy was soon tempered by the story of Aldrich Wiley dying right in front of Samuel. Oh, the horrible things Samuel had witnessed. And she felt so sad for Lieutenant Wiley's widow.

Tabitha didn't think she could bear losing Samuel. She realized more than ever how much she loved him. How long would this cruel war go on? Why couldn't the King just let the colonies have their liberty? If only she could be in Samuel's arms right now. Tabitha wished he had come home on furlough like her sister's sweetheart. But she knew Elisha was only allowed to come home because he was going to marry Martha next week.

Martha was so excited. Excited to be married and excited to be a mother. The town clerk had already posted the wedding date—November 17.

Would Samuel soon propose and come home for good? Tabitha told herself she needed to set aside her worries about Samuel to help Martha plan for her wedding. Tabitha was helping sew her sister's wedding dress and bridal quilt along with her sister Eunice and the family's sewing circle friends. She had already made it a little bigger to make room for her soon-to-arrive nephew or niece.

Martha and Elisha had chosen to get married on a Monday with guidance from the New England wedding rhyme and Reverend Cushing's schedule.

"Monday for health, Tuesday for wealth, Wednesday the best day of all; Thursday for losses, Friday for crosses, And Saturday no luck at all." (85)

Marrying for health seemed to make the most sense given the war, Elisha's captaincy, and the coming baby. Elisha would return to his duty after the marriage was consummated and the new year arrived, which worried Martha terribly.

Reverend Cushing had agreed to marry them at the Livermore home. Even though Tabitha was tucked away in the parlor, the home was noisy. Her six younger siblings were rattling about. The four youngest were chasing each other for tag right outside the window and making faces at Tabitha while Moses and Lydia were arguing about something silly in the kitchen. While it was distracting right now, Tabitha loved the joy and commotion of her younger brothers and sisters. She dreamed of children of her own with Samuel someday.

She read the letter for the fourth time and when finished, carefully folded it back up. She held it to her breast and whispered a prayer.

"Dear Lord, please protect Samuel. I worry about him so much. Please help calm my fears. Please, God, bring him home safely. I will do my best to trust in your will, Lord. In Jesus' name I pray. Amen."

Tabitha lifted her head and realized she was crying again. She dabbed at the tears, stood up, walked to her bedroom, and tucked the letter into her dresser along with the others from Samuel.

She shared the room with Martha, Lydia, and Ruth while the five boys crowded into another. She needed to busy her mind with helping Mother with chores. She also needed to work on Martha's dress. The days passed quickly after Samuel's letter arrived, and a few guests crowded into the parlor along with Elisha and Martha. Today was the day.

Reverend Cushing began, "Dearly beloved, we are gathered together here in the sight of God, and in the face of this company, to join together this Man and this Woman in holy Matrimony; which is commended of Saint Paul to be honorable among all men: and therefore is not by any to be entered into unadvisedly or lightly; but reverently, discreetly, advisedly, soberly, and in the fear of God. Into this holy estate these two persons present come now to be joined. If any man can show just cause, why they may not lawfully be joined together, let him now speak, or else hereafter forever hold his peace."

Reverend Cushing paused. Then he continued.

"Elisha, wilt thou have this Woman to be thy wedded wife, to live together after God's ordinance in the holy estate of Matrimony? Wilt thou love her, comfort her honor, and keep her in sickness and in health; and, forsaking all others, keep thee only unto her, so long as ye both shall live?" asked Reverend Cushing.

"I will," replied Elisha.

Then Reverend Cushing asked, "Martha, wilt thou have this man to be thy wedded husband, to live together after God's ordinance in the holy estate of Matrimony? Wilt thou obey him, and serve him, love, honor, and keep him in sickness and in health; and, forsaking all others, keep thee only unto him, so long as ye both shall live?"

"I will," Martha answered.

"Who giveth this Woman to be married to this Man?" asked Reverend Cushing.

"I do," said Martha's father.

Reverend Cushing took Martha's hand from her father and joined it with Elisha's right hand.

Tabitha began to cry, and more than ever wished Samuel was sitting beside her.

As the vows continued, Tabitha could not help but wish it was she and Samuel exchanging vows right now. After all, she turned twenty in June. She was no longer a child. And she was no longer listening intently to what was being said as her mind wandered to worrying about where Samuel was at this moment. Was he cold? Was he safe? She could see his face, her hands in his, and she remembered what it felt like to have his arms around her. She could feel the warmth of his body, the tenderness of his touch. She ached for him. She had to snap out of it.

Tabitha returned from her thoughts to Reverend Cushing speaking. "For as much as Elisha and Martha have consented together in holy wedlock, and have witnessed the same before God and this company, and thereto have given and pledged their troth, each to the other, and have declared the same by joining hands; I pronounce that they are Man and Wife, In the Name of the Father, and of the Son, and of the Holy Ghost. Amen," Reverend Cushing finished his prayer.

Tabitha was so happy for Martha and Elisha. Please, God, keep both Elisha and Samuel safe.

Chapter 11
From Philadelphia to Valley Forge

Samuel removed his diary from his haversack and prepared his quill and ink. It had been a struggle to keep the small book dry and undamaged, given the rain and snow. The leather cover was now stained from various and assorted assaults. Thankfully, the metal clasp and leather strap held the book, which was barely bigger than his hand, closed. It was about the same size as the Bible he carried. Both were now well worn and greatly treasured. And soon he would need to acquire another book in which to write. He was running out of blank pages.

In a few hours the troops would board the fleet of bateaux and head down the Hudson toward New Jersey. On the twenty-first of November, Learned's Brigade, including Samuel's regiment, arrived at White Marsh in Pennsylvania and set up camp.

They were now just a dozen miles from Philadelphia and the next British general they would face. The King's forces had taken control of the city and sent the Continental Congress fleeing west to York. That made the Susquehanna River a line of defense against the enemy.

Samuel wondered now if Washington would dare face the King's army head on and try to expel the redcoats from Philly. But it became clear to Samuel and the other officers that Washington wanted to dig in along the well-fortified hills and remain on the defensive.

In early December, Washington's spies in the city learned that Howe was readying his army to march against the Continental forces. Washington sent word through the officers to have their troops at the ready to defend the lines.

Captain Cleaveland assembled Samuel and the other officers to pass along the command to have pickets be on the lookout for British scouts.

Early on the morning of December 3, the whole army was ordered to form up for battle. On December 4, word came that Howe's army was on the move toward the patriots. (86)

Musket fire began the next day as the redcoats tested patriot defenses and eventually began firing cannons.

On the sixth, Howe tried to flank the patriot army. But Washington had sent Morgan's rifle corps along with militia from Maryland to head them off in thick woods. Neither Washington nor Howe was willing to risk it all in a full assault, and the back and forth skirmishing finally ended on the eighth.

The redcoats had killed roughly ninety patriots with roughly three dozen missing or captured. The Brits suffered nineteen killed, sixty wounded, and 238 soldiers deserted.

Howe sent his force of 10,000 marching back to Philadelphia for the winter. And Samuel received orders on the seventeenth of December that the entire army would begin marching to Valley Forge.

Samuel had never heard of the place. But it was along the Schuylkill River and within striking distance of Philadelphia and the redcoats.

General Washington also issued an order for the troops to honor a day of Thanksgiving and prayer to be held on the eighteenth. In all the colonies, the Congress had so directed following the patriot victory at Saratoga.

Being from Massachusetts, Samuel referred to it as Pilgrim's Day. But it wasn't much of a celebration. Clouds and rain filled the sky, while there was little to fill the soldiers' bellies. (86) Rainy weather also delayed the march to their winter home.

Finally, on the nineteenth, the sun appeared from behind the clouds and the march began on the Gulph Road with no food or drink for the journey.

Valley Forge was but a few miles from their camp and under better conditions it wouldn't have taken long to get there. But the rain from prior days made the road muddy and ill suited for the wagon wheels.

Samuel knew it would be a long, cold day with some 12,000 soldiers and hundreds of camp followers on the move. Sickness struck many of the men, who were covered only in worn-out clothes. Some had no shoes to protect their feet from the frozen ground.

One would not have imagined this mass of weary and poorly fed souls had beaten the King's army at Saratoga less than three months ago. Samuel feared this winter would challenge the strongest among them.

The 8th Massachusetts regiment reached Valley Forge after sundown. His brother Jonathan's regiment under Colonel Wigglesworth also marched to their new winter quarters. Many other members of the caravan straggled behind in the dark and camped alongside the road.

Hunger and thirst were the enemies this night with only fire cakes to fill the void. Samuel ran into another Samuel, who was a Lieutenant. Lieutenant Armstrong had also been writing in a diary. Both Samuels devoured the fire cakes like wild animals. (87) Then they pitched their linen tents and collapsed onto icy bedrolls. As Samuel's eyes closed, he envisioned Tabitha walking toward him, her arms outstretched reaching for his…

The screech of an owl. The squeal of prey dying in the dark.

Samuel awoke shivering. He heard the owl again. His body struggled for warmth. If the gore of war was not enough, now winter sought to defeat anyone who had survived musket balls and bayonets.

Samuel folded his cold, desperate hands in prayer.

"Dear Lord, would you not spare us now after you have delivered us from so many trials? Please, Father, bring us meat and bread that we might at least not starve as well as be chilled to the bone. Forgive my complaining and ungrateful heart. I thank you for carrying me this far. Please, Lord, let me rest and find hope in a new day. Amen," Samuel uttered in the blackness.

He sank into thoughts of Tabitha again. Oh, how many times his love for her had delivered peace and calm. And soon, sleep returned.

Samuel's eyes opened to the cannon shot from the artillery and the tune of Reveille. Morning light filtered through the opening in his tent. He slowly realized he had fallen back asleep after his prayer. Samuel wouldn't need to get dressed except for slipping on his muddy shoes. He had slept in his wool regimental coat and every other stitch he had worn during the march. He slipped off his woolen nightcap, found his tricorn hat, and slowly crawled out of his tent.

His hands found the ground covered in frost and some ice from the rain that had fallen two days before. His mouth was dry and wanting water. Finding a creek or spring would be the first task of the day. But he knew he shouldn't wander off alone. He would rally a few of his men to venture out of camp and see if there wasn't something closer than the Schuylkill River.

Samuel rounded up five privates to go with him in search of drinking water. They brought extra canteens that had been made by hand much in the same way barrels were made. The canteen maker cut wooden staves on angles so they formed a circle when pieced together. Oak hoops held the staves tight, and beeswax or paraffin prevented water from leaking. A cork was typically made from a tapered piece of wood and attached with a leather fob. Leather or linen straps wrapped around the canteen so it could be carried on a shoulder.

Samuel ordered the privates to return and carry more water back to camp once they had located a source. They would likely have to disinfect the water for drinking by mixing it with whiskey, rum, or vinegar. Next, Samuel and the other officers would assign picket duty, organize foraging parties to look for food, and make sure the men dug privy pits. Then drilling would begin to maintain discipline and readiness.

A supply of meat arrived in camp. But upon inspection it proved rancid and unfit to eat. That made foraging for cattle and other meat crucial to feeding the thousands of soldiers and camp followers.

General Washington also ordered that log huts be built for troops to help survive the winter. Captain Cleaveland showed Samuel and the other officers the order.

> The Colonels, or commanding officers of regiments, with their Captains, are immediately to cause their men to be divided into squads of twelve, and see that each squad have their proportion of tools, and set about a hut for themselves: And as an encouragement to industry and art, the General promises to reward the party in each regiment, which finishes their hut in the quickest, and most workmanlike manner, with twelve dollars—And as there is reason to believe, that boards, for covering, may be found scarce and difficult to be got—He offers One hundred dollars to any officer or soldier, who in the opinion of three Gentlemen, he shall appoint as judges, shall substitute some other covering, that may be cheaper and quicker made, and will in every respect answer the end. The Soldier's huts are to be of the following dimensions—viz.—fourteen by sixteen each—sides, ends and roofs made with logs, and the roof made tight with split slabs—or in some other way—the sides made tight with clay—fire-place made of wood and secured with clay on the inside eighteen inches thick, this fire-place to be in the rear of the hut—the door to be in the end next the street—the doors to be made of split oak-slabs, unless boards can be procured—Side-walls to be six and a half-feet high. (88)

Samuel read the order and knew there would be a lot of hard work ahead finding suitable trees, cutting them down as well as hauling the logs back to camp, and assembling the logs to follow His Excellency's orders. However, the men would be motivated to finish the huts as fast as possible because the weather was turning colder, and in the meantime, they'd all be sleeping in brush huts or wedge tents.

Meat continued to be scarce. Hunger was always nipping at the corners of each soldier's mind. But they wouldn't have long to ponder it.

Late on the twenty-second, Samuel's regiment was ordered to march to join Colonel Morgan's rifle unit. They didn't arrive until the wee hours of the morning. Samuel was told the enemy was testing their boundaries around Valley Forge.

The regiment marched to Springfield outside Philadelphia the next day and camped in Darby less than two miles from the redcoats.

The next morning, Christmas Eve day, redcoats fired on patriot scouts and put the regiment on alert. But the King's forces did nothing more.

Samuel's regiment didn't get a meal until they arrived at the Quaker meeting house in Springfield several hours after the sun set.

The Meeting House was a grand building made of stone that had survived many harsh winters and summer storms. Samuel was thankful for the kindness of the people there, who, while they were against the violence of war, were not against serving the soldiers.

Christmas Day came with no provisions. Samuel chuckled to himself with the thought that perhaps God wanted their stomachs empty so they would be forced to focus on filling their souls with His word instead.

Samuel was put in charge of picket duty while Lieutenant Armstrong and a party of men foraged in the countryside. They returned late in the afternoon with some fresh beef and salted meat, along with flour. Some hunting parties from other regiments had also gone out and brought back some fowl, which, put upon the campfires, was celebrated as if it was the finest Christmas meal the soldiers ever had. But Lieutenant Armstrong's reward was to be sent out on scouting duty until late that night.

The 8th Massachusetts continued to camp near the lines, and a heavy snow fell soon after Christmas. Then Major Hull ordered soldiers into small scouting parties to make sure the enemy wasn't flanking the rebels.

One of the parties was captured by one of the King's Light Horse groups. Some eighty privates became prisoners along with more than a half dozen officers. Only two soldiers escaped.

The King's advanced forces returned to Philadelphia for the winter with their prisoners. In response, Samuel's regiment left Darby and returned to the main camp at Valley Forge.

Now they could finally begin building their log huts. It was a slow effort. They had to haul logs and stone from a mile away. Samuel and several other officers would build their hut, and the privates would be separate.

The year was ending, and the weather was turning colder. Samuel felt blessed to have a tent even though it didn't provide much protection from the cold. Many of the thousands of soldiers slept only under blankets or brush huts made from the boughs of trees. Frost and snow covered the men who could find no relief from winter's icy fingers.

Samuel and his fellow commissioned officers dragged the fallen and trimmed trees through the snow while his thoughts often wandered to Tabitha. He should write her again and wish her a happy New Year. He wondered when he might receive a letter from her? She must have written. But how would she know where to send the letter? The army had been on the move, and until they arrived at Valley Forge, even he did not know how long they would stay put.

It wasn't until the tenth day of January that Samuel would finally abandon his wedge tent and move into the log hut. Samuel would lodge with seven other officers, including those from another company. (89)

They would sleep on beds of straw if they were lucky enough to find it by scouring farms in the surrounding countryside. Each hut had a place for a fire for heat and cooking. The huts often filled with smoke. And if one soldier was sick, the close quarters and dank air proved a perfect place for spreading disease. But what choice did they have? None, thought Samuel. You could take your chances outside in fresh air and risk freezing to death or at least be warmer and hope to survive typhus passed on by the fleas and lice that often invaded the huts.

Flu, typhoid, and dysentery also spread like wildfire among the roughly 2,000 little log buildings and the thousands of soldiers sheltering inside them. Those who were well enough rotated duties as sentries and scouts.

Daily drilling kept the soldiers alert and as ready for battle as was possible considering the dire conditions. Samuel and the other officers struggled to maintain their own morale, let alone encourage the soldiers to endure. Some soldiers slipped away in the night and hoped they were not caught deserting.

Those captured were sometimes hanged as was the case on January 10 with Virginian John Reily. General Washington wanted to send a message to other soldiers thinking about running off. (90) He ordered a detachment of a captain and forty men from each brigade to attend the execution. Some six hundred soldiers witnessed the hanging, including Samuel. His fellow officers didn't say a word about the execution as they returned to their camp. Samuel couldn't forget the image of Reily's body swinging. It was just another layer of horror to add to the stack of memories of fellow soldiers dying in battle. (91)

He forced his thoughts to turn to Tabitha as once again he sought peace in his love for her. Tabitha would save him once again as he lay down to sleep that night, in his new straw bed, in his new log home.

Samuel startled from his sleep. The image of Reily hanging dead from the rope was his first thought. He must have been dreaming. A nightmare, Samuel thought. As he lay there trying to gain his senses, he realized he felt fairly rested. A result of no longer sleeping in the deep freeze of winter on the ground. He wouldn't have to crawl out of his tent only to find even more cold, snow, frost, and ice.

The hut still smelled of smoke from the fire, which had burned out. And while it was not as warm in the hut as it had been earlier, it was much better than the chill of a wedge tent. He looked around in the dim light that bled through the opening in the top of the fieldstone chimney. It seemed he was the only one awake. His thoughts immediately shifted to Tabitha. His candle and flint were nearby. Samuel sparked the candle to flame and decided to write a quick letter before the busyness of the camp day began. He found his quill, ink, and parchment tucked in his haversack.

Camp Valley Forge
January 11, 1778
Dear Tabitha,
I'm writing this by candle as my fellow officers have not yet woke up. We are now able to escape the freezing nights in new log huts that took us more than a week to build. We are at a place called Valley Forge about twenty miles north-west of Philadelphia and the redcoats. General Washington wanted us to be safe from the ravages of winter here in Pennsylvania while we await warmer weather and our next brush with the enemy. I am glad to be out of my tent and removed from sleeping on the frozen ground. It is smoky in our hut once there are flames in the fireplace. But it is better to be warm and free from winter's cold. There are now thousands of us here in this camp. I tell you it is like a little city when the women and children are acounted for. Some of these poor souls who have signed on must be driven by an even greater passion for liberty than I. They come with little clothes and shoes that have long since fallen apart. Some leave bloody footprints behind when they move about camp. My dear it is a sorry sight. I don't know how some of them will survive the winter even with the log huts. I am more than ever thankful for the bounty coat and leather shoes the good Lord has provided. How are things on the farm? Sampson? We sure could have used his strength to drag logs through the snow. I hope he is proving useful to your father in chores. Some of the soldiers here are too weak or sick to be of much use. I fear now that we are all camped together again more will fall ill from dysentery or some other disease. I am much more careful with what I drink following my bout with dysentery. Elisha witnessed my illness before he headed home. It's a good thing he left camp when he did with the baby arriving just two weeks after the wedding. I am eager to

hear about the ceremony and baby Martha from you. It is fitting for her to be named after her mother. Elisha returned to camp with a diferent look about him now that he's married and a father of a daughter. He was so excited to talk about the baby. I wish I could have been there to witness it all. Those must have been happy days—a wedding and birth. I hope you will make me a married man and father some day. Though your sister must be filled with worry now that Elisha has returned from furlough. I see him here in camp from time to time when we drill with his 12th Regiment. Pray that we shall both return home safely once our duty to the army and our new United States is finished. Say hello to your mother and father from me and to all of our friends, and of course please deliver a hug to my mother from me when you are able. Your constantly in my thoughts my dearest Tabitha. You are the joy of my days and the peace in my heart when I lay down to rest each night. I love you beyond measure. Yours forever,

Samuel

Samuel carefully folded and addressed the letter. He brought the candle closer, dripped wax on the letter's flap, and sealed it. He hoped a courier would leave within a couple of days with the regimental mail.

Some soldiers chose to simply sneak out of camp in the dead of night and send themselves home. By the end of January, more than two hundred soldiers had deserted. In some ways, Samuel understood given the cold, the lack of food, and the disease that spread quickly because the soldiers were squeezed into the huts at night.

Adding to the misery, by early February some 4,000 soldiers didn't have warm clothes or shoes. (92) There was also nowhere to bathe, and encouraging the men to be clean was a constant struggle for Samuel and the other ensigns. The officers warned the privates not to throw food into the corners of their log huts. But some did it anyway to avoid a cold trip outside. That didn't help the scourge of disease in the camp. (93)

Despite the challenges, there was an excellent opportunity with the army amassed at Valley Forge to better train the soldiers. The Continental Congress sent Baron von Steuben.

Steuben arrived in America with a letter of introduction from Benjamin Franklin, who met Steuben while serving as Ambassador to France.

Steuben was a highly experienced soldier who had served as an officer in the Prussian army during the Seven Years War and had been an aide-de-camp to Frederick the Great. (94)

Word of Steuben's arrival in camp near the end of February spread quickly. His Excellency had ridden out of camp to personally meet and inspect Steuben.

Washington made him temporary Inspector General and asked him to train the soldiers. Steuben wrote drills that ended up in the hands of each officer, including Samuel. But unlike the earlier practice of having sergeants drill the men, Steuben wanted to conduct the training himself.

Steuben first trained the more than one hundred soldiers in Washington's personal guard to demonstrate proper technique. Then the training would extend to the brigades, regiments, and companies.

Samuel heard Steuben swear up a storm during training, which Samuel learned made him more likeable to the average soldier. His Excellency had scolded and disciplined soldiers who spoke profanities. But the General seemed deaf to Steuben's swearing.

As the weeks went by the army drilled more professionally. Samuel found that discipline improved when the soldiers felt pride in being better trained. And he was amazed at the continued high spirits of most of the men even with incredible challenges from typhus, dysentery, influenza, and typhoid.

Samuel received word that his youngest brother, John, had signed up with the army in February and would likely be heading to the camp at Valley Forge.

With the bulk of his army assembled in one place, General Washington directed commanders to continue smallpox inoculations. He thought it better to have soldiers sick from inoculations during winter camp than struggle with the disease when he would later need his army for battle.

Washington himself knew the horrors of the disease. He suffered from smallpox while in Barbados in his late teens and it left scars on his nose.

If the results of inoculation weren't challenge enough, food continued to be either plentiful or in short supply at Camp Valley Forge. Samuel and the other men quickly learned to eat well when good meat was available. Because the next week they might be back to eating fire cakes and salt beef. But most of the soldiers bore the difficulties well. That is, those who survived.

As spring brought warmer weather, more men were getting sick. Hundreds had already died, including a lieutenant in Captain Keith's company that Samuel had befriended on a foraging mission.

With great sadness, Samuel wrote in his diary on April 6, "Lieutenant Fisk was buried."[20]

Samuel thought it a peculiar set of circumstances that while the cold and snow were fading, and supplies of food and blankets had improved, more soldiers were getting sick.

Soon after Fisk was buried, his brother John arrived in camp as a corporal in Colonel John Crane's artillery regiment. He was assigned guard duty. Now Samuel worried about both his brothers.

As the weeks in April turned to May, Samuel had a hard time shaking off the death of Lieutenant Fisk. It seemed to hang with him

---

[20] Fisk, Ebenezer Lt., US, Revolutionary War Service Records, 1775 to 1783, M881,1775 to 1785, Nara catalog id, 570910, Compiled Service Records of Soldiers Who Served in the American Army During the Revolutionary War, compiled 1894 to ca. 1912, documenting the period 1775 to 1784, and Benjamin's diary dated April 6, 1778

many nights as he closed his eyes to sleep. And it became a familiar foe on nearly as many mornings. Like so many others, Ebenezer didn't die valiantly in battle. He perished at the hands of a disease you couldn't see or kill.

Samuel couldn't wait to leave Valley Forge. But there was something to celebrate. As the first week of May arrived, Congress ratified a Treaty of Alliance with France. General Washington wanted to celebrate. He ordered a feu-de-Joy, or fire of joy, with the whole army to assemble for a grand parade with celebratory cannon and gunfire on the sixth of May.[21]

Samuel awoke that morning to the sound of fifers and drummers across the camp playing Reveille.

After breakfast, the officers were to prepare the troops to line up in battle formation. At ten o'clock in the morning a cannon shot began the ceremony. Samuel hoisted the colors high and began the march to formation at the front of his regiment. Once the regiments were formed up, chaplains read news of the alliance and prayed with the soldiers. The artillery units fired their cannons again. And then the soldiers began firing their muskets and the soldiers shouted, "Long live the King of France!" and "God save the American States!"

Samuel's heart filled with pride as he thought about what the evening would bring. General Washington had also invited all the officers to dine with him.[22] Of course, Samuel accepted along with Lieutenant Armstrong and the other officers of the 8th Massachusetts.

It was a grand meal and certainly the finest Samuel and the other officers had enjoyed during their service in the army. Samuel returned to his log hut along with the other officers after nightfall.

---

[21] Drury, Bob and Clavin, Tom, Alliance Day, May 5, 1778, American Battlefield Trust, Updated July 26, 2024, September 30, 2022, https://www.battlefields.org/learn/articles/alliance-day

[22] Armstrong, Lieutenant Samuel, 1777, Boyle, Joseph Lee (transcribed), Valley Forge National Historical Park, From Saratoga to Valley Forge: The Diary of Lieutenant Samuel Armstrong, Pennsylvania Magazine of History and Biography, vol.121, number 3, July 1997, p. 268

As he prepared for sleep, he wished he could share the whole day's events with Tabitha right at that moment. He would write a letter in the morning. Samuel awoke to the sound of artillery fire to signal the start of the day. He wrote a quick letter to Tabitha before breakfast.

May 7
Camp Valley Forge
My Dearest Tabitha,
I am happy to report we celebrated a Grand Day here at camp yesterday. France has now joined with us in our cause of liberty and his Excellency ordered a celebration. We marched into the finest formation and we prayed for our cause. The cannons fired and thousands of us fired our muskets. And then we all shouted "Long live the King of France" and "God save the American States!" The best of all on the glorius day. General Washington invited all us officers to dine with him for dinner and so we did at his quarters. It was the best meal I've had since this whole war started. His Excellency led us in a toast to our new French alliance. It filled our hearts with joy after a long dificult winter here. But the celebration is over, and I think we shall break camp soon and be on the march. Who knows where? But I will be happy to put this place behind me. Please say hello to all our family and friends for me and share news of our grand celebration here. We are all united in our cause to free ourselves and our colonies from the rule of King George. His excellency also issued continued orders for us to keep our faith at the forefront of our duty which hartens my soul. Here is the admonition he included in his General Orders this month. "The Commander in Chief directs that divine Service be performed every Sunday at 11 oClock in those Brigades to which there are Chaplains—those which have none to attend the places of worship nearest to them—It is expected that Officers of all Ranks will by their attendence set an Example to their men. While we are zealously performing the duties of good Citizens and soldiers we certainly ought not to be inatentive to the higher duties of Religion—To the distinguished Character of Patriot, it should be our highest Glory

to add the more distinguished Character of Christian—The signal Instances of providential Goodness which we have experienced and which have now almost crowned our labours with complete Success, demand from us in a peculiar manner the warmest returns of Gratitude & Piety to the Supreme Author of all Good."[23]

He also ordered no fatigue duty on Sundays. I am sure Tabitha you will find great joy in His Excellency's continued demonstration of faith in God even during this terrible war. You also remain a constant source of peace and happiness for me my dear. I wake each day with a beautiful image of you in my mind. You are the life in each breath I take. And when I lay my head down at night your face is the last joy of the day. I dream of your eyes and lips and the way your hair falls upon your shoulders. I miss the sound of your voice. Pray that some day soon we shall be together forever my sweet Tabitha.

Forever yours,

Samuel

The days of drilling at Camp Valley Forge continued as Steuben wrote new drills and passed them on to the brigades and each officer. Samuel read the new orders with great diligence and was eager to help his fellow soldiers practice. The men grew sharper in their execution each day.

Unfortunately, there was a thorn in Samuel's side. Namely, Lieutenant Jonathan Allen. He became Adjutant for the 8th Massachusetts after transferring from another regiment. He apparently felt the need to force his authority on his new regiment, and soldiers. He was bad-tempered.

---

[23] Washington, George, "General Orders, 2 May 1778," Founders Online, National Archives, https://founders.archives.gov/documents/Washington/03-15-02-0016. [Original source: The Papers of George Washington, Revolutionary War Series, vol. 15, May to June 1778, ed. Edward G. Lengel. Charlottesville: University of Virginia Press, 2006, p. 13.]

Samuel had fallen ill with the same symptoms as Private Peter Bennett from Captain John Burnam's company. Both suffered high fevers from one of the viruses circulating through camp as well as chills, severe body aches, a twisted stomach, and the telltale oozing rash.

They needed bedrest. Adjutant Allen would have none of it and ordered Samuel and Burnam on foraging duty in the countryside. Bennett was later taken to the hospital and died that night. (95)

Samuel had had enough of the Lieutenant's unwarranted disrespect. On the eighteenth of May, he sent a note to Lieutenant Colonel Brooks about the behavior of the regiment's Adjutant.

It read, "As I have been injured by being ordered upon duty out of my tour, and know not any other proper way of seeking redress, but by applying to your Honour, and entering a complaint against J. Allen adjutant of said regiment. Your humble petitioner therefore most earnestly entreats that this may not pass unnoticed. But that you would be pleased to see justice done to your humble servant. Samuel Benjamin, Ensign."

Private Bennett was dead. And Samuel was certain he was much sicker the next morning because of Lieutenant Allen's insistence on ordering him on foraging duty.

There were other soldiers who were not sick who could have fulfilled the need to find new provisions. Ordering the sick to perform duties best kept for the healthy was not helping camp morale.

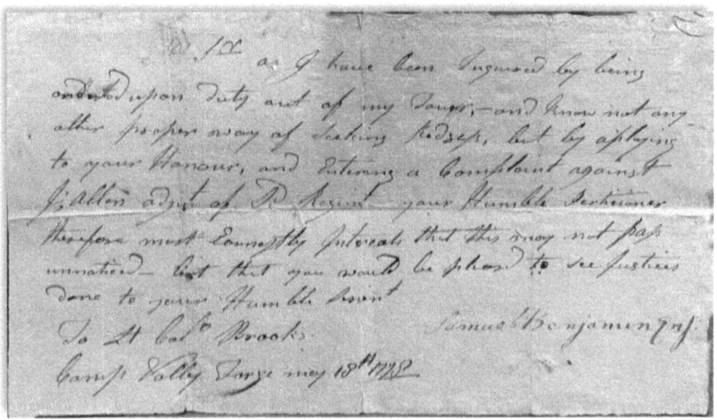

Sir as I have been Injured by being ordered upon Duty out of my Tour,—and know not any other proper way of seeking Redress, but by applying to your Honour, and Entering a Complaint against J. Allen Adjt of Sd Regimt your Humble Petitioner therefore most Earnestly Intreats that this may not pass unnoticed— but that you would be pleased to see Justice Done to your Humble Servt

To Lt Colo Brooks Samuel Benjamin Ensn

Camp Valley Forge May 18th 1778

Samuel Benjamin Papers (MS 75), Manuscripts and Archives, Yale University, 1775 to 1782

The number of deserters had grown dramatically as winter turned to spring. Even with his own mistreatment, Samuel couldn't understand why men would sign up to serve, only to abandon the cause that would free their families from the greedy hands of King George. But Samuel also knew those soldiers had figured out that warmer weather meant marching to the next battle and the risk of dying. More than 1,400 soldiers had deserted by the time General Washington decided to break camp in early summer. (96)

Samuel wasn't sure what discipline Lieutenant Colonel Brooks doled out. But by the seventh of June, Adjutant Jonathan Allen had been discharged. Perhaps Samuel's complaint was not the only one fielded by Lieutenant Colonel Brooks. Thankfully, Samuel had fully recovered, and he and the other officers were getting word that they might be breaking camp soon and be on the march.

Continental spies sent messages saying it appeared the redcoats were preparing to abandon Philadelphia. And they did so on the eighteenth of June. The next day Samuel heard a cannon shot, and per Steuben's new Regulations for the Order and Discipline of the Troops of the United States, the fifers and drummers performed "The General," the signal for the troops to assemble for the march out of camp.

Soon after, "The Assembly" was sounded. And eventually the musicians played "The March," signaling for the whole army to move. (97) Washington began a chase after the British Army.

Chapter 12
The Battle of Monmouth

"BOOM! BOOM! BOOM! BOOM! CRACK! BOOM!"

Samuel thought he might lose his hearing from the back-and-forth thunder of the patriot and redcoat cannons. The artillery units controlled the fight for now. And it was clear the King's forces were trying to drive the left wing of General Washington's main force from the higher ground on Perrine Farm Hill near Monmouth Courthouse in New Jersey.

That's where Samuel's 8th Massachusetts regiment held the ground on Sunday, June 28, 1778.

They were joined by other Massachusetts regiments, and those from Virginia, North Carolina, New Hampshire, Connecticut, Delaware, Maryland, and Pennsylvania.

Ten patriot guns and their crews stood out front in the intense summer heat. Cannonballs soared and so too did the temperatures, which reached near 100 degrees.

Some soldiers passed out after a difficult march to the battlefield with no water and then being immediately pressed into action.

One of the enemy's cannonballs had already killed a man from Gloucester in Samuel's company. Private Jacob Brown lost his life in the first few minutes of the artillery barrage. (98)

Lieutenant James McNair of the 2nd Artillery had met the same fate on Comb's Hill in the morning. A British cannonball took off his head. Word of the gruesome death spread quickly even amid the battle. (99)

Samuel had never witnessed so many cannons being fired from both sides. British infantry had tried to advance, only to be forced back by the rain of patriot cannons.

The redcoats took refuge behind their earthen barricade. Samuel took a knee on the hill but kept the colors flying in front of his regiment. Other Continental soldiers wisely pressed their bellies into the dirt, hoping to be spared a violent death.

The patriot soldiers standing upright squeezed off a few rounds of musket fire before the British cannons made it too risky. Samuel thought he might pass out from the oppressive heat. Jonathan's regiment was also part of the main line. And he wondered how his younger brother was faring in the heat.

He watched the crews of Captain Francis Proctor's 4th Continental Artillery take musket and artillery fire from the redcoats. One of the gunners was wounded and on the ground.

Earlier, Samuel had spotted a woman scurrying back and forth bringing water to the sweltering cannon crew. She must have been the wounded gunner's wife. The woman seemed very emotional as she gave him water and tended to his wound. Apparently satisfied she'd done all she could, she stepped in to help the gun crew keep the cannon firing.

Samuel heard a boom from below and suddenly a cannonball from the enemy passed between the woman's legs and ripped away part of her petticoat. Samuel had never witnessed such a close call that could have quickly ended the woman's life. But she was unharmed, apparently unshaken, and incredibly brave; she continued the task of preparing the cannon for firing. The woman carried gunpowder-filled cartridges to the loader.

Another crew member manned the "wormer." The long pole had a metal corkscrew on the end to clear the barrel. The "wormer" removed whatever rubbish was left in the barrel after the cannon fired. (100)

Samuel was fascinated by the woman and the rest of the artillery crew at work. A wet sponge on the worm swabbed the barrel. Then another man placed the cartridge in the barrel, followed by another man who used a ramrod to shove the powder charge deep into the shaft below the vent hole. One man kept a gloved hand over the vent hole while the powder man stuffed in some paper before others loaded the cannonball. Then the rammer shoved the ball down the barrel.

Samuel heard a shouted command. "Prick and prime!"

The vent tender removed his leather glove and shoved a priming wire down the vent hole to pierce the powder bag. The next step was to pour some powder from a powder horn into the vent hole and shove a matchstick into the vent.

The vent tender then shouted. "Ready to fire!"

With one man down, the gun commander stepped in to also serve as the firer. He grabbed the linstock with the metal fork on the end to hold the burning piece of twine. The commander must have been satisfied with the gun's aim because he didn't have the crew reposition the cannon.

He yelled, "Firing!"

The commander reached out with the linstock and touched the matchstick. The cannon boomed! Smoke exploded into the air and the gun rocked back. (101)

Samuel watched as the ball soared below and tore up part of the bank the redcoats were crouching behind. He also heard a painful yell. The 4th Artillery had just removed another Brit from the battle.

General Charles Lee had tried to hold off the redcoat advance early in the battle. But had eventually retreated when troops commanded by Lord Charles Cornwallis and General Henry Clinton overpowered Lee's forces. General Washington scolded Lee for falling back. In response, Lee reorganized his soldiers.

They returned to the fight and successfully delayed the British advance. That allowed Samuel's regiment and the others under the command of Lord Sterling to take up the defensive position on Perrine Hill.

The artillery battle raged for at least two hours. Samuel and the other soldiers were pinned down in the blistering heat. They lay helpless with only God's mercy to protect them.

As the cannons roared, Samuel eventually spotted four patriot guns at the top of Combs Hill. Those guns apparently belonged to General Nathanael Green's command, including the artillery regiment in which his brother John served. But John's company had been ordered north to North Castle, New York.

The cannons and the artillery in front of Samuel fired ball after ball on the redcoats and kept the King's forces from moving forward. General Clinton must have grown tired of the crossfire from patriot guns. (102) Now his soldiers were being hit by musket fire from the front and raked by cannon fire in their flanks, and the redcoats were forced to abandon with nowhere to go but in retreat. The patriots had outgunned the British artillery. (103) But that wasn't the end of it.

General Washington saw the British cannons being rolled away from the fight and decided to attack. His Excellency had bravely ridden back and forth along the battle lines, and soon Samuel watched as Colonel Joseph Cilley led an advance on the retreating redcoats.

Smoke filled the battlefield from constant musket and cannon fire as soldiers fell either from musket balls or the relentless heat. Samuel breathed in the bitter smell of spent powder knowing dozens would die on both sides.

His regiment would stay put in its defensive position waiting to be drawn into action. But the battle was nearly over as six o'clock arrived and Clinton continued the redcoat retreat.

Samuel thought the next day would bring renewed fighting. He and his fellow patriots spent a restless night sleeping on their arms, out in the open, where they prepared to fight and possibly die on the morrow.

Samuel closed his eyes, wondering if this would be his last night alive. He could hear the agonized cries of wounded enemy soldiers in the distance. Exhausted, he eventually drifted off to sleep.

When Samuel and the rest of the Continental Army awoke the next day, the British Army had disappeared. Scouts reported the redcoats had slipped away in the wee hours of the morning, marching away to Sandy Hook and heading back by boat to New York City—though not all would march or sail away from Monmouth.

The dawn of a new day revealed the hills and lowlands were littered with the dead and wounded. Some of the soldiers on both sides had been pushed beyond their limits. They didn't die from wounds; they perished under the hot summer sun from heat stroke.

It was difficult for commanders to get an accurate count of the number of soldiers killed, wounded, or missing because the fighting took place over several hours and in many different places around the farm fields, woods, and bogs.

Samuel struggled to take in the horror of both sights and sounds as he walked toward the former British lines. Enemy soldiers lay wounded, unable to move, and crying out for water.

He witnessed other Continental soldiers moving grenadiers with broken legs and muscles shredded by musket balls and cannon fire.

He recognized a doctor attending to an injured officer who was gravely wounded at the edge of a bog. The man pleading for help appeared to be almost cut in half—likely by a cannonball. The doctor and another man moved the officer to a nearby tree where, Samuel thought, the man would most assuredly die.[24]

How would Samuel ever get these images out of his mind? General Washington's official report listed sixty rank and file killed, including eight officers and 133 wounded. (104) Roughly three dozen more died from the heat. As for the enemy, more than three hundred redcoats lost their lives. The British commanders left their dead behind to be buried by the patriots. General Washington ordered New York's Lieutenant Colonel Cornelius Van Dyke to organize the burial parties. Some two hundred soldiers gathered the bodies of both redcoats and patriots. That included nearly thirty of Samuel's fellow soldiers, with Jacob Brown among them. The King's forces buried five dozen of their own before retreating. But left nearly two hundred dead on the field of battle to be put in the

---

[24] Gibbes, Robert Wilson, Documentary History of the American Revolution, Reminiscences of Dr. William Read, 1857, 256 – 257, https://archive.org/details/documen-taryhisto02gibb/page/n535/mode/2up

ground by the Continental Army. Locals buried more than two dozen other redcoats. (105)

Some soldiers were laid to rest where they died. Others in the graveyard of the nearby Presbyterian church, which on the inside served as a field hospital.

Samuel thought it one of the great mysteries of mankind. Those who fought each other so bitterly in battle, spilling the blood of men they did not know, ended up being brothers in death, buried side by side for eternity.

A Muster Roll of Capt Ebenr Cleaveland Company in the Massachusetts Regt of foot in the Army of the United States Commanded by Colo Michael Jackson — Taken for the Month of June 1778

Commissd — 1 January 1777 Saml Benjamin Ensn

No	Sergeants	War	3 yrs	Remarks
1	Asa Fitch	1		on furlough
2	John Rose		1	
No	Drums & fifes	War	3 yrs	Remarks
1	Benjn Davis		1	
2	Elit Davis		1	
No	Privates	War	3 yrs	Remarks
1	Francis Lines	1		~~on furlough~~
2	David Parr	1		
3	Joshua Webster	1		
4	Isaac Jacobs	1		
5	Jacob Parr		1	
6	Jacob Young		1	
7	Jacob Danforth		1	Sick on the Road at Newwork
8	Wilm Rose	1		Sick at the Genl hospital
9	Jacob Brown		1	Killed June 28 1778 —

Camp July 22 1778 Mustered then Capt Ebenr Cleavelands Company as specified in the above Roll —

[illegible]

M.R. of Capt. Ebenezer Cleveland's Co. Mass. Regt. Col. M. Jackson for June 78.

Brown, Jacob, US Revolutionary War Rolls, 1775 to 1783, M246, 602384, Revolution ary War Rolls, compiled 1894 to 1913, documenting the period 1775 to 1783, Pub lisher: NARA, Record group 93, p. 83, Massachusetts, 8th Regiment, 1778–80, Folder 11, US

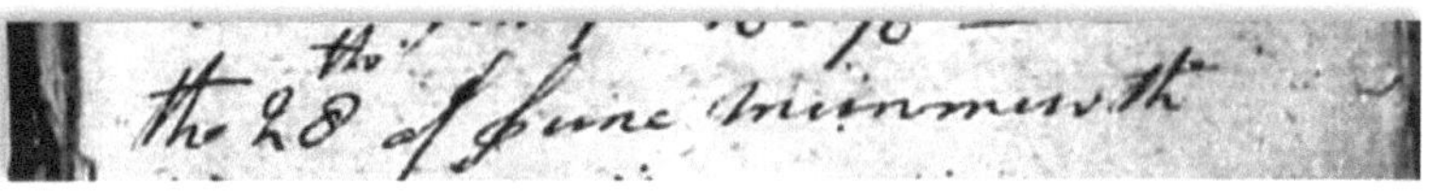

Image from Lieutenant Samuel Benjamin's war diary, Yale University Archives

Chapter 13
West Point

Instructions for the Ensign: "When on that duty they should consider the importance of the trust reposed in them; and when in action resolve not to part with the colours but with their lives."[25]

Samuel read the latest version of Steuben's instructions for the army about the responsibilities for each commissioned officer.

He was proud to know he had fulfilled his duties honorably as an ensign on the field of battle. He kept the colors flying and risked death doing so. He swore he could still smell the acrid smoke from Monmouth and hear the relentless booms of the artillery as well as the shells exploding. Samuel thought of Jacob Brown, who was a good soldier who'd lost his life to a cannonball he never saw coming. He also couldn't help but think of the awfulness of Lieutenant James McNair's death from another cannon, and the other fallen patriots he saw lifeless after the redcoats withdrew. Soberly, Samuel simply wrote in his diary, "the 28th of June Monmouth."

By God's grace he'd been spared in battle again. Would that continue, or would Tabitha eventually get a letter informing her of his death? Those were thoughts that would only get in the way of fulfilling his duty. So, he shoved them aside and moved on with the day's tasks.

Samuel and the other ensigns met briefly to talk about the challenges of getting some of the soldiers to keep themselves clean, let alone not turn their camp into a pigsty. Disease would run rampant

25 Baron Friedrich Wilhelm von Steuben, Regulations for the Order and Discipline of the Troops of the United States, p. 139

if privies were not properly managed and food scraps were allowed to pile up near the tents.

The officers complained about mice and rats being found in precious food stores if the men were not careful to secure the barrels and jars. Each soldier was given a gill of rum as often as it was available. But sometimes Samuel withheld the rum ration from soldiers who were found not practicing cleanliness.

On one hand, he hated to withhold rum because liquor was also used to help purify water. A soldier with dysentery was of little use to the army. But neither was a soldier who didn't follow orders.

Commanders made it clear that they needed every man they could get. But they also needed soldiers who were healthy and obedient. Harsh discipline made it clear that insubordination wasn't tolerated.

Soldiers who were found in violation often received fifty lashings with a cat o' nine tails. If they were caught stealing, they could suffer a hundred lashes.

The company drummers were ordered to carry out the lashings. If a soldier deserted and was later captured, he could be hanged, as Samuel witnessed at Valley Forge.

He also knew if soldiers were fed and uniformed properly, they were more likely to take pride in their enlistment, obey orders, and not desert. Unfortunately, the Continental Army was often wanting for provisions and uniforms.

The troops readied to march to New Brunswick while General Washington ordered Colonel Morgan and his men to shadow the retreating British along with the regiments of Stephen Moylan's light dragoons, the New Jersey Brigade, and militia from New Jersey.

Samuel agreed with His Excellency's decision not to have the whole army chase the redcoats to Middletown, where the enemy would control the high ground. It was better to fight on another day, when the odds were better. Samuel knew better than to speak any of his thoughts about command decisions. But his thoughts were those of an experienced soldier guided by a strong moral foundation.

He knew how to sort the good decisions from the bad and to form his own opinions. He'd also developed his own leadership style. And when he was put in charge, his decisions were a reflection of what he'd learned about human nature as well as his experience in battle.

Samuel was confident in his ability to lead. But he remained patient when a few others around him were promoted. He was sure his time would come. He had proven himself in the heat of battle.

The army camped for a few days in Englishtown and then on to New Brunswick on the Raritan River. There, the river allowed for the soldiers to bathe and clean themselves in an orderly manner. (106)

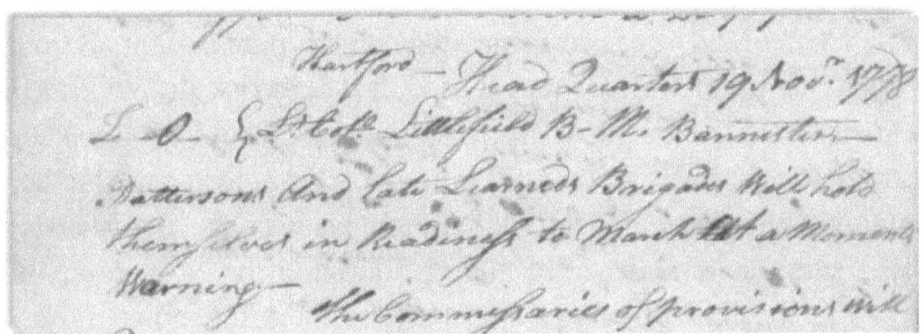
Hartford — Head Quarters 19 Nov.r 1778
[illegible] Lt Colo Littlefield B-M. Bannister —
Pattersons And Late Learneds Brigades Will hold
them Selves in Readiness to March at a Moments
Warning — the Commissaries of provisions will

Tuft, Francis, Orderly book of the 8th Massachusetts Regiment, Nov. 19, 1778 to Aug. 5 to 1779, April 21, West Point, p. 155

The trek away from Monmouth was slow and orderly from New Brunswick on to Scotch Plains and eventually settling in at White Plains, New York by late July.

The Division stayed in White Plains into September and then continued to march northwest to Bedford, on to Danbury, and eventually to Hartford, where they awaited orders about where the troops would

spend the winter.

On November nineteenth, General Washington issued orders for Samuel's brigade to be ready to march at a moment's notice. They began the march west the next day.

They camped at Litchfield, then on to Poughkeepsie on the eastern shore of the Hudson. Unfortunately, several soldiers were caught stealing fowl and other food from local farms and suffered punishment after court martial. Commanders ordered the soldiers be given a hundred lashes on their bare backs at roll call.

The whippings didn't stop all from bad behavior. A couple of soldiers engaged in counterfeiting Continental bills, including a corporal who was reduced in rank and put to the lash. Samuel knew the men whose conduct led to a court martial, and discipline deserved to be punished. But he still felt bad for the soldiers who did not have the good sense to follow orders. The lashings led to bloody backs and injured soldiers with broken spirits.

Saddest of all, deserters faced death as punishment. Samuel couldn't help but wonder why a soldier would risk it. Wouldn't it be better to die with honor in battle than at the end of a noose in shame? But fear was a powerful motivator. And, for some, the here and now of fright pushed rational thought aside and led to desertion.

As summer turned to fall and the boredom of daily camp life drew on, the dull of winter also gave soldiers too much time to think. For some, their thoughts turned dark and desperate.

Samuel himself struggled sometimes to not let the cold and clouds break his spirit. His faith was his hope and the promise of better days. He studied his Bible and busied his mind with memorizing Bible verses, keeping a record in the back of his diary. Today he was studying 2nd Hebrews chapter 2, verses 14 and 15, from his small copy of the King James.

"Forasmuch then as the children are partakers of flesh and blood, he also himself likewise took part of the same; that through death he might destroy him that had the power of death, that is, the devil."

gen - 3 - 15
Heb 2 - 14 - 15
1 John 3 - 3
gen 12 - 1 - 2 - 3
gen 22 - 15 - 18
do - 26 - 3 - 4 - 5

Image from Samuel Benjamin's war diary

His Bible had been imported from England before the rebellion in the colonies. A soldier never knew when death would visit him. It could be illness or a musket ball. Samuel had seen many fall around him and he knew it was only by God's grace that he was still alive.

The Continental and British armies played a game of cat and mouse as the weeks rolled into colder weather. Samuel's regiment spent part of the winter in Poughkeepsie waiting for an opportunity to cross the Hudson. That's where Samuel found himself in a tent on Christmas morning.

He awoke to first sunlight, his warm breath visible in the steam rising in the cold air above his wool blankets. As always, Tabitha formed his first thoughts of the day. He knew she would be with her family celebrating the best foods of the holiday. And he took delight in knowing his beloved would be warm and safe.

New Year's Day arrived like any other day. Duty and drilling kept the troops on task. The court martials continued each day for every kind of offense, from refusing to follow an order to stealing.

In February the army marched south to Fishkill and then to Peekskill. Orders came on March 9 for Samuel's regiment and the others in Learned's Brigade to be ready to march to the landing point opposite West Point and for those trained in manning the boats to be ready for transport. The troops were to be equipped with a week's provisions, including biscuits and pork, along with their arms.

The next morning, they boarded the bateaux and traveled upriver some twenty miles to Newburgh. Samuel's regiment was to escort a shipment of uniforms to headquarters at West Point. By the time they landed, scouts reported the enemy might try to move upriver. So, the troops marched with haste to West Point to defend the river.

And by the third week of March, Learned's and Nixon's brigades were based at West Point to make sure the King's forces could not travel the Hudson and split the colonies. Samuel's brother John had also arrived at West Point to help man the cannons as part of Captain Thomas Wells's company.

"Samuel!" shouted John.

"Benjamin! What are you doing here?" replied Samuel.

"My company left North Castle to shore up the battery here. It's good to see you, brother. I heard about Monmouth and the heat. But it seems you and Jonathan fared well," said John.

"The whole affair was fierce—the heat, the bloodshed from cannon and musket fire. But yes, I did okay. And our brother escaped injury. We chased off the redcoats," said Samuel.

"I have to get back to my duty. But I wanted to give my greetings, Samuel," said John.

"I'm glad you're here, brother. It sounds like all is well in Watertown and Needham," said Samuel.

"Yes, Mother and the children are good. What of Tabitha?" asked John.

"She and her family are well. I miss her terribly. I guess I'm in love, brother," Samuel said with a little chuckle.

"It appears so, brother. She's a fine catch. She could have done better though," John teased.

"I agree. God has shone His grace on me one more time," Samuel said laughing.

They shook hands and parted. Winter was fading in April and by the twentieth commanders ordered the "Great Chain" to be stretched across the river again. Samuel noted it in his diary.

He was amazed by the enormity of the massive links and the design that blocked enemy boats or ships from passing on the river. Large logs were attached to the chain to keep it afloat. Workmen had sharpened the ends of each log so the current would flow easier across them. And the design used tar and oakum to waterproof the logs. The chain was also anchored to large wooden cribs at each end filled with rocks, much like what was used for the floating bridge at Fort Ticonderoga. The chain wasn't pulled tight but was allowed to curve to allow the chain to move with the water. Once the "Great Chain" was back in place, the enemy did not make an attempt on the river. (107)

So, Samuel's regiment settled back into daily drilling and camp life. Some men from each brigade who knew how to fish were assigned the task of catching fish in the river to help feed the garrison.

"I hope you have good luck fishing," said Samuel to one of the privates armed with fishing gear and heading to the water. The man had been picked because of his experience as a fisherman.

"We've caught plenty of sturgeon, rock fish, and black bass before," replied the private.

"Yeah, the sturgeon and rock fish provided a good taste," said Samuel. "Any fresh fish would be better than salt meat and fire cakes." Samuel laughed.

"Agreed," said the private.

"I'll look forward to sharing in your bounty," said Samuel. (108)

Samuel found fresh fish a delicious change to much of the food gathered through foraging expeditions. General Washington had also ordered all the soldiers to save the ashes from their fires so they could be used to make soap. His Excellency made it clear to his commanders that keeping the men clean helped reduce the number of men who got sick from disease. The challenges were great enough with continued lack of arms and ammunitions to properly equip the soldiers.

The warmer weather of spring led the army closer to another battle against the King's forces. In February, Congress approved a bounty of two hundred dollars to each able-bodied soldier who would re-enlist. Congress also promised to officers ten dollars for each soldier they convinced to reenlist.

Samuel had already proven his worth in his time as a recruiting officer. So, he looked forward to earning extra money getting the soldiers in his company to reenlist. He kept a record of the names so no one else could claim what was due to him. The orders promising a bounty came from Middlebrook, New Jersey, where General Washington camped with the main force of the army. Samuel was eating on a May morning when Lieutenant Samuel Armstrong approached.

"Good morning, Ensign Benjamin," said Lieutenant Armstrong.

"Good morning, Lieutenant," replied Samuel.

"You likely heard, Congress approved the creation of a new Light Infantry earlier this year. General Washington wants to follow through on the idea and form a Corps of Light Infantry similar to the unit that served alongside us at Saratoga," said Armstrong. "I think you would be a good fit, Ensign. But His Excellency doesn't want to draw his best soldiers from the regiments without replacing their numbers. So, given your success in recruiting, he's asking you to travel to Springfield to find a hundred men to sign up for nine months of service," said Armstrong.

"Thank you, sir. I'm honored His Excellency has placed his trust in me," said Samuel.

"You're to obtain a horse from the garrison stable and proceed to Springfield. The recruiting bounty will apply, and your expenses will be covered. General Washington made it very clear this is a priority for him," ordered Armstrong.

"Yes, Lieutenant. I'm honored to be selected," said Samuel.

"Captain Keith had already asked me who I thought would be a good choice to help in leadership of a light company from the 8th and you were at the top of my list. Also, given your experience since Lexington, and bravery in battle, I approve of you to not only lead this recruiting mission, but, when the times comes, to also help us select men for the Light Infantry from the Massachusetts regiments," said Armstrong. "Truly, Ensign, I don't understand why you haven't already been promoted to subaltern."

"Thank you for your confidence in me. I'm trying hard to be patient in being promoted," said Samuel.

"Hopefully you don't have to be patient much longer. Carry on," said Armstrong.

Samuel left straightaway for Springfield. His orders gave him five days to complete the journey, a month to recruit, and five days for the return journey. Along the way he wondered how much longer the troops at West Point would be held in reserve without being put to action. But the creation of a Light Infantry was a sign something was in the works.

Another battle was likely the only way Samuel could prove to his commanders that he was worthy of a more trusted leadership role. He liked Lieutenant Armstrong and knew he deserved his rank. He was a trusted officer and liked by the men under his direction. Only the best and most fit soldiers ended up in the Light Infantry. So, it was an honor to be selected.

Samuel's regiment continued their stay at West Point and was given the responsibility of guarding the crucial patriot defense of the Hudson River. But there was trouble elsewhere in the New York territory.

Scouts reported continued trouble with the Six Nations of Indians and loyalists attacking settlers in the northern regions at Wyoming Valley, Cherry Valley, and German Flatts. The Iroquois, Mohawks, Seneca, Onondaga, and Cayuga became the targets of the Continental campaign. And by the end of May, the Indian raids led to an inhuman campaign ordered by General Washington.

In part, Washington's orders for General John Sullivan called for "the total destruction and devastation of their settlements and the capture of as many prisoners of every age and sex as possible," stating that "It will be essential to ruin their crops now in the ground and prevent their planting more....After you have very thoroughly completed the destruction of their settlements; if the Indians should show a disposition for peace, I would have you to encourage it, on condition that they will give some decisive evidence of their sincerity..." (109)

The Oneida and Tuscarora fought on the side of the patriots. Samuel was glad he didn't have to be a part of that campaign and wished the Indians had avoided choosing sides and stayed out of the colonists' fight with the Crown. But he knew the Indians were often just trying to protect their land and their way of life. Sadly, their savage attacks on settlers and taking scalps only inflamed feelings against them.

The awful killing of Jane McCrea remained fresh in the minds of many, and they used it to justify their hatred of Indians. Especially the tribes that sided with the Brits.

The commanders at West Point had more pressing concerns. Namely, that the British Parliament had prodded General Sir Henry Clinton to force General Washington's hand into a battle. English politicians had grown tired of the lengthy struggle against the American colonists and were frustrated their army had not yet defeated the patriot forces. His Majesty's army had already captured New York, Philadelphia, and Savannah. And General Clinton concluded he needed to draw out General Washington's army into a major battle to destroy the rebellion. Clinton brought a force of some 6,000 troops up the Hudson to take control of the crossing at King's Ferry in the last days of May.

The small patriot defenses at Verplanck's Point and Stony Point were easy targets and the Continental troops quickly abandoned. That heightened tensions at West Point, and Samuel's regiment and the rest of the garrison readied for an attack from General Clinton.

The officers talked of marching down and doing battle to reclaim what the redcoats had taken. But Washington refused to be drawn out into a weaker position. So, Clinton withdrew most of his army back to Connecticut and harassed rebels along the coast. That left Stony Point with a smaller British garrison in defense of the rocky outcrop. The officers at West Point wondered if Washington was again pondering attacking the enemy at Stony Point to discourage the British from challenging further up the Hudson again, including West Point. But the plan was kept a secret.

Still, there was growing excitement in camp as His Excellency asked his commanders to keep the troops at the ready. The other officers made sure the soldiers were disciplined in every way, from cleanliness to maintaining their arms.

Chapter 14
A Daughter Of Liberty

The morning sun shone bright as Tabitha sat in the parlor of her family's home in Waltham. The warm glow of a new day lifted her spirits as she put the last stitches in a patch she was sewing on a pair of her father's work britches.

She closed her eyes and saw Samuel's face in that same morning sun. His deep blue eyes stared into hers with a look that spoke not only of love but of devotion. She could feel his hands in hers. Then she felt his arms reach around her as he pulled her close. His face against her cheek. The rhythm of his breathing on her neck that seemed to match the beating of her heart. The smell of his soap. She imagined the excitement of one day lying with him as husband and wife, finally able to make their dream of children come true. Her body tingled and her face felt flush. Then she heard her mother's footsteps in the kitchen.

She opened her eyes and returned to the here and now. Samuel was still far away, and danger lurked. She closed her eyes again and prayed. "Dear God, I humbly plead, please keep Samuel safe. Forgive my selfishness. But I promise if you return him to me, I will devote our love, our lives, our children to your service. Father, you have spared him thus far and I thank you. Please, Lord, bring him home unharmed. I pray in the name of Christ, Amen."

"Tabitha," her mother called.

"Yes, Mother. I'm coming," replied Tabitha.

Tabitha opened her eyes, knowing her mother wanted help preparing the stove for breakfast. As she walked toward the kitchen, Tabitha noticed tears had fallen from her eyes. She quickly dabbed at them with her apron and arrived in the kitchen finding her mother's arms open wide for a hug. Her mother gave her a knowing look and received her daughter's head on her shoulder.

"I see you have been crying, my dear daughter," said Mother. "I have already prayed this morning for Samuel and all those brave men who are putting themselves in harm's way for us. I hope along with you that Samuel returns to your arms safely when this horrible war is over."

"I prayed the same this morning, Mother," said Tabitha.

"Dry your tears now, girl. Worry is not our friend, and it won't protect Samuel. Let's get on with our chores," said Mother.

Tabitha turned her thoughts to gathering wood for the stove. Sometimes the best medicine for an ailing heart was focusing on the task at hand. She was also thinking of the spinning bee in a few days organized by the Daughters of Liberty.

Tabitha loved the company and conversation of the other women. All would gather at First Parish in Waltham on Saturday. She looked forward to seeing her sister. Now that Elisha had left the army and was home, Martha was her joyful self. The next couple of days seemed to pass quickly and finally Saturday arrived.

"Hi, Martha!" shouted Tabitha as she spotted her sister walking outside the meeting house.

"Tabitha, I have much to tell you," Martha answered back.

Tabitha rushed to meet her sister's arms and hug her little niece as well. Little Martha loved seeing her Auntie Tabitha, whom she called "Tabba." It was the best the toddler could make of her aunt's name.

The sisters had left their spinning wheels at the meeting house from the last spinning bee, so they didn't have to drag them back and forth from their homes. Tabitha noticed Martha's face had a mischievous look about it.

"Dear sister, what is on your mind? You have a curious look on your face," replied Tabitha.

"You're going to be an aunt again!" said Martha excitedly.

"EEEEE!" squealed Tabitha. "That's wonderful news!"

"We worked on it when Elisha got a few days away from his command last spring," said Martha.

"I'm not sure 'working' is the right word, Martha!" said Tabitha laughing. "You didn't have to 'work' too hard to have little Martha. When are you expecting?" asked Tabitha.

"It appears late September or October," replied Martha.

"You're going to have a little brother or sister. Isn't that wonderful!" said Tabitha as she tickled baby Martha under her chin.

Little Martha giggled as Tabitha took her niece into her arms and snuggled her.

"Someday I hope to give you many cousins, adorable little Martha. Let's head inside," said Tabitha.

The sisters walked together in a way only sisters can. There was a bond unspoken. But clear as day. Tabitha playfully bounced little Martha up and down as she climbed the stairs of First Parish Church and walked through the front door.

"Tabitha!" exclaimed a cheerful young woman with rosy cheeks and ebony hair.

"Why Martha Stearns, aren't you the belle of the ball!" replied Tabitha as she continued. "I love your dress. Have you been sneaking in here just to show how you can out-spin and out-sew the rest of us?"

"Maybe," chuckled Martha. "Do you like it?"

"It's perfect, of course," said Tabitha.

Martha and Tabitha had been friends since they were little girls growing up in Waltham. Tabitha loved her friend's charm and wit. And instead of being jealous of her friend's talents, Tabitha was simply proud to be Martha's friend.

"Have you heard from Samuel?" asked Martha.

"I have. He writes as often as he can. I'm amazed his letters get through at all," replied Tabitha. "I worry whether he will ever come home and I worry about some of the things he tells me he's seen. This war is just awful. I'm just glad Martha's Elisha is back home."

"Yes. Samuel is in my prayers, Tabitha. As are many others from our village."

"Well, let's get to spinning, Martha. I need to take my mind off the dangers Samuel faces and do my part for the cause," said Tabitha.

She walked over to her spinning wheel, which sat alongside the others in the aisle between the pews. Reverend Cushing had been kind enough to bring chairs for the ladies.

Tabitha sat in the spindle-back chair beside her wheel. The chair had no arms and worked well for spinning. It had a sturdy wooden base. She held the single strand coming through the orifice between her index finger and thumb and loosened the fibers just enough so she could attach the fibers of the unspun linen. She carefully twisted the two ends together. Once she was satisfied the twist would hold, she placed her right foot on the treadle and pushed it down to get the footman moving back and forth as the wheel began spinning.

Tabitha loved the rhythmic motion of her foot rising and falling and the smoothness of the fibers as the bobbin gathered the linen yarn. Her mind drifted to images of her father harvesting the flax, which ultimately produced the linen after soaking and pulling apart the fibers.

Her father was a hard worker and a good provider with a tender heart. He made her feel loved as a daughter. Even if he didn't outwardly express his love that often. Tabitha knew that love was also in the doing. Not just the saying. For words without action, without sacrifice, were empty. She hoped that was a lesson she and Samuel could one day pass along to their children.

She hoped to spin enough yarn to make a dress that she could wear for Samuel the next time he returned home. Once again, she said a quick little prayer in her head. "Lord, please bring Samuel home to me."

Lossing, Benson J., West Point 1780, The Pictorial Field-Book of The Revolution; or, Illustrations By Pen and Pencil, Of the History, Biography, Scenery, Relics, and Traditions of The War For Independence. Vol. I, 1860

Chapter 15
Stony Point And The Light Infantry

West Point was a good place to train for a mission. The fort was high on a bluff on a curve in the Hudson and artillery crews held a commanding view of the river from the west bank. The "Great Chain" stretched across the water, promising to slow or block enemy ships.

The orders to form a Corps of Light Infantry finally came on the twelfth of June while Samuel was away recruiting in Springfield. In part it read:

> The companies of Light Infantry are to be immediately drawn out agreeable to this proportion; The officers commanding regiments will be particularly careful in the choice of the men, which is a duty, the good of the service, and the credit of their respective regiments equally demand; When it is considered that in every army the honor of a regiment and that of its Light-Company are intimately connected, the officer commanding it cannot but be solicitous to furnish men that will support the reputation of his regiment. (110)

To begin, the first troops were to be chosen from Virginia, Maryland, and Pennsylvania regiments. To be picked, a soldier had to demonstrate strength and bravery, and must have served at least a year in the army.

But a few days later orders came for Major William, of Samuel's regiment, to select men from seven of the Massachusetts regiments to form a battalion of Light Infantry.

Samuel returned from Springfield the first week of July after successfully recruiting the one hundred soldiers General Washington had ordered. He was sitting on a stool cleaning his musket outside the barracks when he spotted Captain James Keith walking toward him. The Captain looked stern as usual. Samuel stood, tipped his hat, and bowed in salute.

"Ensign Benjamin," Captain Keith addressed Samuel in a voice that sounded an octave lower than most other men.

"Yes sir," replied Samuel.

"Congratulations on your success in Springfield. His Excellency is pleased with your results and now I can officially assign you to the new Corps of Light Infantry. You will maintain your rank for the time being. But there could be an opportunity soon for you to receive a promotion," said Keith.

"Thank you, sir!" said Samuel with excitement in his voice. "I will make you proud, sir."

"I know you will, Ensign. I am choosing you because you have proven yourself many times in battle. And Major Hull mentioned you by name to be selected," said the Captain.

"I am honored, sir. When do my new duties start?" asked Samuel.

"Immediately, Samuel. You've no doubt heard murmuring that His Excellency ordered the creation of the Light Infantry for a special mission. We need to make sure General Clinton is persuaded to not make any attempt further up the North River. I expect you to bring the same discipline and order you have helped maintain in the 8th to this new Corps of Light Infantry. The training is already underway. Here's a list of the soldiers chosen from your regiment. And I'd like your input as you help in their drilling," replied Keith.

"Yes sir," said Samuel.

"Carry on, Ensign," said Keith.

"Sir," replied Samuel.

Samuel tipped his hat, bowed his head in salute, and watched Captain Keith walk away. It was finally happening. Samuel swelled with pride. Samuel joined the new Corps of Light Infantry the following day to help with the soldiers' training. Samuel awoke to the sound of Reveille and was excited. The men had been ordered to muster on the parade ground with bayonets mounted on their muskets. And then he spotted an old friend among some new officers chosen for the Light Infantry.

"Thomas!" Samuel yelled. They'd gotten separated years before into different regiments and had lost track of each other.

"Samuel!" Thomas shouted back in surprise. They hurried for a handshake.

"I see you're wearing a captain's uniform," said Samuel in admiration.

"Yes, I am, Ensign Benjamin. You've also done well, I see," replied Captain Hunt.

"It's good to see you, Thomas. It'll be an honor to serve with you again," said Samuel.

"And you as well, Samuel. It looks like we'd better return to our duty. We'll have to get caught up over a meal sometime," said Captain Hunt.

"That would be great," said Samuel.

Samuel, Thomas, and the other officers quickly found themselves under the command of Major General Baron von Steuben along with Major Hull. Von Steuben first instructed the troops on the bayonet at Valley Forge. On his own time, Samuel memorized the written instructions to make sure he could help hold the men in his company accountable. In part, the instructions read:

> Charge—Bayonets! Two motions:
> 1st. The same as the first motion of the secure.
> 2d. Bring the butt of the firelock under the right arm, letting the piece fall down strong on the palm of the left hand, which receives it at the swell, the muzzle pointing directly

> to the front, the but pressed with the arm against the side; the front rank holding their pieces horizontally, and the rear rank the muzzles of theirs so high as to clear the heads of the front ranks, both ranks keeping their feet fast.
> The redcoats used bayonet charges with precision early in the war to overwhelm the untrained patriots with gruesome success. The Continental soldiers often fought with muskets that were hunting guns and had no bayonet mounts. After Valley Forge, Samuel and many other soldiers had grown confident in their ability to return the favor to the redcoats with the point of their bayonets mounted on their French Charleville muskets.

"Step forward as you lunge with your musket!" shouted Samuel as he instructed one of the younger members of the regiment. "Don't just use your arms to drive your musket forward. Use the momentum of the step to put more force into the effort. And make sure you have a solid base as you lunge," instructed Samuel.

"Yes sir!" replied the private. (111)

General Anthony Wayne was chosen to be the senior commander of the new Corps of Light Infantry.

Samuel discovered that Elisha had decided to leave the service on July 6. He left Samuel a note in the barracks explaining that, with another baby on the way, he thought it best to not test God any further. Elisha had already served his new country and now his duty was to his new wife and children. Samuel was sad to see Elisha go. But he respected his decision and knew there might come a time when he might have to make the same choice.

Samuel's thoughts returned to training. The new Light Infantry regiments were ordered to march roughly five miles south to Fort Montgomery. They were to set up separate camps to avoid suspicion.

North Carolina Major Hardy Murfree also formed a unit to be part of a fourth Regiment of Light Infantry that included the Massachusetts troops.

Two years earlier, the redcoats had taken Fort Montgomery from outmanned patriot forces in a fierce battle. Seventy-five Continental soldiers died or were wounded. The British also removed the first chain patriots had erected across the river near Fort Montgomery.

It was an excellent place for the Light Infantry to train for a future attack along the steep banks of the river. Samuel suspected they were preparing for an assault on Stony Point. But he kept his thoughts to himself.

The British-held outpost sat more than a hundred feet above the Hudson and was protected by more than a dozen cannons and mortars and roughly six hundred soldiers from the King's 17th Regiment of Foot and two grenadier companies. The British soldiers continued to improve their fortifications. (112) That made it a threat.

The Continental Light Infantry regiments of more than 1,200 soldiers continued practicing for a surprise attack using only bayonets. The Massachusetts soldiers were told they would be marching with unloaded muskets to make sure no one panicked, fired a shot, and ruined the element of surprise. Samuel and the other soldiers practiced running up hill with their bayonets mounted.

The training at Fort Montgomery continued as the heat of summer grew more intense. The men were eager to learn what they were training for. If it was an attack on Stony Point, it would require a longer march down the banks of the river another nine miles below where they were drilling as the crow flies. But the winding trails and hills would make it a fourteen-mile trek.

On July 14, General Wayne gathered his commanding officers and revealed the plan to attack Stony Point in three columns. Wayne would attack at midnight leading a column on the right, from the south, of roughly seven hundred soldiers. That column would consist of the first and third regiments of Virginia, Pennsylvania, and

Connecticut soldiers as well as the Massachusetts soldiers led by Major Hull.

That meant Samuel and his fellow soldiers from the 8th would be attacking from the south, wading through the river and a marsh before climbing the hill below Stony Point. Major Murfree's North Carolina troops would join Colonel Richard Butler's Pennsylvania Light Corps, which included the Marylanders in a second column attacking from the left, or the north.

Eventually Murfree would break off to form a third column, traveling from the west over the inland causeway with loaded muskets. Murfree's light companies would fire on the British regulars, drawing attention away from the soldiers attacking silently with only bayonets. The soldiers of Lee's legion, Colonel Ball's regiment, and Brigadier-General Peter Muhlenberg's brigade would be held back in case the attack was failing.

The soldiers were ordered to shave, powder their hair, and ready themselves for action. The men were told to pack light and leave their muskets unloaded.

The Light Infantry began the march over difficult ground around noon on July 15. The soldiers found themselves sometimes forced to walk single file on narrow trails through thick forests. Anyone the soldiers encountered during the march was to be taken into custody and held until the attack was over.

Whatever their mission was, it was close by. Eight hours later the troops arrived at a farm owned by David Springsteel. Finally, the soldiers were told they would be attacking Stony Point, less than two miles away. General Wayne issued strict orders with dire consequences: "If any soldier presumes to take his musket from his shoulder, or to fire or begin the battle until ordered by his proper officer, he shall be instantly put to death by the officer next to him; for the misconduct of one man is not to put the whole troops in danger or disorder and be suffered to pass with life."

The orders also contained the full measure of trust the General had in the soldiers assigned to the task: "The General has the fullest confidence in the bravery and fortitude of the corps that he has the happiness to command." (113, 114, 115)

Commanders asked for volunteers who would be out front with axes to break through enemy defenses. The volunteers of the "Forlorn Hope" would likely be the first to die. Wayne knew money would also provide motivation. The first five men to reach the summit would be paid extra. Five hundred dollars to the first, four hundred to the second, and so on down to the fifth. Washington signed off on the idea. (116)

Each column had twenty volunteers who would chop through the enemy's defenses made of fallen logs with pointed ends called the abatis. They would also have to overcome sentries.

Samuel was amazed at the bravery and brazenness of the volunteers, most from Virginia, who would lead the attack. They would be led on the right by Lieutenant Knox of the 9th Pennsylvania. The soldiers of the "Forlorn Hope" on the left were led by Lieutenant James Gibbons of the 6th Pennsylvania. They would be followed on the south by 150 soldiers commanded by Lieutenant Colonel François de Fleury and on the north by Maryland's John Steward.

General Wayne ordered the soldiers to stick white paper in their caps so that, in the dark and confusion, the Light Infantry could distinguish friend from foe. Samuel and the other soldiers began the march from the south. But the tide was still too high, and they had to wait for it to recede before they could wade through the marsh below the fort. The noise of hundreds of soldiers splashing through the marsh and river must have alerted the British sentries.

"Crack, crack."

Samuel ducked as he heard musket fire ahead. But there was no more gunfire for a few minutes. Samuel and the others reached dry ground. Then the still of night erupted into musket fire on top of the hill.

"That has to be Murfree's men," whispered Samuel to the soldiers around him.

"Must be," replied someone else in the dark.

"Attack, men!" Major Hull shouted.

Samuel began climbing the hill as quick as his feet and muscles would allow.

"BOOM! BOOM!" roared cannons above.

The flashes of exploding gunfire exposed Samuel and the others to the British soldiers on top of the hill just as they passed through the first abatis. And now the King's regulars fired their muskets down the hill. Samuel saw General Wayne break through the second log fortification and then heard him cry out. He'd been hit in the head.

Then Samuel heard the Major's voice.

"Forward, my brave fellows, forward! Carry me into the fort. If I am to die, I want to die at the head of my column!"

But the soldiers around him thought better of it. One stayed behind to treat Wayne's wounds and the rest continued up the hill. Samuel could hear Wayne still yelling orders as he reached the top, breathing hard, his musket horizontal with the bayonet leading the charge.

Suddenly a redcoat tried to run him through. Samuel stepped aside, turned, and thrust his bayonet at the soldier's side. The Brit crumpled to the ground with the groan of a dying man. The fight was on.

Samuel rushed forward and ran head on into another red-coated soldier. Again, Samuel thrust his bayonet into the man's belly with devastating effect. There was no time to think, only time to attack. Fight or die.

The smell of exploding gunpowder filled the air, along with the cries of the wounded and dying. Samuel lunged again, and again spilled the blood of the enemy. Then he and several others reached the enemy's fort.

A few members of the Light Infantry lay dead or mortally wounded. French Lieutenant Colonel de Fleury was holding the British flag in his hands and proclaiming victory as all the Continental soldiers began yelling, "The fort's our own!" But the fighting was not done.

The redcoats refused to surrender and more of them raced toward the Light Infantry soldiers. Samuel was overwhelmed by two red-coats for a moment, dodging blows from both when his musket was knocked from his hands. A bayonet nearly pierced his side as it sliced through his wool coat. Samuel drew his sword and slashed at one of the redcoats, then the other. Both fell in pain. Samuel re-trieved his musket and continued forward.

The bloody hand-to-hand fighting went on for several more minutes before the British commander Lieutenant Colonel Henry Johnson ordered his men to surrender and lay down their arms.

The Continental soldiers spared any redcoat who asked for mercy. Samuel and a few others clambered back down the hill to check on General Wayne. He was bleeding from his head. But alert. They helped him slowly climb up the hill and into the fort to the cheers of the Light Infantry.

"Huzzah! Huzzah!"

The general soon dictated a dispatch to send to General Wash-ington. It simply said, "Dear Gen'l: The fort and Garrison with Col. Johnston are ours. Our officers and men behaved like men who are determined to be free."

But it was not without sacrifice and sorrow. Fifteen Continental soldiers lay dead with more than eighty wounded, including his friend Thomas. Thankfully, it appeared Captain Hunt's wound was not that serious. As for the King's soldiers, twenty died, more than seventy were wounded, and nearly sixty were missing. (117)

"Compatriots. We must honor those who will not return alive with us," said Samuel. "Please kneel with me and pray for their souls."

Samuel took a knee near some of the fallen members of the Light Infantry and led those around him in prayer.

"Dear God, we pray for the souls of those who have perished here. May your grace and mercy lead them to heaven to be with you. And comfort their families as they grieve their loss for the cause of liberty. Thank you, God, for sparing those of us still standing. Amen," prayed Samuel.

The men stood and began to gather the bodies of the dead for burial. It took several hours to dig thirty-five graves and properly honor the dead. The Light Infantry took some five hundred British and loyalist soldiers as prisoners.

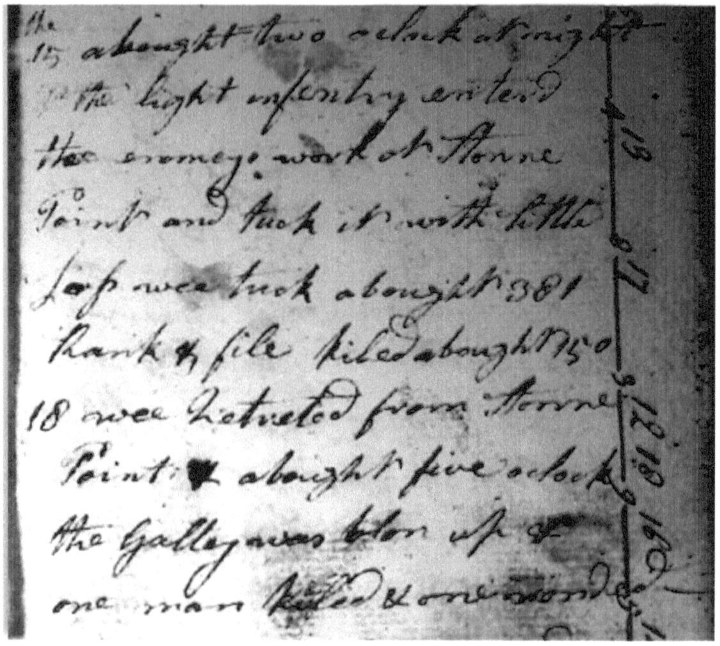

Image from Lieutenant Benjamin's Revolutionary war diary, Yale University Archives

Transcription:

> The 15 about two oclock at night the light infantry enterd the enemys work at Stonne Point and tuck it with little loss. We tuck about 381 rank & file killed about 150 18 we re-treated from Stonne Point about five oclock the galley was blown up & one man killed & one wounded

The next day, General Washington rode with General Nathanael Greene and Baron von Steuben to Stony Point. His Excellency gave thanks to God for sparing his Light Infantry from an even greater loss. While reluctant to give up the captured fort, Washington determined it would be too dangerous to try to keep it with Clinton's main army and ships easily heading up the Hudson.

Washington ordered the troops to seize the cannons, gun powder, and stores. He also ordered the soldiers to destroy the fort as best they could before ordering a retreat.[26]

Tragically, careless use of gun powder caused an explosion that killed one of the Light Infantry and wounded another.

Wayne had promised the soldiers before taking the fort that whatever they seized would be used to reward the soldiers in payment. Samuel had never heard of such a thing. But His Excellency was told of the promise and informed the officers at Stony Point he would recommend to Congress to approve Wayne's promise. (118) Samuel recorded the events in his diary and when he returned to West Point wrote a letter to Tabitha.

---

[26] Sheehan, Michael, Stony Point Battlefield State Historic Site, Battle of Stony Point, https://www.mountvernon.org/library/digitalhistory/digital-encyclopedia/article/battle-of-stony-point#:~:text=The%20Battle%20of%20Stony%20Point,British%20fortifications%20at%20Stony%20Poin.

West Point
July 19, 1779
My Dearest Tabitha,
I have survived yet another daring and bloody raid on the enemy at a place called Stony Point along the Hudson River. The light infantry marched under the cover of night. And very dark it was. Those of us from Massachusetts followed behind Major Hull of our 8th Massachusetts and Gen. Wayne along the river. I can tell you now what I would not have wanted to tell you before our action lest you worry. We marched toward the enemy with our muskets unloaded. We were to remain quiet. Bayonets being our only defense. White paper was handed around to fix in our hats so that in the dark and confusion of battle we would know who was friend or foe. After a march of roughly 14 miles, we reached a marsh below the enemy's works and waded through waist deep water before again reaching dry ground. The enemy's pickets saw us and fired away then retreated to the high ground. We had heard the enemy thought of their outpost as impregnable and called it their "little Gibraltar." As we scrambled up the hill from the river the enemy alarmed and began firing on us with great fury with ball and buckshot. Their cannons boomed with grapeshot which mostly went over our heads. As we stormed the enemy's works Gen. Wayne was shot in the head with a musket ball and fell. But I'm happy to report he survived the injury with little blood loss. I tell you Tabitha the enemy would not give way even though overwhelmed, and we caried on with the slaughter with our bayonets thanks to the training of Gen. von Steuben. Within minutes we overran their works shouting, "the fort is our own!" and shouts of "Huzzah" quickly folowed. Our bayonets dripped deep red. Finally, hundreds surrendered. The next day His Excellency General Washington visited

our victory. "He offered his thanks to Almighty God, that He had been our shield and protector amidst the dangers we had been called to encounter." I too am thankful for God's grace upon our effort. We have since withdrawn from Stony Point and are awaiting orders. Sadly one of ours was killed when we blew up their galley. This is a brutal effort and I wish I could hold you in my arms. Please greet your parents for me as well as your brothers and sisters, and our neighbors. Tell Martha I miss her delisious jumbles. Until I can hold you again my beloved, I am truly yours,

Samuel

CHAPTER 16
How Much Longer?

Tabitha recognized Samuel's handwriting on the outside of the folded letter and was beyond thrilled to hold it in her hands. She carefully pulled apart the wax seal and began reading.

Once again, she found herself crying. Elisha had come home to Martha. Why couldn't she have her Samuel home and out of harm's way?

She found Samuel's gruesome descriptions about the battle hard to read on the one hand. But on the other, she was glad Samuel was honest with her about the horrors he was facing. She silently asked God why he allowed the evils of war. Then her thoughts quickly turned to thanking God that her beloved Samuel was alive.

Evil was just a fact of this world. The colonists could either surrender to the King's tyranny or fight against it. But if they didn't succeed, Samuel's sacrifice, her sacrifice, and that of thousands of others would be for nothing. Losing could also mean the loss of everything she held dear. They had to win, didn't they? They had to believe that good and liberty would survive where evil could not.

She read the letter three times wondering if Samuel would still be the man she loved when he returned. Surely, no matter what he endured, his gentle, honest spirit would survive. Samuel loved people. Shedding the blood of others must have been so hard for him. Even if they were trying to kill him.

"What did Samuel write?" Tabitha's mother asked as she walked into the parlor.

"Another horrible battle, Mother. He is unharmed. But he watched others die around him and he had to kill several British regulars. It's just awful, Mother. Awful," replied Tabitha.

Mother used her apron to dab at Tabitha's tears.

"I'm not sure any of us knew what we were getting into when we decided to fight back against the Crown," said Mother.

"I certainly didn't think the war would last this long. I thought King George would realize our willingness to shed blood, accept our independence, and eventually leave us alone. I see now that was a foolish thought," said Tabitha.

"Is that a letter from Samuel?" asked her younger brother David.

"Yes, it is, David," replied Tabitha.

"Don't be sad, Tabby," he said.

"I know you miss him. So do I," said David.

He was just five when Samuel first fought at Lexington. David and Samuel had a special connection. David always got excited when Samuel would come for a visit. And Samuel loved throwing David in the air and making him squeal in delight as Samuel caught him on the way down.

"Hopefully, Samuel will be home soon, David," said Tabitha.

"I hope so," replied David.

"I could use your help in the kitchen, dear daughter. It'll get your mind off the war," said Martha.

"I'll be right there, Mother," replied Tabitha. "Come along, David. Let's go help Mother."

Tabitha knew she must write Samuel a letter tonight to encourage him.

Waltham
August 2, 1779
My Dearest Samuel,

I just received your latest letter with great joy. Thank you for letting me know you are in good health. It is difficult to read of the bloody battles and what you are called upon to do fighting for our freedom. But I thank you for being honest with me about the difficult trials you are facing. I and many others continue to pray for your safety. All is well here at home. The crops look good and father is hoping for a hearty harvest. We had a thunderstorm that rained down hail last week. But thankfully no serious damage to our corn. I have passed along your greetings to all who know and love you. My little brother David asks often about you. He's gotten a lot bigger and he'll be harder for you to toss about. One day he might be able to toss you. I continue to praise God for keeping you safe. We just held another spinning bee at the meeting house. It was great fun. The Daughters of Liberty are doing our part to oppose the tax. I hope to have a surprise to wear for you when next we see each other. All the ladies said a prayer for you in the army and militia. So many from Waltham, Watertown, and surrounding towns signed up to serve. We are very proud of all of you and the patriot resistance remains strong here. News of the British attacks in the southern colonies is heartbreaking. It seems as if the King's commanders think that's where they shall gain an advantage. We hear New York City is still in the grasp of General Clinton. Thankfully our Boston remains in the hands of patriots. It should give you great comfort to know we feel safe from the regulars here in Waltham. I love you beyond measure my dear Samuel. I lay my head on my pillow each night thinking of you and longing for when I can hold you again. Know that after I fold my letters, I lay a kiss upon the seal that your lips might meet mine when you receive it. All my love and devotion,

Yours Truly,

Tabitha

Tabitha dropped a little rose water on the paper, hoping that the aroma might arrive along with her words. She folded the letter and sealed it with wax and a kiss.

She would ask Father to deliver it to the tavern, where the courier would pick up the mail and deliver it to Postmaster Hastings in Cambridge.

Tabitha set the letter on the kitchen table and quietly climbed the stairs leading to the second floor. She was already in her nightgown and ready for bed.

All was quiet in the house now. Her brothers and sisters had long since been told by Mother to go to sleep. But she heard some giggling as she stepped down the hall to her room. She couldn't wait to lay her head on her pillow. She was exhausted.

CHAPTER 17
The Battle Of Paulus Hook

Soon after the attack on Stony Point, Wayne, Fleury, and Steward received gold medals. Knox and Gibbon, who led the two Forlorn Hopes, were promoted to captain.

Samuel heard talk in the officers' barracks that General Washington was looking for a way to repeat the success of the mission somewhere else and might need a few members of the Light Infantry. Then Major Harry Lee visited West Point at Washington's invitation to talk about a plan Lee had proposed. (119)

Samuel heard the pounding of horse hooves and saw Lee ride into camp as the Light Infantry was drilling on the parade ground. Samuel and the other soldiers saluted the Major as his horse galloped past them.

They all admired his courage, skill, and fearless nature.

A few days later, Samuel and some others from the Massachusetts Light Infantry were asked if they were interested in another mission. There would be no official order for their involvement. They were told Lee had used his best scout, Captain Allen McLane, to survey Stony Point's defenses before the attack and used McLane again to inspect the British defenses at Paulus Hook. They were also told McLane didn't think an attack would be successful. That made an attempted assault on Paulus Hook a dangerous mission.

That's apparently why Lee wanted to include some experienced soldiers from the success at Stony Point in his plan against Paulus Hook.

Major Lee was based at Paramus, about twenty miles north of Paulus Hook, and had assembled a force of Marylanders with

Captain Levin Handy in command as well as two hundred Virginia infantry and McLane's cavalry. McLane's dragoons would be on foot.

Samuel and a few others of the Massachusetts Light Infantry volunteered to take part in the attack. On August 18, Samuel and the others were ordered to ride on horseback some forty miles from West Point to New Bridge to join Major Lee and roughly four hundred other soldiers. Then around four in the afternoon they all began a sixteen-mile march to Paulus Hook.

Mountainous trails and thick woods made it a difficult trek. And along the route, Samuel overheard Virgina Major Jonathan Clark arguing with Major Lee. It sounded like they were arguing over who should be in command. It was now dark.

Soon after the ruckus and the confusion about which trail they should take, about a hundred of the Virginians had separated from the main group.

Clark stayed with the main body, while Lee seemed unfazed by the dispute and marched forward. It was a long and grueling journey, much like the march to Stony Point, and now they had a smaller force.

More than ten hours had passed and some of them were fatigued. A rising tide meant the soldiers had to wade through marshes while trying to keep their powder dry. It turned out dry powder wasn't much of a concern.

About two miles from the fort, Lee ordered the soldiers to fix their bayonets and to keep their muskets unloaded. Now it became clear why Lee wanted the Light Infantry used at Stony Point for this attack.

The soldiers formed three columns and when they got closer, Lee ordered a few men to clear the abatis just outside the fort. Soon Samuel and the others waded through chest-high water and now their powder was soaked. The march had gone on much longer than anticipated. First morning light revealed their approach and the redcoats opened fire.

"Attack!" yelled Lee.

Undaunted by the gunfire, Samuel and the others realized their best defense was to run forward quickly.

"Attack, men!" shouted Samuel as he rushed forward with the others in his column. The rebels climbed over the fort walls and put their bayonets and swords to work.

"Die, rebel!" one of the redcoats shouted at Samuel as he charged forward. Samuel dodged to his right and shoved his bayonet in the man's left side as he slid past.

"Not today," replied Samuel.

The enemy soldier didn't hear Samuel's words over the sound of his own cry of pain as he slumped to the ground.

Samuel had fought like this before, and his training took over. Lunging and stabbing. Dodging and ducking. A dangerous dance with death. In minutes, it was done.

The Continental troops had quickly overwhelmed the regulars in the fort. Most had been asleep. Some fifty redcoats lay on the ground dead or wounded. Two patriots dead. Three wounded.

The surprise attack mostly worked. Women and children in the camp awoke from the noise, peered outside, and to their horror saw enemy soldiers rounding up prisoners. Lee saw the women and children and abandoned his plan to burn the barracks and spoil the cannons.

Receipt for a Horse.— —

Receipt for a horse from Samuel Benjamin's documents at Yale University Archives

The soldiers gathered more than 150 redcoats and began the retreat to New Bridge. The return trip was just as grueling, and now they had redcoat prisoners to manage.

A party of British regulars rushed out of the woods a few miles into the retreat and opened fire on the rear of the rebel column. Thankfully, Lee's experience had taught him to have a covering force guard the retreat, and the Brits quickly abandoned their attack.

Samuel was exhausted by the time they reached the New Bridge camp. First, he checked on his horse to make sure the mare had oats and water. He'd already pitched his tent. But his uniform was damp from wading through the marshes. So, he had to start a fire and strip down to dry everything and sneak inside his tent. Samuel was thankful he'd left his diary behind in camp. It would have been ruined in the water. He found his quill and ink. The march to Paulus Hook started on the eighteenth, so that's how Samuel entered it into his diary.

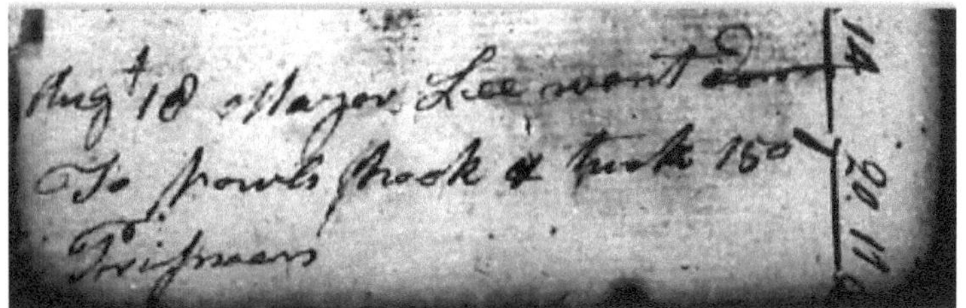

Image from Lieutenant Samuel Benjamin's war diary, Yale University Archives

"Aug 18 Major Lee went down to Paulus Hook & tuck 150 Prisoners."

Tabitha would have been furious if she knew he had volunteered for the task. But what good was it being a soldier if you were unwilling to follow your sense of duty? Samuel corked his ink bottle and tucked away his quill. He laid his head down on his bedroll with an image of Tabitha filling his thoughts. She was so beautiful. He loved her eyes the most, and then he was asleep.

Chapter 18
Heading Home

The fifer and drummer played Reveille as they did each morning. Samuel awoke to the music. He wasn't just tired. He was drained. There was a difference.

He usually felt rested after sleeping. This morning, he felt…empty. Was it marching and fighting wet? More killing? Maybe all of it? He missed Tabitha. He missed home. He would apply for a furlough.

He was surprised at how quickly he'd come to the decision. Home was some two hundred miles away and he doubted his commanders would allow a member of the Light Corps to leave with the British continuing to test the Continental defenses in the Hudson River Valley.

Samuel didn't even feel like breakfast. He would eat a biscuit and salt meat later. He just wanted to get dressed, clear his camp, and ride back to West Point. He climbed out of his tent and found the others from the Light Infantry already up and breaking camp.

"What say you, boys, should we get out of here and head back to the Highlands?" asked Samuel.

"Yeah," they all said nearly in unison. Their captain gave them permission to return to their headquarters. They got their horses ready and were on their way.

The journey was unremarkable. But it was sill late afternoon before they arrived at West Point. Samuel turned in his horse at the stable, got a receipt, and walked back to his barracks. He was starving. But determined. His first order of business was writing a note requesting a furlough and then to get it to Major Hull. He dropped the note off with Hull's adjutant. Would they allow him to leave? Was there another fight around the corner? The questions swirled in his mind as he asked the other officers what the quartermaster had provided for dinner.

There was fresh fish from the river and squash and carrots from local farmers. The man designated to cook tonight always performed admirably. That was not usually the case. Other cooks burned the meat or left it undercooked, which sickened the soldiers who ate it. Some of the beef or pork was already of questionable quality. It didn't help to have it poorly prepared. Still, Samuel thought, it was not nearly as bad as the food the men and camp followers had to eat at Valley Forge. He had lived the highs and lows of the army.

"This fish is delicious," said Captain James Keith.

"It all tastes great!" replied Samuel. "I've never had better squash."

"So, tell us about what happened at Paulus Hook, Ensign Benjamin?" asked the Captain. Samuel kept chewing and thought about the question. He liked Captain Keith. He was from Easton, about thirty miles south of Boston. He was married and had a child. An experience Samuel hoped to enjoy in time. Samuel answered when he finished a bite of fish.

"The regulars didn't put up much of a fight. I tell you, the march through the mountainous woods and wading through the water was the toughest part. Major Lee had hoped to repeat the success of the Stony Point surprise, arriving in the dark and attacking with unloaded guns. But the tide had come in by the time we neared the fort, and our approach was slowed by several hours. We'd already had to wade through some marshes. Then the water was chest high near the redcoats' works. Our powder was wet. The bayonet was our only option, which was Lee's plan all along. First light revealed us, and we ran through the Brits' gunfire, and took them with little effort. Only two of us fell. Three others wounded," replied Samuel.

"You look worn out, Ensign. You've done more than your part. Why don't you take some time away?" asked Captain Keith.

"I've put in for a furlough, sir. It'd like to see my sweetheart," answered Samuel.

"I'll encourage Major Hull to grant it when I see him," said Captain Keith.

"Thank you, sir," replied Samuel. "You must miss your family?"

"I do. But my wife is a gracious woman, and she believes in our cause," said Captain Keith.

"So does Tabitha," replied Samuel.

"Tabitha?" inquired the Captain. "I assume she's your sweetheart."

"Yes sir. I plan to marry her when this is all over. If she'll have me and her father gives the okay," said Samuel.

"Lieutenant, I'm sure her father would be proud to have a valiant soldier join their family. And of course she'll say yes. Just ask her and hold your sword like this!" laughed Captain Keith. He pulled his sword from the scabbard and held it as if he was going to attack.

Samuel chuckled. "I'm hoping she'll say yes without fear of injury," he said, laughing. The officers at the table all joined in the laughter and continued to enjoy cordial conversation for several more minutes.

Samuel finished his meal and headed back to the barracks, still smiling at Captain Keith pulling his sword as part of a marriage proposal.

Samuel wanted to read his Bible outside while there was still summer light. He loved the heat of summer when it was tolerable. But for a moment, he thought about the horrible heat of Monmouth, and the men who had died from heat exhaustion as well as his own struggle with incredible thirst that day.

He sat on a bench outside the barracks, the sun's rays warm against his face. He closed his eyes and thought of Tabitha. Would she say yes? She had to, or his heart would be forever broken. He had seen love in her eyes, and she certainly saw it in his. His feelings for her were so strong, so overwhelming, that he couldn't have hidden his love for her if his life depended on it. Now he wanted to go home more than ever.

He prayed. "Dear God. Thank you for Tabitha. I do not deserve her love. But I am thankful for it. I humbly ask, please protect her from all harm. Protect all those who I love. I pray I will be able to return to her, and be her husband one day, when this war is through with me. And please bless us with children. As you have commanded God in Ephesians, I promise to bring up our children in the nurture and admonition of you. I thank you for keeping me alive thus far. And ask for your continued blessing. I pray these things in your name, Father. Amen."

Samuel opened his eyes and took in his surroundings. The sun shone brightly on the beautiful wooded hills and valleys around West Point. He reached for his Bible on the bench next to him and opened it to the Psalms. He leafed through till he found chapter 9. He read verse 2.

"I will say of the LORD, He is my refuge and my fortress: my God; in him will I trust."

Samuel found comfort in that verse. Although he knew it was no guarantee. He could be killed in battle, or by disease, or some mishap.

But he was confident. His faith assured him that if he was killed, he would go to heaven. He only hoped he would live long enough to be Tabitha's husband and the father of their children. If he was blessed with children. He didn't want them to be without their father like he was without his. Samuel wondered how different his life would have been if his father had not been killed serving in the King's militia. The sun was sinking lower in the sky, and he needed to dry, clean, and oil his musket and prepare some more cartridges.

He'd already thrown out the waterlogged gun powder from the attack on Paulus Hook. The sun set by the time he had finished his nightly chores, and he headed off to bed. The Light Infantry continued with daily drilling and all the customs of life in camp.

The days seemed to drag on as he waited for word on his furlough request. He had recovered some from the fatigue that followed the fighting at Paulus Hook. Still, he continued to feel as if he had not recovered. He awoke on the morning of September 6 and once again wondered if he'd hear anything about a new battle. He was having breakfast with the other officers when Captain Keith approached.

"Ensign Benjamin, I have good news," said the Captain.

"Yes sir. What is it?" asked Samuel.

"Your furlough has been approved. Also, I have a note from His Excellency's aide-de-camp this morning reimbursing you for the expenses you incurred for your mission to recruit the men in Springfield who enlisted for nine months of service. As for your furlough, you're to leave right away as soon as you can arrange for a horse and supplies for your trip. You're already very familiar with the route through Springfield, having just recruited there. See the quartermaster for the money owed to you for recruiting. That should help pay for your travel home. I assume you're going to see that girl you told me about? She's in Waltham, right?" replied Captain Keith.

"Yes sir," answered Samuel.

"I hope she says yes, Ensign. Remember to bring your sword," the Captain said laughing.

"I will, sir. Thank you, sir!" Samuel replied smiling.

"You can thank Major Hull when you see him. I told him you wanted to ask some girl to marry you," said Captain Keith.

"She's a patriot, sir. She joined the Daughters of Liberty," said Samuel proudly.

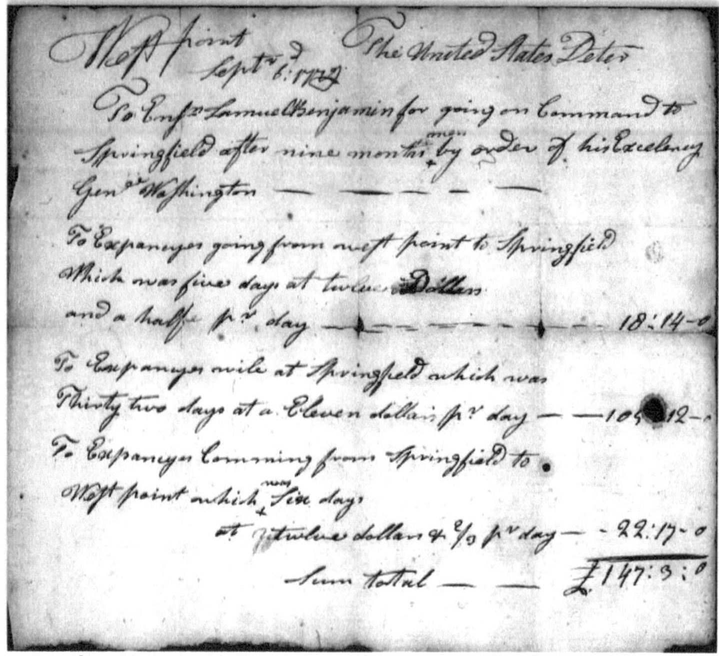

West point Septr 6: 17[illegible] The United States Dtor

To Ensn Samuel Benjamin for going on Command to Springfield after nine months men by order of his Excellency Genl Washington — — — — —

To Expanses going from west point to Springfield which was five days at twelve Dollars and a halfe pr day — — — 18:14-0

To Expanses while at Springfield which was Thirty two days at a Eleven dollars pr day — — 105:12-0

To Expanses Comming from Springfield to West point which was Six days at twelve dollars & 2/3 pr day — 22:17-0

Sum total — — £147:3:0

Image from Lieutenant Samuel Benjamin's documents at Yale University Archives

Samuel tipped his hat to the Captain, turned, and hurried over to the fort stables to make sure he could secure a horse for his journey to Massachusetts. Samuel would need a strong and healthy steed for the long ride.

"Hello, friend. I need another good horse you can spare for about a month," said Samuel to the stable master.

"Where are you headed this time, Ensign? I didn't expect to see you so soon," said the soldier.

The two had become familiar over the summer. And, of course, Samuel had just returned the horse he'd ridden to New Bridge.

"I'm headed home to Waltham just outside of Boston," responded Samuel.

"I'm familiar. That's some two hundred miles. I've got just the fellow for you. He's a dapple-grey Arabian. We acquired him after a skirmish. Apparently, he belonged to a fallen British officer. No one knew his name. So, I've christened him after His Excellency's horse—Nelson. He seems okay with it. He hasn't complained," laughed the portly soldier.

He walked Samuel down the stable corridor and stopped in front of Nelson's stall. The stallion was a somewhat stately animal a little more than fifteen hands tall. Nelson looked at Samuel with a wary eye. Samuel returned the stare.

"Let's be friends, old boy," said Samuel as the gate opened with a squeak.

Nelson snorted. But didn't draw his head away when Samuel reached out to pet the side of Nelson's face. "That's it. I promise to take good care of him," said Samuel.

"When are you leaving?" asked the stable master.

"I hope to be on my way in an hour," said Samuel.

"Let's get you a saddle, blanket, and bridle then, shall we," said the soldier.

"You can walk him back to the officers' barracks and tie him outside until you're ready to ride," said the private.

Samuel would also need a good map to guide him on his way. He also thought he should check with a couple of the other officers from Massachusetts about innkeepers who were friendly to the cause.

Continental soldiers needed to be careful about staying away from loyalist-leaning establishments lest they be spies for the King.

His mind was racing. Samuel had no way of letting Tabitha or his family know he was returning. He'd arrive home as fast as or faster than a letter courier who would have to make multiple stops along the way. Samuel figured he'd average about thirty miles a day on horseback if the weather cooperated. It would take him roughly a week to make the trip.

The weather was clear. There was still plenty of daylight and he decided he would leave in an hour. He could put in at least twenty miles before sunset. Finding water for his horse along the way was fairly easy. But he'd need a bag of feed to cover a couple of days. A hungry horse was a stubborn horse.

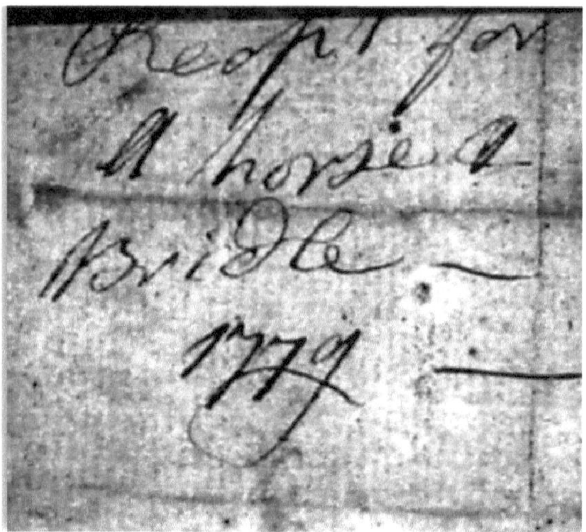
Recp't for
a horse a
Bridle —
1779 —

Image from Lieutenant Samuel Benjamin's documents

He tied a blanket onto the dragoon saddle, which had a lower pommel and cantle. Samuel also swapped his longer musket for a smoothbore carbine with a shorter barrel that would fit the saddle scabbard. He wanted to travel light to make better time without tiring out his horse. If he couldn't easily find a tavern or inn to sleep, he would do so on the ground. He was used to sleeping that way on the battlefield. It would be much easier to fall asleep on the ground without the fear of an attack. Of course, there was always the danger of a rattlesnake or a bear. Catamounts or lions weren't much of a threat because they seemed to be afraid to encounter people. Samuel had heard the Mohawk call the big cats Kenreks, which he had a hard time saying. Starting a fire would scare off wild critters for most of the night. He made sure he had his flint, steel, and char cloth.

September weather remained mild. He wouldn't wear his regimental wool coat and waistcoat. And he wouldn't need his leather Light Infantry helmet. Instead, he chose his cocked hat and hunting frock along with his linen breeches and leather riding boots. He'd brought his spurs along from home and buckled them onto his boots. It would be less risky to travel not looking like a Continental officer.

He packed some salt meat and biscuits in his haversack, filled his canteen with water, and headed outside where his horse was tied up. He grabbed the double leather reins of the snaffle bridle, put his left foot in the left stirrup, rose up while swinging his right leg over the saddle, and mounted his horse.

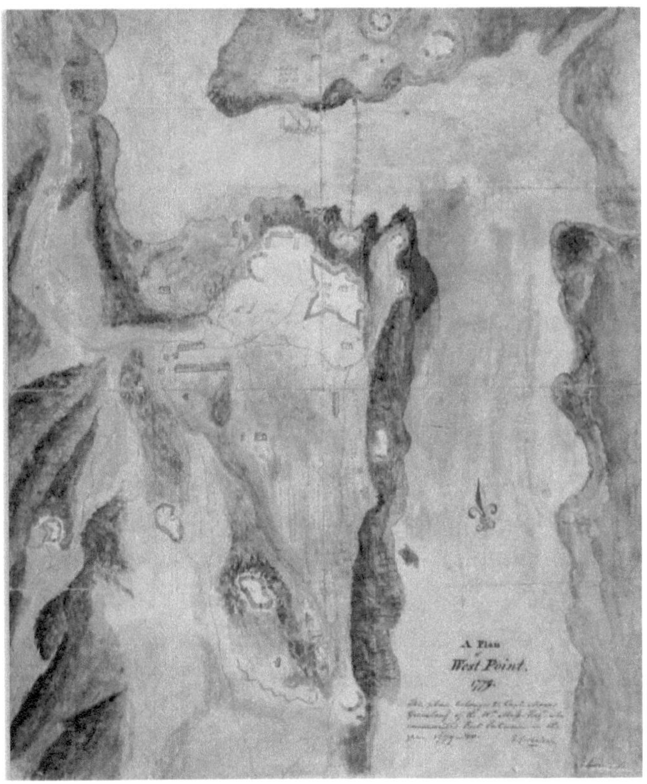

Manuscript Plan of West Point Drawn by Moses Greenleaf, 1779, Paper, Ink, Watercolor, Collection of the Massachusetts Historical Society

The spirited stallion moved his hind legs back and forth. Then snorted. But quickly settled under Samuel's weight as horse and rider considered each other for a moment and then settled into the relationship.

Samuel rode out of West Point in little more than an hour after his talk with Captain Keith. He couldn't cross the river at King's

Ferry because it was back under the threat of the King's soldiers after they retook Stony Point. And Dobbs Ferry was too far down river. He would ride north and find a smaller ferry crossing upriver from the Great Chain that could carry his horse, likely near Fishkill.

Samuel was on the lookout for small critters and snakes that could spook his horse and cause the animal to rear up and throw him. The trail near West Point was well worn and easy going for several miles moving north. He'd have to practice patience and not overwork his new four-legged friend when the trail got more challenging.

It would take him a week to make it to Waltham with proper overnight rest and decent weather. He'd had a lot of time to think.

Now that Samuel could put his military duty behind him for a few days, his mind was filled with how it would feel to hold Tabitha in his arms, to smell her hair, to breathe the same air as her. He decided he would offer a proposal of marriage. His heart would give him no other choice.

His mother had given him a small locket that had passed from his paternal grandmother after his father's death. He would retrieve it from the belongings he'd left in Watertown.

Samuel treasured the locket, and it would serve as a perfect token of his love and commitment to Tabitha if she said yes. He thought it a better gift than the Puritan tradition of a thimble that would then have the top cut off to serve as a wedding ring. (120) Samuel decided he wanted to buy Tabitha a real wedding ring one day that she could wear proudly.

He rolled these thoughts over and over as he filled the long hours of riding. Occasionally he'd pass another rider on the road or perhaps an oxen or horse drawn cart. He'd offer his greetings.

Thankfully, the days passed peacefully, and he only had to sleep on the ground for one night. The one night of rain, he'd been able to find lodging at a tavern.

His heart beat faster as he reached the South Parish of Worcester at sunset on the twenty-first, less than a forty-mile ride to Waltham.

Nonetheless, it was too late to push through and risk his horse stumbling in the dark.

He stopped for the night at the Drury Tavern. Samuel knew of the Drury family as die-hard patriots. Thomas served in the militia and answered the call at Lexington and Concord. The family let him spend the night without payment when he told them he was an ensign from Watertown. One more ride, and Samuel would be in Tabitha's arms. (121)

He awoke before sunrise on the twenty-second, a fine Wednesday morning full of promise. Samuel closed his eyes and thanked God for bringing him safely thus far, asking for his grace and mercy for the final stretch of his journey. He watered Nelson and gave him some oats the Drurys had been kind enough to share. He threw the saddle blanket over the stallion's back, lifted the saddle on, and cinched it tight. Then he untied Nelson and grabbed the reins.

"We're almost there, Nelson. You'll soon get a few days' rest, my friend," said Samuel reassuringly.

He lifted his left foot into the stirrup and climbed aboard his newfound compatriot. It was almost as if Nelson knew the way to Tabitha. Samuel barely had to tug at the reins, and the horse was trotting east.

The ride took Samuel and Nelson through Westborough and Southborough through Weston. He was almost there. Two miles out, Samuel spurred Nelson into a gallop. His four-legged friend seemed to sense he was almost done for the day. Two hundreds yard out, and Samuel could see the top of the Livermore home through the distant trees. His heart pounded.

It was dinner time and he knew Tabitha and her entire family would be home, likely still gathered around the table. He could see smoke coming from the chimney. He could smell something delicious as he drew near the house. Nelson slowed to a stop. Samuel slid off the saddle and tied up his horse to the hitching post.

He hurried to the kitchen door and knocked loudly. The door opened and Samuel saw Tabitha's father with a surprised look on his face. Samuel gestured a shush with the index finger of his right hand. Mr. Livermore smiled and shook Samuel's hand.

"Who is it, Nathaniel?" asked Martha from the dining room.

"Nathaniel, who is it?" Tabitha's mother asked again.

Samuel walked quickly to where the Livermore children were all seated eating their dinner. Tabitha squealed in delight.

"Samuel!" she shouted in surprise.

"Oh my goodness, you're home!" she said in surprise as she ran to his open arms.

"I am!" Samuel exclaimed, chuckling.

He held Tabitha tightly in his arms and breathed in the smell of rosewater and joy. It felt like a dream for both of them as if it couldn't be real that they were together again.

"You're not in uniform. Are you home for good? Please tell me it's so," said Tabitha.

"No. I'm home just for a few days. And I am blessed that Major Hull granted me these days to be home. Let's just enjoy our time together, my dear Tabitha, and not worry about the days to come," replied Samuel.

He strengthened his grip on her for a moment to emphasize the point.

"Oh, I've missed you so," said Tabitha.

The children had all pushed away from the table. Now they gathered round Samuel and Tabitha, tugging at Samuel's hunting frock as if to signal they too wanted hugs. Which he granted one by one. David waited till the last to get his hug. And when it came, he didn't want to let Samuel go.

"Tell me about being a soldier!" said nine-year-old David with excitement as he removed his arms from Samuel's waist.

"There is much to tell," said Samuel.

"Please, Samuel, sit down and I'll prepare you a plate. You must be starving?" said Martha.

"Indeed I am, Mrs. Livermore. I have been dreaming of eating one of your delicious meals for two hundred miles, ever since I left West Point," said Samuel.

"Nathaniel has just butchered one of our Devon steers. You can enjoy fresh beef before it is potted, Samuel," said Martha.

"David, would you please get Samuel a chair," said Nathaniel.

"Yes sir," answered David obediently.

David returned from the parlor with a ladderback chair and slid it right next to his chair at the table.

Samuel laughed. "Somehow I knew I'd end up sitting next to you, David," he said, smiling.

Martha brought Samuel a plate of roast beef, fresh turnips, carrots, and Indian Corn. Tabitha's chair was directly across the table from David's place and, of course, now Samuel. She sat staring at Samuel, still in disbelief that her sweetheart was home.

"Have you had to kill any redcoats?" David asked.

"David, give Samuel a moment to breathe and eat some food," said Martha. "I'm sure Samuel will be glad to share stories with you, son, once he's done eating."

Samuel stabbed a piece of beef with his fork and slid it into his mouth. The savory juice spread from side to side as his tongue lifted the warm liquid to the roof of his mouth. He held the deliciousness there for a moment as he closed his eyes and took in the flavor of the mouthwatering, slightly salty, and rich meat.

"Mm…incredibly good, Mrs. Livermore," uttered Samuel.

He swallowed and opened his eyes, which were met by the deep blue eyes of Tabitha. There it is. Pure, sweet, magical love.

He knew in that moment he would die for her, do anything for her, except the one thing she dare not ask him to do—resign from his commission in the army. Tabitha knew how strongly Samuel felt about the cause of liberty. She also shared the passion as a patriot. And she was torn between her love and concern for Samuel and what she knew would be the only way they could truly be happy together. To fight against and be free from the Crown.

"I received your letter after you fought at Stony Point, Samuel. I shared it with Martha and Elisha. They share my concern about the dangers you face serving with the Light Infantry. Elisha tells me the

Light Corps often fights with smaller numbers and in much riskier situations," said Tabitha in a worried voice.

"It's true. But it is a great honor to be chosen for the Light Infantry, and I serve with some amazingly good and brave men. If I may quote General Wayne after Stony Point. He said, 'Our officers and men behaved like men who are determined to be free,'" said Samuel.

Nathaniel lifted his glass of cider and spoke, "Here, here. I raise my glass to Samuel and the others of the Continental Light Infantry. May the Lord's favor shine upon Samuel and his fellow soldiers who fight for our liberty."

Samuel joined him, as did Tabitha and the older children, Moses, John, and Lydia.

"Thank you, sir. We look out for each other. My fellow soldiers are my brothers in arms. We are all deeply committed to the cause," said Samuel.

Tabitha looked at Samuel.

"I am proud of you, my dear," said Tabitha. "Just worried. That's all."

"I understand," replied Samuel.

"After dinner, if you two would like some privacy, you have our permission to retire to the parlor," offered Nathaniel.

"I think we should very much like that sir," said Samuel.

"Yes, Father. Thank you," parroted Tabitha.

Her younger siblings mocked them with smooching noises and giggles.

"Enough, children," scolded Martha.

"Can you tell me just one story?" begged David.

"Certainly," said Samuel.

Martha looked at him with caution. Samuel understood her glance and had no intention of sharing stories of the horrors of war. Instead, he chose to talk about the "Great Chain."

"The most amazing thing I have seen at West Point, David, is what we call the 'Great Chain.' Imagine links that are two feet across made of iron each weighing more than your father. Now imagine a chain of those links stretching for six hundred yards across the mighty North River. It is so heavy, the only thing keeping it afloat are massive logs tied to the chain, so that it won't sink. It's a testament of man's ingenuity. And you might ask David why someone would build such a thing? Let me tell you. It keeps the ships of the King's Royal Navy from moving freely on the Hudson. And the King's Navy has not dared challenge it. Because we have great guns, mighty cannons, pointed down from on high at West Point. The ships would have to slow and turn their broadsides to fire their cannons in an effort to blow it apart. And then our cannons would blow those ships apart!" Samuel said excitedly.

"Wow!" said David. "Have you seen those cannons fire?"

Samuel responded, "Many times, David. As a matter of fact, my brother John is a corporal in Colonel John Crane's Third Artillery and now mans some of those cannons at West Point."

"They must be loud?" asked David.

"The boom of a cannon is very loud. Especially if you're close by," answered Samuel.

"Clean your plate now, David," said his mother.

"Yes ma'am," replied David obediently.

"Mother and Father, can Samuel and I be excused?" asked Tabitha.

"Certainly. Children, stay out of the parlor," said Tabitha's father.

Samuel and Tabitha retreated to the parlor and sat in the chairs on either side of the whale oil lamp on a small, circular walnut table. Samuel could smell the pungent scent of the burning whale oil. It wasn't as displeasing as the burning fish oil often used in Betty lamps he'd carry around in the barracks and in his tent. The light in the parlor lamp would flicker from time to time. But he paid it no attention as he focused on Tabitha—her beautiful blue eyes and the sound of her voice.

"Tell me about West Point and your journey home, Samuel?" asked Tabitha.

"West Point sits on a flat plain settled into the hills and overlooks the Hudson River. It's really quite beautiful. The fort is surrounded by forested mountains. Each day I try to take a moment to breathe in the serenity of the place when the air is not filled with musket or cannon fire. Thankfully, the gunfire has been for practice, not attack," said Samuel.

"And what of your journey home, Samuel?" asked Tabitha.

"I was given a fine horse. And we got along quite well. I was only forced to sleep on the ground one night and the weather was pleasing. The rest of the time I found lodging at taverns or inns. I met some fine people during my stays. Most are vocal patriots. And when they discover you are a soldier for the cause, they treat you quite warmly and generously," said Samuel.

"That's wonderful! I still cannot believe you are home. It seems like a dream, Samuel. I've missed you so much and worry so greatly. I pray for you several times a day. I'm grateful I have my chores, helping Mother, sewing, and helping with the children to occupy my thoughts. Otherwise, I think I should go mad with worry," said Tabitha.

"God has so far shown me favor. I'm trying to live according to His purpose. I have been faithful to our love, my dear. You are also a constant fixture in my thoughts and prayers," Samuel said earnestly.

He slid his chair close enough so that he could hold Tabitha's hands in his. And for a moment, they took enjoyment in just being close to each other, the warmth of each other's hands, and for the first time in a long time, Tabitha did not have to wonder if Samuel was safe.

"How can I let you return to the army, Samuel? I wish you could just stay home like Elisha," said Tabitha with sadness in her voice.

"Our circumstances are different, my dear. And I must continue so that men like Elisha can come home and know their fellow soldiers will continue the fight. So that we may all, one day, enjoy a newfound freedom," answered Samuel.

"I know what you say is true. But my heart struggles to accept it. What if you are killed or maimed, as has happened to so many of our wonderful men? I will grieve forever what we could have had," said Tabitha.

Samuel paused before answering. He knew what she said was true. And that his life could end on any given day whether from gunfire or disease when he returned to his duty. But in his heart, he knew he had no choice. His resolve for the cause was resolute.

"I hear the passion in your voice. And I dream of the day when this terrible war will end, and I can come home to your arms once and for all. But I am committed to help end this struggle with victory for those of us who have already sacrificed so much for our new nation. I sacrifice for you, your family, my family, and for God. My heart will tell me when it's time to come home. And I pray the Lord's protection until such time as my mind and heart change. For now, I only ask that you should trust that God has called me to this duty. And pray for my safety and success," said Samuel tenderly.

"You know I have and will. I love you, Samuel, with all my heart and soul. I only hope that God's plan is for you to come home and not die for the cause," said Tabitha.

"Me too, my dear. You know how I feel about you. I shall ask your father for your hand in marriage. Let's not worry about what might not happen. And instead direct our thoughts to the dream of our future and family," said Samuel as he caressed her hands.

They spoke for a few minutes more, exchanging funny stories about this or that, and then parted for the night. Samuel needed to head to his home and see if the boarders had been taking care of the place. He would no doubt have to shake the dust off his bed before he'd be able to sleep. He carried a candle lantern outside and made a quick stop at the Livermores' stable to check on his old friend Samson. He was greeted by the earthy and sweet smell of fresh cut hay.

"How are you, old boy?" Samuel said to the horse he'd left behind.

He received a soft whinny in return. Samson's eyes seemed to light up when he saw Samuel and heard his voice.

"I hope you have been earning your keep around here. You have to promise me you'll stay well till I return home from this war, my friend," said Samuel.

He rubbed the side of Samson's head a few times and fed him a handful of corn he found in a bucket inside the barn. When Samuel turned to leave he heard another whinny directed at his back, which made him smile.

He had left the saddle on Nelson and was thankful the moon would provide light for his three-mile ride east to the Benjamin farm in Watertown.

Samuel awoke the next morning determined that today he would return to the Livermores' farm and ask Mr. Livermore for his daughter's hand. He wasn't sure he'd receive a yes.

Perhaps Tabitha's father would not allow him to ask until he returned from the war. Nathaniel might want to protect Tabitha's heart should Samuel be killed. Samuel knew her heart would be broken even if there wasn't an intention of marriage. They were madly in love and formalities could not protect them from grievous loss.

Samuel didn't grab anything for breakfast. He retrieved something much more important—his grandmother's locket. He stuffed it into the right pocket of his breeches, walked outside, saddled up Nelson, and rode west to the Livermores'.

When he arrived, he found Mr. Livermore feeding his dairy cow in the barn.

"Good morning, Mr. Livermore," said Samuel.

"Top of the morning to you, Samuel. I expected I might see you first thing today. How did you sleep?" asked Nathaniel.

"I slept well, sir. Although it took me a bit to get my chamber ready for bed. It's been a while since I was home, as you know," replied Samuel. Nathaniel finished his chore and turned to face Samuel.

"You look like something's on your mind, Samuel," said Nathaniel.

Tabitha's suitor found this moment nearly as nerve-racking as preparing for battle. He paused for a moment, stood tall, and then the words came out.

"There is, sir. I would like to ask for your daughter's hand in marriage, sir, if you'll allow it," said Samuel.

"I wondered when your question would come, son. It's apparent to everyone around you that you belong together. I have worried about my daughter should something happen to you. Her heart already belongs to you, and she is of age to make her own decisions. But I am honored that you respect my role as her father. You have my consent, Samuel. Just try not to get yourself killed," said Nathaniel.

He stepped toward Samuel and extended his hand. Which Samuel grasped with a strong grip.

"Thank you, sir. I will treasure her all the days of my life. And hopefully we'll give you some grandchildren to spoil," said Samuel.

"When are you going to ask her?" said Nathaniel.

"I planned on today, sir, if I received your permission," replied Samuel.

"Did you really think I'd say no, young man?" asked Nathaniel.

"The military service has taught me not to presume, sir. I only hoped," said Samuel.

"Your hope is realized, Samuel. Tabitha is in the house helping Mary with chores. You best get inside. I'm sure she heard your horses' hooves pounding outside and she's probably wondering why you haven't come to see her yet," Nathaniel said.

"Yes sir. Thank you again, sir!" Samuel exclaimed.

Samuel quickly walked to the house and knocked on the back door off the kitchen.

"Samuel. You're here bright and early. Come inside," Mary said.

"Thank you, Mrs. Livermore," Samuel replied and stepped through the door.

"Tabitha! Samuel is here!" Mary said in a loud voice.

Samuel heard Tabitha's footsteps coming down the hall and then she entered the kitchen with a big smile on her face.

"Good morning, Samuel. Are you hungry?" asked Tabitha.

"I am. I was in a hurry to get over here and didn't have anything to eat at my house since I just got home last night," Samuel replied.

"I saw you head to the barn to talk with Father after I heard your horse trot up. You've got a devilish look in your eye," said Tabitha.

"I have something I want to ask you if we can talk in the parlor," replied Samuel.

"Sure. But do you want to eat first?" asked Tabitha.

"Let's talk first. Then I will take you up on breakfast," Samuel responded.

He grabbed Tabitha's hand and walked with her to the parlor. The morning light was peeking through and creating shadows on the walls opposite the window.

"What is it, Samuel?" asked Tabitha.

Samuel held her hands and faced her. He reached into his right pocket for the prized gift and slowly knelt on one knee.

"Eeeeh!" Tabitha squealed in excitement as tears began streaming from her eyes.

"Tabitha, my love, will you marry me?" asked Samuel as he placed the family heirloom into her hands.

"Yes, yes, yes, a thousand times yes," she replied, more excited than she had ever been in her whole life. Samuel continued to kneel and looked deeply into her eyes.

"My grandmother's locket is now yours, sweetheart. You are my life, my breath, my everything, Tabitha. I am convinced God wants us to be together forever," said Samuel as he rose and quickly pulled Tabitha to his chest, wrapping his arms around her.

He inhaled the smell of her lavender perfume. And Tabitha felt as if she couldn't get close enough to Samuel. Neither wanted to ever let go. Samuel's eyes had also filled with tears of joy. They now had a purpose for their hearts.

Tabitha was twenty-two years old. She had dreamed of this day since she was seventeen, when she had first felt butterflies being in Samuel's company at a church gathering. That was months before that dreadful day at Lexington and Concord when Samuel marched off to battle. Tabitha quickly snuffed that out of her mind and focused on the beauty of the moment. She imagined years of these moments and would hold on to those thoughts as best she could.

"It's awfully quiet in there. What's going on in there, you two?" Mary inquired.

"Mother, come here. I have wonderful news to tell you," she answered, beaming.

They could hear Mary's footsteps coming from the kitchen and then she stepped into the parlor.

"Samuel and I are engaged to be married!" Tabitha said with the most excitement she had ever shown her mother.

Mary rushed to embrace her daughter.

"Oh, dear girl. I know how much you have hoped this day would come. Congratulations to the both of you!" Mary said with a smile. She grabbed Samuel's right hand and that of Tabitha.

"Mother, look at the locket Samuel gave me. It belonged to his mother's mother. Isn't it the most beautiful thing you've ever seen?" Tabitha exclaimed.

"It is, Tabitha. I wish you many wonderful years together, and please promise me you'll bring me grandchildren! But not as quickly as Martha," she said laughing.

"We will, Mother," said Tabitha.

During those beautiful September days, Samuel and Tabitha walked and talked, dreamed and laughed, and fell more deeply in love.

"Samuel!" Elisha said loudly as he walked through the front door of the Livermore home.

"It's good to see you, old friend. I see you have been enjoying Martha's cooking. You're not as skinny as when I last saw you in camp," joked Samuel.

"Indeed. Her meals are certainly better than salt meat and fire cakes. I hope I never have to eat those again," replied Elisha.

"Congratulations on your marriage. Did Martha tell you Tabitha and I are now engaged?" asked Samuel.

"Yes, I did," said Martha as she stepped inside, adorned with a big smile and little Martha in her arms.

"Who is this beautiful little creature?" asked Samuel.

"This is little Martha," said Martha.

Little Martha took one look at Samuel and buried her face in her mother's neck.

Martha directed her voice to her daughter, "Martha, this is Samuel. He's Aunt Tabitha's fiancé. Don't worry. He won't bite," she said playfully.

Little Martha turned her face back to Samuel and gave him a timid smile.

"I hear a brother or sister is on the way?" inquired Samuel.

"Yes. We are so excited. Martha will have someone to share her room. I'm so glad they let you come home for a little while, Samuel. I know my sister would be happier if you would stay," said Martha.

"Someday I will return for good. And Tabitha and I will give little Martha and your other children cousins to play with. But my duty continues for now," said Samuel.

"Dinner is ready, everyone!" called Mary from the kitchen. Samuel was hungry and eager to avoid any more talk about his return to West Point. Sitting at the table with his sweetheart at his side, and the company of friends, filled Samuel's heart with joy. He watched Elisha and Martha with their little girl and dreamed of the same for Tabitha and himself. The love in the room. The comforts of home. Thinking of those things would make Samuel's return to military duty more difficult and more meaningful.

The days for Tabitha and Samuel to spend time together were too short. On the morning of the twenty-second, Samuel stopped at the Livermore home one last time before heading back to West Point. He knocked on the kitchen door. It swung open and he found Tabitha in tears.

"I have dreaded this day, Samuel," said Tabitha.

"I have as well, my love. But my duty as a soldier calls," replied Samuel.

"I know. But I can still hate that you're leaving, can't I?" she said, not really asking for permission.

"I will miss you beyond measure and you will be my first and last thought of each day," said Samuel.

"And you mine," Tabitha replied and continued. "I will pray for your safe return more than ever now. Promise me you will not be too brave. You don't have to win the war all by yourself, you know."

"I fight alongside many great men. We look out for each other. And I will fight wisely. I shall write when I can. Please take care of Samson for me. Will you?" said Samuel.

"Of course. When I feed him each day, I always tell him that you won't be gone forever, and that someday you will bring him home to the Benjamin farm," she answered.

"You mean bring him home to our farm?" replied Samuel with a smile.

"Oh, yes. Our farm," Tabitha said. The hint of a smile appearing.

They wrapped their arms around each other and did not want to let go. Eventually, Samuel removed his arms and held Tabitha's hands in his. He looked into her eyes.

"I must go, my dear. I love you more than life itself," Samuel said.

He forced a smile to hide his sadness. Tabitha couldn't muster a goodbye. It took all her strength to not cry again.

Samuel lifted himself onto Nelson's saddle and gave Tabitha a last look before turning the horse and trotting away.

Samuel's heart was heavy. It was the hardest goodbye he'd ever given. He took special notice of familiar landmarks as he bobbed up and down on Nelson's back.

There was the tall and stately oak at the end of the Livermores' path. The tree's uniform shape stood apart from the others, which could only grow in admiration of their neighbor. The oak's trunk and branches seemed to have been fashioned by God's own hands. The morning sun's rays danced on the foliage flashing multiple hues of green. A soft breeze rustled the leaves and delivered the familiar smell of breakfast coming from chimneys on neighboring homes. Soon the colors would change to yellow, orange, and red.

He adored his Massachusetts. He was willing to die for it and the fellow patriots who called this land home. Would he lay eyes on this place again? Or would news of his death fill Tabitha's eyes with grief and despair?

The rhythm of Nelson's prancing stride helped fill the hours of his journey and helped guide his thoughts to the duty that lay ahead. He made it as far west as Shrewsbury on that first day and stayed at the Cushing-Haven Tavern. It was a well-known patriot meeting spot.

He had pushed Nelson pretty hard and decided he would take it a little easier the next day. But the weather had been good, and he wanted to take advantage.

On the second day, Samuel rode to Spencer and found lodging at Jenks Tavern. The establishment was known for good beds and hearty meals.

He rode the next day until after dark and made it to Springfield on the twenty-fifth of September. He stayed at an inn near the armory. He climbed the stairs to the second floor and found his room at the end of a long hallway lit by candle lanterns.

Septemr 13 1779 I got home
& the 22d day I Set out for Camp
25th I arrived at Springfield from
Waltham — — —

Image from Lieutenant Samuel Benjamin's war diary, Yale University Archives

Once inside, he remembered that in the excitement of being home, he'd forgotten to write in his diary. He was too tired to write much. So, he sat at a desk in the room and grabbed his quill and ink. He simply jotted:

September 13 1779 I got hom
& the 22nd day I set out for camp
25th I arrived at Springfield from Waltham

Samuel was more than a third of the way back to West Point. He still had nearly 130 miles to go, including a ferry crossing.

God willing, he'd live to take Tabitha as his wife. He just had to not get killed. That was in the Lord's hands. Samuel would not change how he fought as a soldier. Being too careful, or timid or cowardly, could get you killed as easily as recklessness in battle. A healthy sense of fear helped a soldier fight smartly and allowed training to come to the fore. Yes, in facing the enemy, his heart raced along with his breathing, his body tensed, and his vision narrowed. But his focus remained clear. That's what had kept him alive. That, and luck, and God's grace. He hoped all those things would deliver him home to Tabitha at the end of this damnable war.

Samuel rode into West Point on the last day of September. He'd resume his duties as an ensign on the first day of October, a Friday. Thankfully, his one saddle sore was minor. Still, he'd be nursing it for a few days.

Chapter 19
A Just Reward

First light. The familiar melody. Samuel had missed waking to Reveille. It was an old friend that reminded a soldier he was still alive. Tabitha. God, he missed her so much.

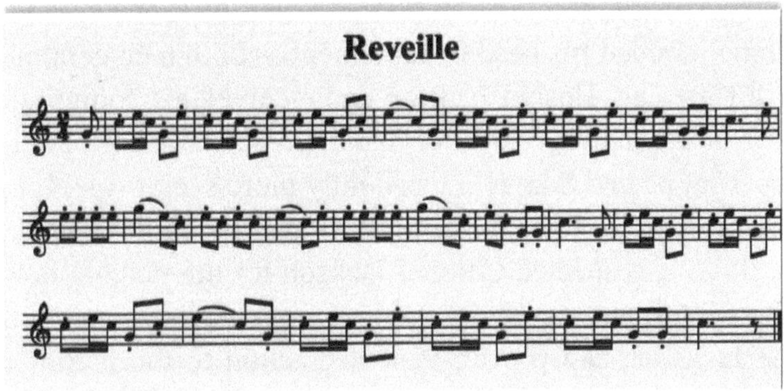

The day would bring a return to drilling and the duties of an ensign. It had been six weeks since the Battle of Paulus Hook. Six weeks since he'd taken another man's life. One of many over the past four years of being a soldier. Some faces he remembered. Others only the sound of their cries. Why did he have to wake with death on his mind? He prayed. "God help me to face this day with hope and courage. Thank you for Tabitha and the time we had together. I pray you will one day deliver me back to her arms. Amen."

Samuel rolled out of his bunk onto the hard wood floor of the officers' barracks. He pulled on his breeches as well as his linen socks with seams in the back where they were stitched together.

Samuel's mother had taught him how to sew. Now, he mended his own clothing. It was a necessary skill for a soldier, especially repairing holes in socks. Thankfully, Tabitha had gifted him a new pair when he was home. He slipped on his boots, waistcoat, and regimental coat, all the accoutrements of an officer, as he prepared for his day.

"Good morning, Samuel," said fellow ensign Michael Jackson.

"Good morning, Michael. Anything significant happen while I was away?" Samuel asked.

"Nothing much, Samuel. Drilling and the daily struggle to get some of our privates to maintain cleanliness. My father has been a little out of sorts these past few days. His old wounds have really been giving him fits. So, stay clear of him if you can. Maybe he's just surly with me because I'm his son," said Jackson.

Samuel nodded his head in agreement as both men continued to ready for the day. Ensign Jackson had received his commission in October, more than a year after Samuel received his promotion to ensign. That placed Samuel in a slightly more senior role. He liked Michael and had noticed his father was awfully hard on him sometimes. Still, he respected Colonel Jackson for not playing favorites with his offspring.

The Jacksons had proven their dedication to the patriot cause long before. Samuel was still amazed the Colonel had his whole family serving at Saratoga, even the ten-year-old. His father's wounds at Breed's Hill and Montresor's Island left the Colonel with a permanent limp and pain. That made him a tremendous example to the men in his regiment even if the Colonel wasn't fully capable of the rigors of the field.

Samuel sought orders from Captain Keith after breakfast. He found the Captain inspecting the muskets of several privates he had ordered into formation near their tents.

"Good morning, Captain," Samuel said.

"I'm glad you came to me, Ensign. You saved me a trip to find you. Colonel Jackson wants to see you in his quarters," said Captain Keith as he continued to look over a musket.

Samuel's stomach started to churn. The Colonel's son had just told him to stay clear of his father and now he'd been ordered to appear in front of the Colonel.

"Yes sir. Do you know what this is about?" asked Samuel.

"Don't worry, Ensign. I think you'll be pleased with your meeting. I'd get over there straightaway," said Captain Keith.

"Yes sir," Samuel replied.

Samuel couldn't imagine why the Colonel would want to see him. Orders usually came through Captain Keith and rarely directly from the Colonel. He reached the Colonel's headquarters and knocked on the door. His aide-de-camp pulled the door open, and Samuel could see Colonel Jackson sitting at his desk. The Colonel looked up and waved Samuel inside.

"Ensign Benjamin, come in," said Colonel Jackson.

Samuel issued a salute with his hat and bowed.

"I'm happy to report to you, Benjamin, you'll no longer be referred to as ensign. But rather as Lieutenant Benjamin. Your new commission papers arrived yesterday by courier," said the Colonel.

"Sir, thank you, sir," replied Samuel.

"You are welcome. Frankly, your promotion is long overdue. And your actions at Stony Point and Paulus Hook added urgency to the matter," the Colonel exclaimed. "I should have asked for a lieutenant's commission for you after you proved yourself at Saratoga. I understand you have a young woman you are sweet on back home?" asked the Colonel.

"Yes sir. She said yes to my proposal of marriage when I was home," Samuel answered.

"What's her name, Lieutenant?" Colonel Jackson asked.

"Tabitha Livermore, sir," replied Samuel.

"I'm familiar with the Livermore name. Some were chosen as selectmen, if I recall," said the Colonel.

"Yes sir. Tabitha's father served as a selectmen a few years back, as did her grandfather. They are a good Christian family and respected members of the community," said Samuel.

“You best write your Tabitha a letter and inform her of your promotion. You are dismissed, Lieutenant Benjamin,” said the Colonel.

“Thank you, sir,” Samuel replied and bowed his head in salute.

“Oh, one more thing, Lieutenant. You’ll be needing this,” said the Colonel as he handed Samuel a newly published copy of von Steuben’s “Regulations for the Order and Discipline of the Troops of the United States.” (122)

“Thank you, sir. I shall commit it to memory, sir,” Samuel said and again saluted.

Samuel kept his composure in the Colonel’s presence. But after the Colonel’s aide closed the door behind him, Samuel uttered a sound of excitement and walked with a spring in his step. It had finally happened. The Colonel didn’t need to tell Samuel to write a letter. He couldn’t wait to tell Tabitha about his promotion.

> October 3, 1779
> West Point
> My Dearest Tabitha, I have the most glorius news. I have received my lieutenant’s commision. I am greatly pleased by my new roll. Colonel Jackson informed me of the commision himself. Obviously since you are reading this you know I arrived safely to West Point without incident. His Excellency has now made West Point his headquarters. His aid-de-camp, Alexander Hamilton, is a man that is greatly respected by all here. I have little else to tell you since I’ve only just returnd except that which is most important—I love you above else.
> Yours forever,

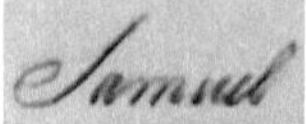

The days of October looked to be uneventful at West Point. That would give Samuel time to study his new duties as a lieutenant.

He had observed Lieutenant Armstrong and others of the rank of subaltern during his several years in the army. But now he must assume those duties and commit them to practice, perfection, and execution.

Earlier in the year, General Washington had requested from the Board of War that von Steuben's "Regulations for the Order and Discipline of the Troops of the United States" be published.

Inſtructions for the Lieutenant.

THE lieutenant, in the abſence of the captain, commands the company, and ſhould therefore make himſelf acquainted with the duties of that ſtation; he muſt alſo be perfectly acquainted with the duties of the non-commiſſioned officers and ſoldiers, and ſee them performed with the greateſt exactneſs.

He ſhould endeavour to gain the love of his men, by his attention to every thing which may contribute to their health and convenience. He ſhould often viſit them at different hours; inſpect into their manner of living; ſee that their proviſions are good and well cooked, and as far

Image from an original copy of Friedrich Wilhelm von Steuben's "Regulations for the Order and Discipline of the Troops of the United States," p. 141, 1779

Congress approved the request in late March, and the first copies were published in Philadelphia. These first copies had been a result of trying to conserve paper amid a shortage. The cover was a board covered in blue paper and the pages were half bound. (123)

Samuel was particularly impacted by von Steuben's instructions that a lieutenant should "gain the love of his men, by his attention to everything which may contribute to their health and convenience."

Samuel thought von Steuben's instructions mirrored how Jesus led his disciples. The General's instructions called for an example of servant leadership and caring for the needs of the privates. But those instructions also called for a lieutenant to discourage complaining about frivolous things and ensure that the rules of subordination were followed.

As a lieutenant, Samuel helped train the new recruits, or "awkward squads." New soldiers had to first learn the basics—how to come to attention, to shoulder their firelocks as well as learn how to carry out the right face and left face, and how to march and halt in an orderly fashion.

Samuel and the other lieutenants' responsibilities also included selecting soldiers for guard duty and making sure they stayed alert and responsible. On Thursday of the first week of October, Samuel was given an even more important task. He was summoned to Colonel Jackson's headquarters.

The Colonel ordered him to gather a dozen fellow members of the 8th Massachusetts Light Infantry and once again travel to Springfield, where he was to take command of a new group of recruits and gather a wagon load of French Charleville muskets and cartridges from the armory.

He'd receive additional orders in Springfield from Captain Samuel Page, the Commanding Officer of Recruits.

Thankfully, the trip to Springfield was without incident. Samuel and his fellow Light Infantry soldiers arrived at the Springfield Armory late on the afternoon of the twelfth. Samuel checked in at the office of the Armory Superintendent, Lieutenant Colonel David Mason. The other soldiers waited outside, surveying the grounds. The armory wasn't in one building, but rather several buildings, some rented. There was the magazine for storing gun powder, muskets, and cartridges as well as a barracks and a laboratory. (124)

Continental magazine at Springfield in 1782, drawing by Samuel Davis

"Good afternoon, Lieutenant Colonel. I'm Lieutenant Samuel Benjamin. I'm here to collect..." Samuel was interrupted by the senior officer.

"No need to introduce yourself, Lieutenant. I've been waiting for you. His Excellency's aide-de-camp sent a courier a few days ago alerting me to your pending arrival. The wagon and muskets are in the barn next door under guard. I've also told the stable master to provide you with two of our best horses for the wagon. Just sign this Bill of Lading, Lieutenant Benjamin. I understand you're also to see Samuel Page about taking command of some recruits," said the Lieutenant Colonel.

"Yes sir. Those are my orders, sir," replied Samuel.

"Make sure you and your men see our quartermaster to replenish your supplies. You are welcome to spend the night in our barracks, and our cook will give your men supper. Lieutenant, you are welcome to dine with me tonight in my quarters," said the Lieutenant Colonel.

"Thank you, sir. I am honored by your invitation, and I will see you for dinner. Thank you, sir," replied Samuel.

"You are dismissed, Lieutenant," answered Lieutenant Colonel Mason.

Samuel and his men walked to the barn, opened the door, and found the wagon as promised. It was already loaded with the Charleville muskets. Samuel told the two men experienced with horses that in the morning they were to head to the stable, gather the two draft horses already assigned to the task, and hitch up the wagon for transport. Meanwhile, Samuel and the other soldiers would organize the recruits for the march.

"For now, men, you are to see the quartermaster to get supplies for our return journey. We've been offered to stay in the armory barracks tonight, and the cook will provide you an evening meal. I expect some rum will also be offered. You are dismissed. I will see you in the barracks after dinner," said Samuel.

He then walked to the recruiting headquarters, where he found a man sitting at a desk inside the front door.

"Good morning, sir," said Samuel. "I'm Lieutenant Benjamin reporting for further orders. I'm supposed to see a Captain Samuel Page of the 11th Massachusetts."

"Yes, Lieutenant. I am he. I have the orders for your return right here per General Washington's instructions. I have another one hundred new recruits who have enlisted for nine months. Roughly half of them are good men who were in their town militias and have some training and experience. The others are quite green, Lieutenant," replied the Captain. Captain Page handed a piece of paper to Samuel.

"Thank you, sir. You're with Tupper's 11th, aren't you?" asked Samuel.

"Yes, Lieutenant. I'm from Danvers. How about you?" replied Captain Page.

"I'm from Watertown, sir. I've been in since Lexington. I saw some of your Danvers men die at the hands of the redcoats in Menotomy," said Samuel.

"Horrible thing. I was there too. Seven of our militia men died that day. My father is Captain Jeremiah Page, who commanded our company, and I served under him," responded the Captain.

"Good to meet you, Captain Page. We Samuels from Massachusetts must stick together, don't you think?" said Samuel cheerfully.

"Indeed we must, Samuel Benjamin. Good to meet you, Lieutenant. Have a prosperous trip," said Captain Page.

"Thank you, sir," replied Samuel.

Samuel stepped outside and began reading the orders. They listed Samuel's new rank as a lieutenant and there was an urgency to the instructions. That meant His Excellency knew about his promotion.

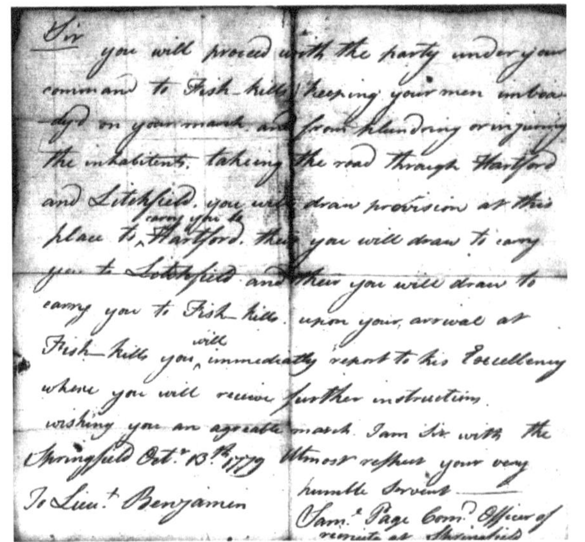
Sir
you will proceed with the party under your command to Fish-kills keeping your men imbodyd on your march and from plundering or injuring the inhabitents, takeing the road through Hartford and Litchfield. you will draw provision at this place to carry you to Hartford. then you will draw to carry you to Litchfield and then you will draw to carry you to Fish-kills. upon your arrival at Fish-kills you will immediatly report to his Excellency where you will receive further instructions. wishing you an agreeable march. I am Sir with the
Springfield Oct.r 13th 1779
Utmost respect your very humble Servent
To Lieu.t Benjamen
Sam.l Page Com.d Officer of recruits at Springfield

Image from Lieutenant Samuel Benjamin's documents, Yale University Archives

And the orders clearly indicated Samuel was to immediately report to General Washington upon his arrival at the Fishkill Supply Depot.

The orders were somewhat cryptic. Why was he to receive further instructions directly from His Excellency? Samuel suspected there was some secret purpose to the next part of his journey.

General Washington must not have wanted to write it into the orders lest the note fall into enemy hands. The orders told Samuel to take the route through Hartford, where they were to resupply. Then march on the trail to Litchfield, where they would again resupply before heading to Fishkill. The orders accounted for the general unruliness of untrained recruits. Samuel was ordered to keep them embodied so they wouldn't be prone to steal or harm any civilians along the way. The march would cover the one hundred miles from Springfield to Fishkill. Thankfully, the next morning the weather was clear, even if a little cold for an October morning. The trail to Fishkill was well worn from years of Continental troop movements and would likely be uneventful.

Samuel ordered his troops to refill their canteens. The horsemen had already secured a bucket so they could water the horses along the way. The march took three days, and at times Samuel was frustrated by the undisciplined and crude behavior of some of the recruits. He had to scold them a few times in camp, telling them that General Washington, or any of his officers, would not allow any crude or profane language in their presence.

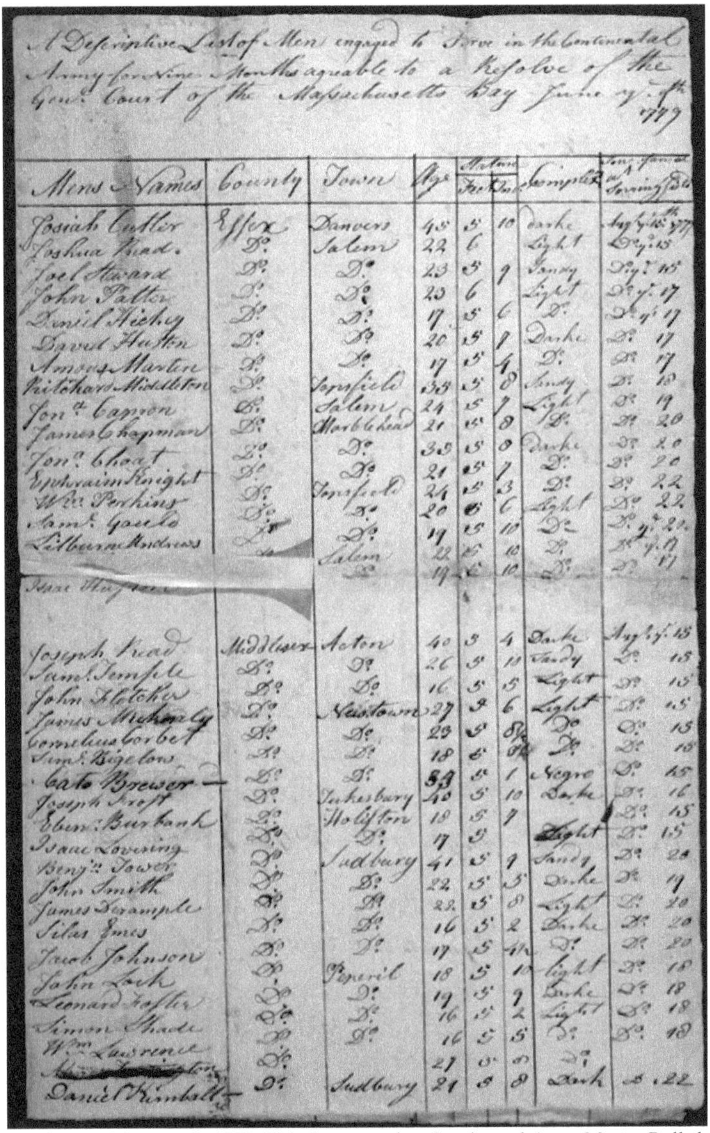

A Descriptive List of Men engaged to Serve in the Continental Army for Nine Months agreable to a Resolve of the Genl. Court of the Massachusetts Bay June 9th 1779

Mens Names	County	Town	Age	Stature Feet	Stature Inches	Complexn	Time of Arrival at Springfield
Josiah Cutler	Essex	Danvers	45	5	10	Darke	Augst 15th 1779
Joshua Read	Do	Salem	22	6		Light	Do 15
Joel Haward	Do	Do	23	5	9	Sandy	Do 15
John Patten	Do	Do	23	6		Light	Do 17
Daniel Hickey	Do	Do	17	5	6	Do	Do 17
David Hutton	Do	Do	20	5	7	Darke	Do 17
Amos Marten	Do	Do	17	5	4	Do	Do 17
Pritchard Middleton	Do	Topsfield	33	5	8	Sandy	Do 18
Jona Cannon	Do	Salem	24	5	7	Light	Do 19
James Chapman	Do	Marblehead	21	5	8	Do	Do 20
Jona Choat	Do	Do	33	5	8	Darke	Do 20
Ephraim Knight	Do	Do	21	5	7	Do	Do 20
Wm Perkins	Do	Topsfield	24	5	3	Do	Do 22
Saml Gould	Do	Do	20	6	6	Light	Do 22
Lilburn Andrews	Do	Do	19	5	10	Do	Do 21
	Do	Salem	22	5	10	Do	Do 17
		Do	19	5	10	Do	Do 17
Isaac Thayer							
Joseph Read	Middlesex	Acton	40	5	4	Darke	Augst 15
Saml Temple	Do	Do	26	5	10	Sandy	Do 15
John Fletcher	Do	Do	16	5	5	Light	Do 15
James Mahonaly	Do	Newtown	27	5	6	Light	Do 15
Cornelius Corbet	Do	Do	23	5	8½	Do	Do 15
Saml Bigelow	Do	Do	18	5	8½	Do	Do 15
Cato Brewer	Do	Do	33	5	1	Negro	Do 15
Joseph Frost	Do	Tewksbury	40	5	10	Darke	Do 16
Ebenr Burbank	Do	Holliston	18	5	7		Do 15
Isaac Lovering	Do	Do	17	5		Light	Do 15
Benja Tower	Do	Sudbury	41	5	9	Sandy	Do 20
John Smith	Do	Do	22	5	5	Darke	Do 19
James Dalrymple	Do	Do	23	5	8	Light	Do 20
Silas Ames	Do	Do	16	5	2	Darke	Do 20
Jacob Johnson	Do	Do	17	5	4½	Do	Do 20
John Lock	Do	Pepperil	18	5	10	Light	Do 18
Leonard Foster	Do	Do	19	5	9	Darke	Do 18
Simon Shade	Do	Do	16	5	2	Light	Do 18
Wm Lawrence	Do	Do	16	5	5	Do	Do 18
[illegible]	Do		21	5	8	Do	
Daniel Kimball	Do	Sudbury	21	5	8	Dark	Do 22

Continental Army Muster roll, 1779. This document is a Continental Army Muster Roll showing recruits from Springfield, Massachusetts in 1779. The roll documents the one hundred men who signed up to serve in the army for nine months. It lists hometown, country, age, stature, complexion, and time of arrival. https://www.mountvernon.org/education/primary-source-collections/primary-source-collections/article/continental-army-muster-roll-1779

Most of the recruits strongly believed in the cause of liberty, and if they were willing to get shot at by redcoats, then Samuel would leave further discipline to the sergeants who would train them. It was a somewhat ragtag group that marched into Fishkill after a three-day journey. He ordered his men to find the quartermaster and turn over the recruits for distribution into the regiments. Samuel was told His Excellency used the Van Wyck House at Fishkill as his headquarters when he was there. (125)

So, Samuel headed straight to the Van Wyck House when he and the men under his command arrived shortly after sundown. He showed the guards outside the home his orders and climbed the short stairs to the front door and knocked. Washington's aide-de-camp, Alexander Hamilton, answered the door. Samuel tipped his hat and bowed in salute. Before he could introduce himself, Hamilton spoke.

"Judging from your uniform and the epaulette on your left shoulder, you are Lieutenant Samuel Benjamin, I presume?" inquired Hamilton.

"Yes sir, Lieutenant Colonel Hamilton," replied Samuel. He thought the Lieutenant Colonel's accent was like something he'd never heard before.

"You are here, Lieutenant, at the request of His Excellency, who has judged you to be a trusted and loyal member of the Light Corps. The General wants to personally give you instructions for the next part of your journey. And he's extended an invitation for you to dine with him this evening. He remembers you, Lieutenant, from the supper at Valley Forge. And he spoke of your gallantry at Stony Point and Paulus Hook," said Lieutenant Colonel Hamilton.

"I remember the supper fondly, sir. It was a great honor to dine with His Excellency, and I look forward to supping with the General tonight," answered Samuel.

"General Washington has several meetings today. He'll no doubt work through his three o'clock dinner. He will give you your instructions tonight at the late supper. Please feel free to have your men get a meal at the central mess tent. I think we have boiled beef today. We'll see you for supper tonight at nine. Thank you, Lieutenant. You are dismissed," said Lieutenant Colonel Hamilton.

"Thank you, sir," Samuel replied.

Samuel bowed his head in salute, turned, and headed for the door.

His thoughts were swirling. What instructions did His Excellency want to give him? Why so secret? He'd find out in a few hours. Samuel found his men outside the quartermaster's office checking down each name in the muster roll with a sergeant who was to take command of the group.

As soon as each man was accounted for, they would be given a supply of clothing from the quartermaster including a bounty coat, breeches, and a pair of shoes, if the recruit's needed replacing.

The shoes were made on a straight last and did not have a left and right. A soldier would soak the shoes in water and wear them wet so the leather would form to each foot.

They'd also be issued a haversack for food, a canteen for water, and a pack or bedroll for spare clothing. Additionally, each soldier would be supplied with one of the muskets they brought from Springfield, a cartridge box, a bayonet carriage, and a scabbard.

Samuel oversaw the process deep into the afternoon and after sundown before he returned to his temporary quarters to clean up for supper with His Excellency.

He returned to the Van Wyck House shortly before nine o'clock, making sure he was not uncomfortably early and certainly not late. You did not want to keep His Excellency waiting. He again found General Washington's Life Guards outside the front door. They exchanged greetings, and Samuel ascended the steps to the front door and knocked. The door opened to His Excellency's valet, William Lee, who greeted Samuel.

"Good evening, sir. The General and his aide are expecting you. I will show you to the dining room," said Lee.

"Thank you, Mr. Lee," replied Samuel.

Samuel knew Mr. Lee's name from other interactions when the General was headquartered at West Point. Lee was His Excellency's constant companion.

He followed Lee down the central hallway to the dining room, where he found General Washington seated with Lieutenant Colonel Hamilton. Both were in their finest uniforms, and each had a glass of madeira wine. A large bowl of walnuts was on the table next to General Washington. (126)

Samuel immediately removed his Light Infantry helmet and bowed in salute. He wasn't surprised to find His Excellency munching on a mouthful of walnuts. It was common knowledge that General Washington loved them.

"Good evening, Lieutenant Benjamin. Thank you for joining us for dinner. We are pleased to have you with us. I thank you for bringing this latest batch of recruits from Springfield and congratulate you on your earlier successes in recruiting men to the cause," said General Washington.

"Thank you, sir, for your kindness. It is my honor to serve," replied Samuel. He was surprised to hear His Excellency speak more softly than expected. Samuel found the General's voice to be commanding but weaker than he expected.[27] As anticipated, His Excellency appeared tall even while seated.

"You are a great patriot, Lieutenant. That's why I asked you to dine with me here tonight. I understand you are from Watertown and served with a minute company," said General Washington.

"Yes sir, I was eager to join the cause for liberty and have been in the service ever since Lexington," said Samuel.

"I understand your father was a soldier?" said General Washington.

"Yes, he was in a Boston militia Company of Foot and died shortly after the Battle of Quebec while fighting for His Majesty's Service," answered Samuel.

---

[27] Long, Susan Brynne, George Washington's Voice, George Washington's Mount Vernon, https://www.mountvernon.org/george-washington/facts/washingtons-voice

"So, he died in service to the King. Did that influence your decision to fight with us?" asked General Washington.

"Greatly, sir. My family had no interest or quarrel in Canada. But Father was following orders and died. I barely remember him, sir," said Samuel solemnly.

"I'm sorry you lost your father at such a young age, Lieutenant. That must have been terribly difficult for your mother and your siblings. But you have become a fine soldier, Samuel, and your father would be proud of you," said General Washington.

"Thank you, sir. I hope to have sons of my own when this war is over," said Samuel.

"Are you married?" inquired General Washington.

"Only engaged, sir," said Samuel.

"Who is the blessed young woman?" asked General Washington.

"Tabitha Livermore, sir. She's from Waltham. She's a fine woman and a member of the Daughters of Liberty," replied Samuel.

"Excellent. I'm sure you make a dashing couple. Well, before we get on to dinner, I want to talk to you about your next assignment, Lieutenant. Alexander, could you please make sure there are no ears nearby?" General Washington said to the Lieutenant Colonel.

"Yes sir. I think the staff are still preparing the meal. I'll make sure they stay out of earshot," replied Lieutenant Colonel Hamilton.

"So, here's what I want you to do, Samuel. I have some papers of the utmost importance that I need delivered to Major Benjamin Tallmadge in Bedford. Tallmadge is the Director of Military Intelligence. Do you know where Bedford is, Lieutenant?" asked General Washington.

"Yes sir. It's about thirty-five miles south of here. My regiment marched through there after Monmouth, sir," answered Samuel.

"Yes, of course. We have reason to believe the enemy has spies along the route and may try to intercept our messages. As you're likely aware, British Lieutenant Colonel Banastre Tarleton attacked Colonel Sheldon's forces in Bedford in July and burned the town. (127) Major Tallmadge has set up camp there with his dragoons.

And I need you and your Light soldiers to get the papers there safely. Under no circumstances are you to allow the papers to fall into enemy hands. Destroy them if you must. Have I made myself clear, Lieutenant?" asked the General.

"Yes sir. I will defend them with my life, sir," replied Samuel.

"Good, Lieutenant. I know you will. That's why I've assigned you to this task. Hopefully it won't come to that. Lieutenant Colonel Alexander will give you a satchel with the papers inside. If you have to destroy them, you'll notice they are addressed to a Samuel Culper, Sr. Make sure to burn the papers to ashes if you must so that the Culper name is destroyed," demanded the General.

"Yes sir. I understand," said Samuel.

Lieutenant Colonel Hamilton had returned to the doorway and was keeping watch.

"That's all of it, Lieutenant. Under no circumstances are you to write anything of our conversation down or any details of your mission. You are allowed to tell two of the most trusted men in your detail that Major Tallmadge should receive the satchel should something happen to you. You should also direct those trusted men to destroy the papers lest they fall into enemy hands during an attack. Understood?" said General Washington.

"Yes sir," replied Samuel.

"Alexander, you can tell the staff they can now serve the meal," said His Excellency.

"Yes sir. I'm hungry. How about you gentlemen?" inquired the Lieutenant Colonel.

"Indeed!" said General Washington. "I'm particularly hungry eating so late. Please join me, gentlemen, in offering thanks to God for this meal.

General Washington bowed his head.

"Heavenly Father, we thank you for the food we are about to eat. Please bless it to our bodies and us to your continued use. Amen," the General finished and lifted his head.

"I love fish, Samuel. How about you?" asked General Washington.

"I share your love of fish, sir. And we've certainly had many fine meals of fish while stationed at West Point thanks to the bounty provided by the Hudson," answered Samuel.

"Then you'll love tonight's meal, Samuel. I'm told we have some brook trout from Fishkill Creek along with mutton, potatoes, and cabbage. Eat well, Lieutenant. I want you well-fed for your journey tomorrow," said the General happily.

"Thank you again, sir, for placing your trust and your food in me," laughed Samuel.

General Washington enjoyed the humor and joined in the laughter.

"Good one, Lieutenant. We must laugh when we can. For surely, we have all known enough heartache with this awful war," said the General.

Samuel sampled everything on the table and found himself over-eating. But once you've had nothing but fire cakes for a week, you can't eat too much of a good meal.

Samuel and his men slept in the large barracks at the Supply Depot, which was a large complex of housing, workshops, storehouses, and stables as well as a prison, a hospital, an armory, blacksmith shops, stables, and a parade ground.[28]

They awoke to the sound of fife and drums mustering the soldiers for duty. Samuel was ordered to retrieve the satchel from Lieutenant Colonel Hamilton at the Van Wyck House that morning first thing along with the men under his command.

The march would take all day. There was a light rain falling about five miles into their journey when Samuel spotted some suspicious movement in the brush along the side of the trail.

He silently held up his hand for his men to stop their march. There were several flashes in the brush and the cracks of muskets firing. One of Samuel's men cried out in pain. It was Ensign William Hildreth.

---

[28] Friends of the Fishkill Supply Depot, Saving America's Last Great Revolutionary War Site, https://www.fishkillsupplydepot.org/depot.html

"Take cover, men!" Samuel shouted.

Samuel heard another crack of a musket firing and a thud in the tree he was hiding behind. Two of his soldiers dragged their wounded compatriot into the brush. Thankfully, the injured man was only grazed on the side of his left arm. He'd recover.

Samuel caught a glimpse of a cocked hat above the brush. He raised his flintlock pistol and fired. He heard a cry of pain and the sound of a body hitting the ground. Then more musket shots coming from the same direction.

By this time, all the Light Infantry soldiers had raised their muskets, aimed toward the brush, and were waiting for Samuel's command to fire.

"Fire, men," he said in a whispered tone hoping the enemy wouldn't have time to duck down.

It worked. There were groans of agony followed by what sounded like two more men falling to the ground in muffled thuds. Then Samuel heard running footsteps.

"Chase, men! Some left, some right," he shouted.

The highly trained Light Infantry soldiers split and ran after the fleeing attackers, spotting three men in civilian clothes dashing through the woods. Two of Samuel's men took aim and fired, hitting two of the enemy. Another caught up with the final attacker, drew his sword, and when the man turned to fight, impaled the man with his saber. A half dozen men lay dead or dying on the ground. Samuel found one of the men bleeding badly but still conscious.

"Who sent you! Who are you with!" Samuel shouted.

"Damn you, rebel!" the man weakly mumbled, then breathed his final breath.

"I think that's the last of them, men. We don't have time to bury them. Let's hope there aren't more enemy along the way. I'm not sure how we would have fared if they had matched our numbers. How are you doing, Will?" said Samuel to Ensign Hildreth.

He'd removed his wool coat to find his left shirt sleeve torn up and bloody from the passing musket ball.

"I'm good, Samuel. It hurt when it hit. But it only took a little of me. I think the Good Lord was looking out for me," said Ensign Hildreth.

"Indeed he was, Will. Let's get you patched up and keep moving. I don't like sitting here like targets," Samuel ordered.

Samuel tore off the lower part of Will's shirt sleeve, rolled it up, and tied it over the wound with a piece of leather string he always carried with him just for this purpose. War was a cruel teacher, and Samuel had learned the lesson about how to treat a field wound long before.

The men helped Ensign Hildreth to his feet and resumed their march. They reached the Bedford camp just before nightfall. If there weren't any spare tents, the men would just sleep on the ground. Samuel asked where Major Tallmadge's tent was and headed straight there. He found the Major standing next to a campfire drinking something from a cup.

"Major Tallmadge?" Samuel inquired.

"Yes. That's me. Are you Lieutenant Benjamin?" replied the Major.

"Yes sir. Here's the satchel from His Excellency," Samuel said, eager to hand off the papers that had led to the recent danger.

"A courier let us know to expect you. Good work, Lieutenant. Any trouble along the way?" asked the Major.

"Yes, as a matter of fact. We came under fire from a half-dozen men in civilian clothes. One of my men was wounded. But we killed all of them," said Samuel.

"I'm glad you and your men survived. The woods are crawling with enemy spies right now. That party you encountered was probably the work of Adjutant General John André, who is the head of the Brits' spy network. He knows I'm here and he's been trying to intercept our communications from New York. You did us a favor by eliminating some of his men. That should make the route safer for a while," said the Major.

"I hope so, sir. My men and I will spend the night here before heading back to West Point," said Samuel.

"Good. We have some extra tents for you. Make sure you see our cook about a meal. I'm sure all of you are hungry after the excitement of the day," said Major Tallmadge.

"We are, Major. I'll make sure my men get fed and draw provisions for our return to Fishkill," said Samuel.

Samuel and his men would return through Fishkill before heading on to West Point. He'd also report to His Excellency on his return. He would be proud to tell General Washington of successfully repelling the enemy attack. At least for a day, Samuel was part of His Excellency's spy network.

Chapter 20
The Terrible Winter

Freezing weather soon led to the end of any military campaigns. Camp duties at West Point shifted to preparing for the coming of winter, including harvesting trees for firewood and repairing shelters. Snow arrived early and heavy.

"Attention! Rest. Good morning, men," said Samuel to his group of new recruits.

"Good morning, sir," replied most of the dozen fledgling soldiers.

"This morning, we need more firewood for our stoves and fireplaces. So, I need you to get saws and axes from the quartermaster. Who is experienced with work horses here? A show of hands, please," ordered Samuel.

Four soldiers raised their hands.

"Alright, you four need to go the stable and requisition a horse, harness, and sled and return here. The others, get the tools necessary for sawing and chopping down the trees. The snow will make it harder to find the trail through the woods. So, I'm sending Sergeant Jackson with you. He knows the way and will supervise your work. You will obey Sergeant Jackson without question. I see all you soldiers are wearing your wool bounty coats. Make sure you also have wool or leather mittens. Talk to Sergeant Jackson if you don't have a pair. We want to make sure you don't get frostbite or die before you get to fire a shot at a redcoat. The wood you harvest will be used to keep you warm and cook your meals. So, work hard, don't chop off a foot, and do your best, soldiers. Make sure to grab your muskets and cartridges. Always be ready to defend yourselves. Sergeant Jackson, they are yours. Have a care, men!" Samuel shouted.

Samuel watched some of the new soldiers' next actions. He could already tell the ones who would be good men and potential leaders. The others stood there wondering what to do next until Sergeant Jackson told them. It would be a cold day in the woods and Samuel was glad he would miss out on the foraging mission.

Later that day a courier arrived in camp delivering a message that Congress was calling for a Day of Thanksgiving and Prayer to be observed on December 9.

Nearly a foot of snow fell at West Point on November 26. If that kept up, it would make it difficult for the soldiers to have thankful hearts.

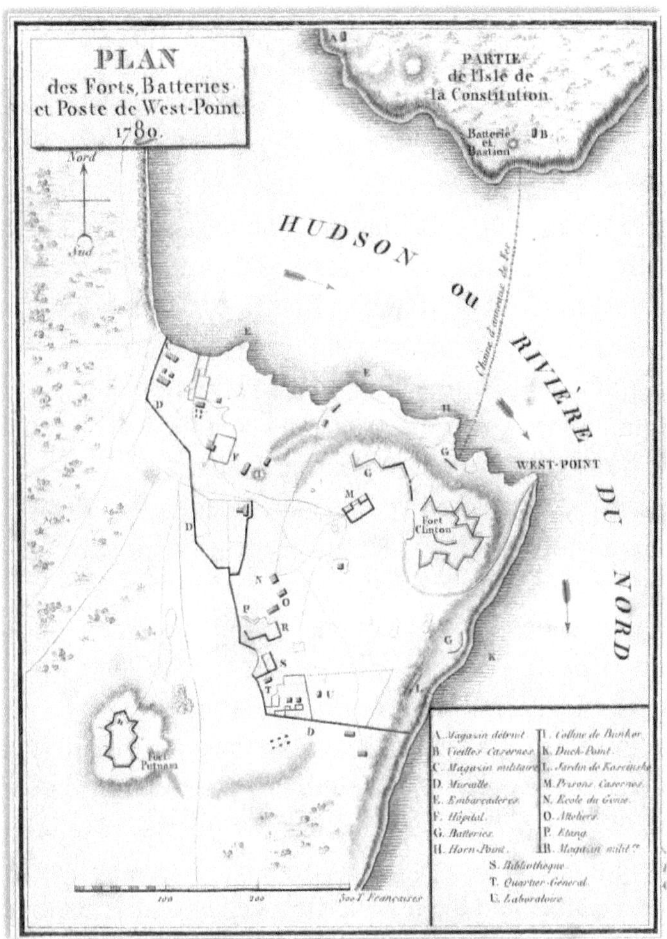

"Plan des Forts, Batteries et Poste de West-Point, 1780," eighteenth-century French-engineered military plan of West Point

General Washington soon decided he needed to be closer to the Continental Congress and his main army. His Excellency's last day of being headquartered at West Point was the twenty-eighth. He stopped briefly at Cortlandt Manor on the east side of the Hudson and then made his winter headquarters at the mansion of Theodosia Ford in Morristown, New Jersey.

Mrs. Ford was the widow of militia Colonel Joseph Ford, who had hosted Continental troops before he died of pneumonia. The location of the Ford Mansion allowed General Washington to be closer to the American capital of Philadelphia and to keep watch on the British Army headquartered in Manhattan. (128)

Snow and bitter cold continued to descend on West Point and made the Day of Thanksgiving and Prayer difficult.

Another eighteen inches of snow fell on December 18, followed by more bone-chilling cold. Samuel, and the others on duty at West Point, weren't surprised to receive word that the winter was proving especially cruel for the roughly 10,000 Continental soldiers stationed near His Excellency's headquarters in Morristown.

The Continental Army had turned a farm in Jockey Hollow into their winter home. The heavy snow and cold made it extremely hard labor for the soldiers to build their log shelters.

It didn't help morale that General Benedict Arnold was court-martialed at Morristown in December for misusing his position for profit. His heroism on the battlefield didn't stop Arnold's critics from trying to destroy his command. His bitterness grew when Washington punished him with a harsh rebuke. Old Man Winter seemed the enemy of the whole of the Northeast.

Another severe snowstorm struck on the twenty-eighth. Then on the first day of the new year—mutiny at West Point.

Samuel was furious. Roughly a hundred soldiers, including some from his regiment, marched away from camp saying they were going home. Samuel and the other officers chased after them and convinced them to return.[29] Commanders punished some of the soldiers. But most were pardoned.

The winter didn't relent. The next day another blizzard created massive snowdrifts. The intense cold increased suffering. Scouts reported New York harbor had frozen solid. So had the Hudson at

---

[29] Orderly book, West Point (N.Y.), 13 September 1779 to 31 January 1780, 8th Massachusetts Regiment, Continental Army Record Keeper: Francis Tufts, Also, Heath, William, Memoirs of Major-General Heath. Containing anecdotes, details of skirmishes, battles, and other military events, during the American Revolutionary War, p. 226, Published according to act of Congress, https://quod.lib.umich.edu/cgi/t/text/text-idx?c=evans;cc=evans;rgn=main;view=text;idno=N25514.0001.001

West Point and soldiers still in tents couldn't find warmth. Some remained buried in snow for two days. (129)

The irony was that the West Point fortress was stronger than ever. Polish engineer Tadeusz Kościuszko and the troops under his command were completing several fortifications. And more than six hundred soldiers now manned Fort Arnold, which ruled over the west bank with enough firepower to destroy any ship trying to get beyond the chain.

There was a twenty-four-pound cannon accompanied by a half-dozen eighteen-pounders, a twelve-pounder, a four-pounder, a trio of three-pounders, and nearly a dozen mortars. In addition, the stone-walled Fort Putnam, built by Colonel Rufus Putnam and his 5th Massachusetts troops, guarded the other part of the river, including the "Great Chain."

But winter proved more powerful than the stone walls of West Point. Samuel's brother Jonathan decided to muster out of the army in January. He told Samuel he had never been so cold and desperate. Samuel was sad to see him go. But their family needed him home to help with the farm and the harsh winter.

The season was worse than Samuel's time at Valley Forge but without the rampant disease of those months in Pennsylvania. More than two dozen snowstorms plagued the army along with days of starvation at Morristown as supplies ran short. Icy roads made it nearly impossible to deliver supplies of food and clothing.

There were stories of men roasting old shoes to eat just to quell their hunger pains. Hundreds of soldiers deserted. Dozens died. (130)

Starvation continued into the spring and some of the Connecticut soldiers staged another mutiny. They threatened to march out of camp in search of food. Thankfully, the soldiers calmed down and remained.

Samuel was thankful most of the soldiers at West Point had not grown that desperate. But warmer weather could not arrive quickly enough.

In April, Samuel's other brother, John, had also seen enough. He also left the army, joining Jonathan back home in Massachusetts.

Samuel's brothers were not alone in resigning. More than two dozen officers from the Massachusetts line resigned by the end of April. (131) Once again, Samuel decided he needed to remain committed to the cause and his duties as an army officer. But he was discouraged by the resignations of some fine officers.

Then a courier brought news that General Benjamin Lincoln had been under siege by Lord Cornwallis for six weeks at Charlestown, South Carolina and eventually surrendered his army of 5,000 men on the twelfth of May. (132)

It was a horrible blow to the Continental cause. The King's generals made it clear that they were committed to their "Southern Strategy." They had already taken Savannah late in 1778. The Brits believed they would find more loyalist support in the south.

A few weeks later, British commander Banastre Tarleton slaughtered Abraham Buford's Patriot army at Waxhaws, South Carolina. General Washington received reports that Tarleton's men massacred Continental soldiers who had tried to surrender. More than a hundred patriots died.

Samuel and the other officers wanted to go after Tarleton, who was dubbed a butcher after Buford's massacre. But Samuel understood His Excellency's dilemma.

The Continental Army faced shortages of nearly everything, including food and clothing. The Continental currency was nearly worthless, and Congress wasn't paying the soldiers for their sacrifice. The situation was dire and threatened the entire effort to be free from the Crown.

The British still held New York City and were a continued threat to capture the Hudson River and control the Highlands. So, in June, General Washington ordered most of the army to march out of Morristown toward West Point. His Excellency wanted to attack the British in New York City and take back control of the vital port.

General Washington had changed his views on people of color serving as soldiers. Samuel was pleased there was a growing number of free men of color serving in the Continental Army. It aligned with his abolitionist views. Thousands of negroes and Indians had enlisted.[30] Thankfully, the French continued their commitment to the Patriot cause by sending 5,000 soldiers to America. They arrived in Newport in July under the command of Comte de Rochambeau. The French arrival led to a stalemate with the British forces in New York that extended through the summer.

---

[30] U.S. Army Center of Military History, Life of the Continental Soldier, https://history.army.mil/Revwar250/Continental-Soldier/

Chapter 21
A Hellish Plot

There was rot undermining West Point.

In August, General Washington had entrusted the fort to the command of General Benedict Arnold. Samuel didn't understand why the great tactician of the battlefield would choose to command a fort. But at the same time, he was proud to serve under a man he had personally witnessed fight with incredible bravery at Saratoga.

During the fleeting days of summer, it seemed less likely that the British would challenge West Point. So, on the twenty-second of the month, Samuel's regiment received orders from General Washington, along with the bulk of the army, to ready for a fifty-mile march to Teaneck, New Jersey. There, they would confront the enemy, which had been conducting raids from New York City.

Samuel marched with the Light Infantry two miles out in front of the main left column. The Continental force numbered 14,000 by the time they reached Teaneck. Washington was aware of the danger of attack by British forces and wrote the following in his orders for August 23, 1780:

> The Army being now very near the Enemy. The Genl flatters himself every Officer and Soldier will make it a point of Honor as well as duty to keep constantly in Camp and to be at the shortest notice ready to Act as circumstances may require. He is at the same time persuaded, should an opportunity be afforded us that every part of the Army will vie with each other, in the display of that conduct[,] fortitude and bravery which ought to distinguish troops fighting for

their Country, for their liberty, for everything dear to the Citizen, or to the Soldier.[31]

The army stayed at Teaneck until the third of September, then moved inland a few miles to Steenrapie. General Washington made his headquarters in the confiscated home of loyalist Jan Zabriskie. The army stayed through the twentieth of the month, then moved north to Orangetown. (133)

The redcoats never challenged the Continental Army during those several weeks near New York City. And with General Washington's attention on the British forces in New York, it proved a perfect opportunity for Benedict Arnold. And then it became clear to Samuel why Arnold wanted command of West Point.

Word of Arnold's treason spread quickly through camp. Samuel was with Adjutant Francis Tufts when Tufts wrote in the Orderly Book of the 8th Massachusetts Regiment of His Excellency returning to West Point from Hartford to "unravel fully so Hellish a Plot":

Treason of the blackest dye was yesterday discovered. General Arnold who commanded at West Point, lost to every sentiment of honor of private and public obligation was about to deliver up that important post into the hands of the enemy.[32]

---

[31] Orderly book of the 8th Massachusetts Regiment, 1780, Aug. 10 to Oct. 27, Orangetown, Teaneck, Steenrapie, Totowa, p. 30, 89–91

[32] Tufts, Francis, Regimental orderly book of the 8th Massachusetts Regiment, written by Francis Tufts, adjutant, p. 89, Huntington Digital Library, https://www.huntington.org/collections/lib-p15150coll7-43716?img=93

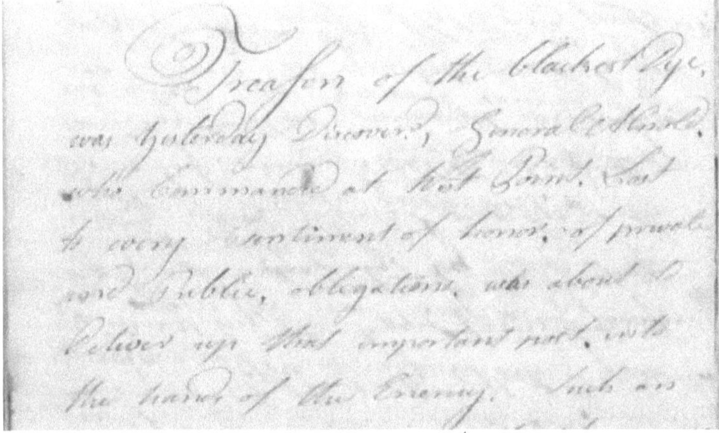

Treason of the blackest Dye,
was yesterday Discovered, General Arnold,
who Commanded at West Point, lost
to every sentiment of honor, of private
and Public obligations, was about to
deliver up that important post, into
the hands of the Enemy. Such an

Image from the Regimental Orderly Book of the 8th Massachusetts Regiment

General Arnold had conspired with British Adjutant General John André to surrender West Point. The commander Samuel so greatly admired and had fought alongside, had now committed the most shameful and disgraceful act against His Excellency, the very army he fought for so bravely, and the new United States Samuel so dearly loved. It was an unspeakable sin and showed a depravation of spirit so grave that Samuel could barely tolerate the thought of it. Samuel documented the treason in his diary with great sadness. Last year, André's men had nearly killed Samuel and the soldiers under his command while delivering those papers for His Excellency.

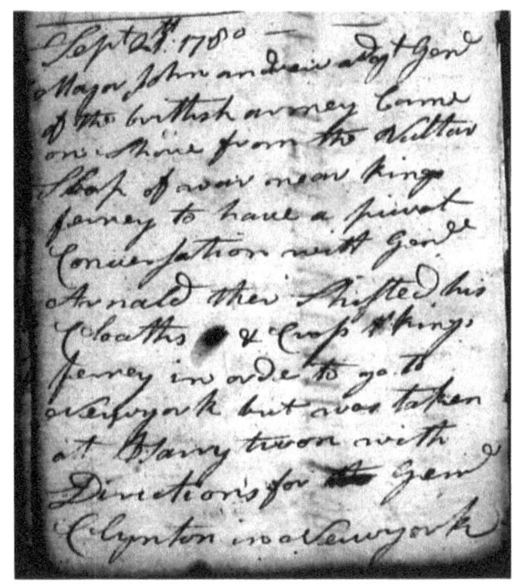

Sept 21. 1780
Major John andrew adjt Genl
of the british army Came
on Shore from the Vultur
Sloop of war near kings
ferrey to have a privat
Conversation with Genl
Arnald then Shifted his
Cloaths & Crost kings
ferrey in order to go to
Newyork but was taken
at Tarry town with
Directions for Genl
Clynton in NewYork

Image of Lieutenant Samuel Benjamin's war diary, Sept. 21, 1780

> Transcription
> Sept 21, 1780 –
> Major John Andre adjt Genl of the british army came on shore from the Vulture sloop of war near Kings ferry to have a privat conversation with Genl Arnold then shifted his clothes & cross at Kings ferry in order to go to New York but was taken at Tarrytown with Directions for Genl Clynton in New York

Unfortunately, General Arnold made his escape to the enemy on the same ship that delivered André. Samuel and the other officers could only hope the traitor would be captured and held to account.

The British spy was taken from Tarrytown to North Castle. The commander there didn't know of Arnold's treason and sent him a message about the papers that were found in André's boot. The message only served as a warning for Arnold. Thankfully, when Major Tallmadge learned of the papers found on André, he messaged His Excellency. General Washington immediately understood Arnold's actions were treasonous and quickly ordered an investigation. (134)

André was eventually moved to West Point. And it didn't take long to decide he would be executed. The only question was how André would be killed. The prisoner was moved to Tappan, just two miles from where Samuel's regiment was headquartered.

Samuel was saddened by the thought that Major André, who he knew was a gallant officer, could be treated as a spy and die at the end of a rope. If he was executed as an officer, he would die by firing squad. But André was operating behind enemy lines under the false name of John Anderson and was wearing a disguise when he was captured. He

was acting as a spy.

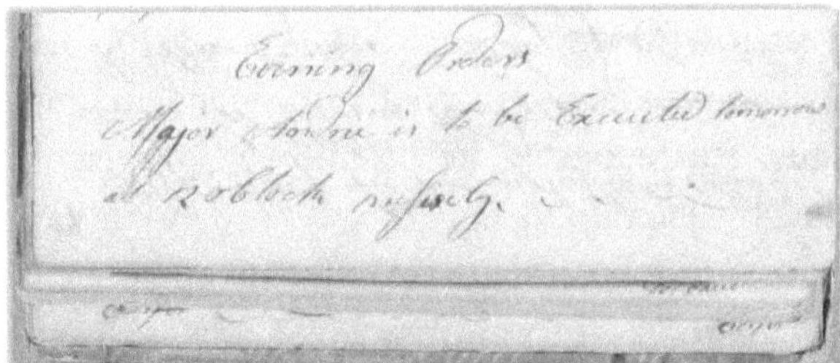
Evening Orders
Major André is to be Executed tomorrow
at 12 oclock precisely.

Orderly book of the 8th Massachusetts Regiment, 1780, Aug. 10 to Oct. 27, Orangetown, Teaneck, Steenrapie, Totowa, p. 98

General Washington had to send a message. Four years earlier, the British hanged the Continental spy Nathan Hale. Washington ordered the execution for October 1. But the execution was delayed until noon on the second, after a flag of truce arrived with a message from General Sir Henry Clinton asking for André to be released. The general did not yield and ordered André to be hanged at Tappan. Samuel and the other officers of his regiment arrived on horseback, as ordered, to witness the execution. They were among a crowd of roughly 2,000.

The Unfortunate Death of Major John André, by John Goldar (engraver), after William Hamilton (painter), for Edward Barnard's The New, Comprehensive, Impartial and Complete History of England (London, 1783)

It was a sorrowful day. André was known for his charm and many talents. He was an artist, poet, and musician, and spoke several languages. He requested he be allowed to wear his uniform. And his request was granted.

Samuel saw André bow to several men he apparently knew as he was led from his place of confinement to the gallows. His bows were returned with great respect. The British officer paused when he first saw the hanging place. Samuel could not hear what the officer at his side said when he paused.

But he then heard André say, ‘‘I am reconciled to my death, but I detest the mode.” André was then led to a wagon, and he stepped up and inside, sulked for a moment, and then said, ‘‘It will be but a momentary pang.” He took two white handkerchiefs from his pockets. The provost marshal tied his arms with one. André removed his hat and tied the other kerchief to cover his eyes. André reached for and found the heavy rope, and in noble fashion, slipped the noose over his own head and tightened it. Colonel Scammel told André he could speak if he so desired. André lifted the handkerchief from his eyes and spoke. “I pray you to bear me witness that I meet my fate like a brave man.”

Many in the crowd wept. Samuel thought the struggle for liberty had reached a new level of misery. He bowed his head in prayer and asked God to spare André’s soul. The wagon was pulled away and André hung in the air. The life of a great officer and a gentlemen was over at the age of thirty.

General Arnold sought to inflict a fatal blow against the patriot cause. Instead, he had condemned André.

Soon after the execution, Samuel was put on command at Dobbs Ferry. General Washington learned the crossing point had served as a key point in General Arnold’s treasonous plot.[33]

As a highly trusted officer, Samuel was chosen to keep watch on the post. Arnold’s treason also included leaving West Point

---

[33] Koke, Joshua Hett Smith, Smith later recounted how Arnold and André’s “original interview” was intended to take place at Dobbs Ferry, N.Y. (Smith, Narrative, 180 to 82).

unprotected by ordering a New York regiment out of the garrison. He sent other soldiers away from the fort to cut wood. Samuel thought it was General Arnold's treachery that had placed the noose around André's neck, leaving His Excellency with no other choice than to execute André as a spy. (135)

US Revolutionary War Rolls 1775 to 1783, M246, 602384, Revolutionary War Rolls, compiled 1894 to 1913, 1775 to 1783, NARA, 93

Chapter 22
Desperation and Mutiny

October ended and November arrived with Samuel's regiment still headquartered at Camp Totowa, New Jersey. Morale suffered following Arnold's treason, and it was affecting the discipline of some of the troops.

Samuel got wind that a corporal in the 8th Massachusetts Regiment had complained about the lack of food and had wandered off and killed a sheep belonging to a local farmer. Samuel confronted the corporal, who was eating mutton along with some of his fellow soldiers when he found the men in their barracks.

No lamb or mutton had been supplied that week. Samuel knew the corporal was lying when he said a sheep must have wandered off because he found the animal dead on the edge of camp. Samuel told the corporal he was going to recommend a court martial. The man continued with his lie and the next morning Samuel received a letter from the corporal challenging Samuel to a duel.

The man was a non-commissioned officer and therefore incapable of challenging a commissioned officer of a higher rank. In addition, the Articles of War prohibited Continental soldiers from dueling.[34] They would face a court martial if caught. Custom allowed a senior officer to respond by caning the challenger to humiliate them.[35] Samuel had no intention of

---

[34] Article VII: Art. 2. No officer or soldier shall presume to send a challenge to any other officer or soldier, to fight a duel, upon pain, if a commissioned officer, of being cashiered, if a non-commissioned officer or soldier, of suffering corporal punishment, at the discretion of a court-martial., Journals of the Continental Congress—Articles of War; September 20, 1776, Yale Law School, Lillian Goldman Law Library, The Avalon Project, https://avalon.law.yale.edu/18th_century/contcong_09-20-76.asp

[35] Irish Code Duello, A series of rules devised at Clonmel, Co. Tipperary, in 1777 to cover the practice of dueling by "Gentlemen delegates," Oxford Reference, https://www.oxfordreference.com/display/10.1093/acref/9780199916191.001.0001/acref-9780199916191-e-2659

doing so. But he threatened it when he quickly replied with a written response.

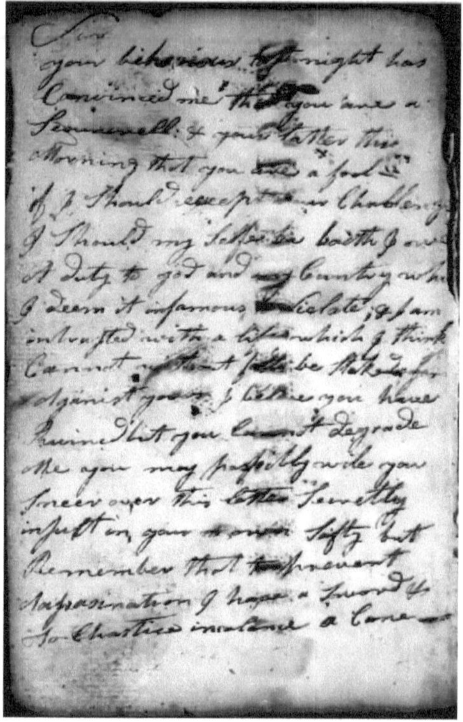

Retouched image from Lieutenant Samuel Benjamin's documents at Yale University. The wording is unaltered.

"Sir, Your behavior last night has convinced me that you are a scoundrel & your letter this morning that you are a fool. If I should accept your challenge I should myself be both. I owe a duty to God and my country who I deem it infamous to violate, & I am entrusted with a life which I think cannot without folly be staked against yours. I believe you have ruined. But you cannot degrade me. You may possibly while you sneer over this letter secretly insult in your own safety. But remember to prevent assassination I have a friend to chastise insolence—a cane."

The corporal was shown mercy and not convicted. But he was reduced to the rank of private. That satisfied Samuel.

He had experienced overwhelming hunger himself during these difficult winters. And understood how it could alter a soldier's thoughts. The corporal had otherwise been a loyal patriot.

Soon General Washington received intelligence that enemy troops might be foraging in the area, and he wanted his Continental troops ready to challenge the redcoats.

The Light Infantry under the Marquis de Lafayette continued to drill and be ready for action. Samuel was proud of his new role as a lieutenant in the Light Infantry.

The Marquis de Chastellux visited and inspected the Light Corps. The French Major General spoke fluent English and served as the liaison between his superior General Rochambeau and His Excellency. General Chastellux wrote of the Continental Light Infantry:

> This troop made a good appearance; were better clothed than the rest of the army; their uniforms, both of the officers and men, were smart and military, and each soldier wore a helmet made of hard leather with a crest of horsehair. The officers are armed with espontoons, or rather half pikes, and the subalterns with fusils; but both were provided with short sabres brought from France and made a present to them by M. de la Fayette.[36]

But with winter approaching, General Washington wanted to march the army to West Point and the Light Corps was dissolved for the winter on November 26.

The march to West Point covered nearly sixty miles and Samuel and his regiment arrived by December 1. Samuel lay his head down to sleep that first night and couldn't help but think about how close Arnold had come to dealing the Continental Army a deadly blow.

It was good to be back at West Point. For one, it was warmer and, so far this winter, lacked the incredible snow of the last. The challenges came mostly from lack of pay and supplies. Christmas

---

[36] Travels in North-America, in the years 1780 to 81 to 82/By the Marquis de Chastellux; Tr. from the French, by an English gentleman, who resided in America at the period, with notes by the translator; Also, a biographical sketch of the author, letters from Gen. Washington to the Marquis de Chastellux, and notes and corrections by the American editor. http://www.loc.gov/resource/lhbtn.06665

came and went without any gift except the doldrums of being cooped up in camp. Samuel had time to write Tabitha a letter.

December 26, 1780
Garrison West Point
My Dearest Tabitha,
I hope my writing finds you in good health and having celebrated a happy Christmas with your family. I dream of one day never being away from you as we celebrate the birth of our Lord and Savior. As for me, I am well. I am sure you heard of General Arnold's treason and escape to the enemy. I still despair at his treachery. I had hoped the farther the days from the dark event would provide some peace. But alas, I am still haunted by the evil of their deceit. Our only celebration is that we can claim victory that this vital garrison is still in patriot hands. So for that, I am glad to be back at West Point for the winter. Although I had to fend off a challenge to a duel from a scoundrel. He had no standing to threaten me. I look forward to receiving another letter from you my bride to be. It brings me great joy to set ink to those words. We have not faced much danger this year other than a brush with the enemy at Elizabethtown in early summer. The British are mostly fighting our cause in the Carolinas. So we have skirted danger and sufered no loss of life to speak of. The Light Infantry is disbanded for now. But I am confident we will be called upon in the new year and perhaps sent south. Please write when you have a moment. Give my best wishes to your parents, brothers and sisters, along with Elisha and Martha. I miss all those I love. I am glad my brothers have left the army and are out of harms way.

I send you my love,

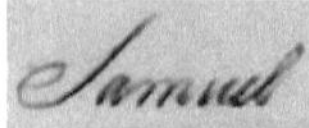

Samuel sealed the letter and wondered when he could stop writing letters and simply be home. But his duty to the cause of liberty was not finished.

The new year arrived with word that the Pennsylvania troops had mutinied. They had not been paid, and clothes and provisions were also sorely lacking. Many soldiers wanted to be released from their enlistment contracts. They marched to Princeton to bring their grievances to political leaders.

General Wayne, who commanded the Pennsylvania line, negotiated with the leaders of the mutiny. The British tried to take advantage of the situation by encouraging the soldiers to defect. But the Pennsylvania men remained loyal to the cause.

After several days, General Wayne negotiated a peaceful end. More than half the Pennsylvania soldiers left the army, leaving little more than a thousand men still enlisted. (136)

Then the New Jersey troops also mutinied. This time, His Excellency was having none of it and decided to use force to stop the spirit of rebellion.

Samuel's regiment was ordered to march through heavy snow some forty miles south to surround the New Jersey camp at Ringwood. Major General Robert Howe led the expedition. (137)

Three of the New Jersey ringleaders thought they would repeat the success of the Pennsylvania mutineers and negotiate terms.

By the twenty-sixth of January, Howe received a report that some of the Jersey troops were refusing take orders. His Excellency arrived by sleigh to add pressure to his demand that the Jersey men end their mutiny without compromise.

A force of five hundred soldiers—Samuel's regiment and the Massachusetts 9th, along with several others—surrounded the mutineers' camp.

Howe ordered the artillery trained on the tents. In the first light of day, the mutineers found they had no avenue of escape. Still, some of the Jersey troops refused to surrender. Howe ordered the Massachusetts troops to move forward and force the issue. He gave the mutineers five minutes to submit, or he'd order the loyal troops to open fire.

Samuel agreed with the demand. Everyone had suffered and sacrificed the same as the New Jersey and Pennsylvania men. Discipline had to be restored.

The Jersey soldiers came out of their tents unarmed and surrendered. But that wasn't the end of it.

Howe ordered the senior New Jersey officers to point out the ringleaders for punishment. He held a court martial right there in the snow. Three of the ringleaders were sentenced to death. And Howe ordered a firing squad be formed from the troops that had mutinied. It was a brutal affair that led to some of the Jersey boys crying as they lifted their guns to fire at their own.

Sergeant David Gilmore was forced to his knees. The sound of a weeping New Jersey firing squad was drowned out by the thunder of musket fire. Gilmore lay dead from six shots to his head and heart.

Sergeant John Tuttle died next. But the supposed ringleader, Sergeant Major Grant, was spared when his senior officers learned he had been coerced into going along with the awful plan. (138)

It was another dark day for the patriot cause and Samuel was saddened by the way it all played out. He wrote in his diary about his regiment's involvement in the affair.

> January 1781 The Pennsylvania and Jersey troops mutinied. The Massachusetts troops had to go[37] & quell them—Shot two of them that was the ringleaders of them.

---

[37] Entry from Lt. Samuel Benjamin's diary

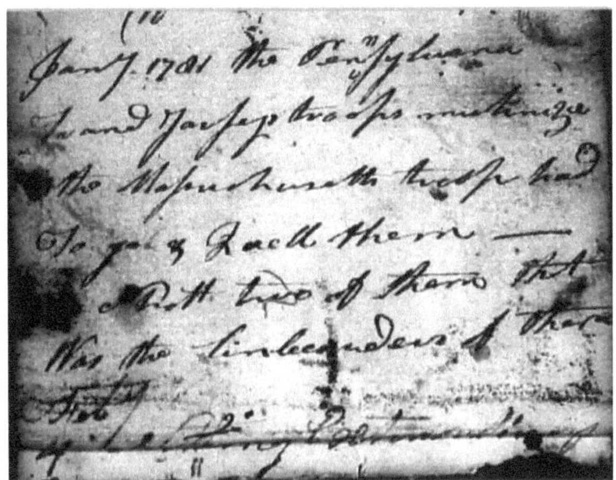
Image from Lieutenant Samuel Benjamin's war diary, Yale University

Samuel hoped that was the end of soldiers thinking about mutiny. But he'd learned that was unlikely. Desertions had been a problem from the very beginning of the patriot cause.

Many men thought they could be heroes until the bullets started flying or they didn't get what they were promised. They chose comfort and cowardice over courage and commitment. The real test of patriotism was staying true to the cause even in the toughest of times.

He didn't feel like writing again in his diary for almost two weeks. That's when the French statesman, the Duc de Choiseul, arrived at West Point to visit with His Excellency.

The Duc de Choiseul had long been a supporter of the patriot cause. But it was mostly out of seeking revenge against King George after the French lost hold of America. Samuel didn't understand why a statesman who had been dismissed by Louis XV would still be trying to insert himself into the Patriot cause. But Samuel documented the visit in his diary during the dull days of February.

The Light Infantry was ordered to march for the lines for inspection. Commanders needed to keep the troops alert on the boring days of winter lest the redcoats spring a surprise attack.

March arrived with new recruits. They'd be needed once the snow melted and military action resumed. Colonel Goose Van

Schaick also arrived at West Point with his First New York Regiment. St. Patrick's Day came and went with little to do except for normal drilling and the daily chores of military life at the garrison. A few prisoners of war arrived for temporary confinement.

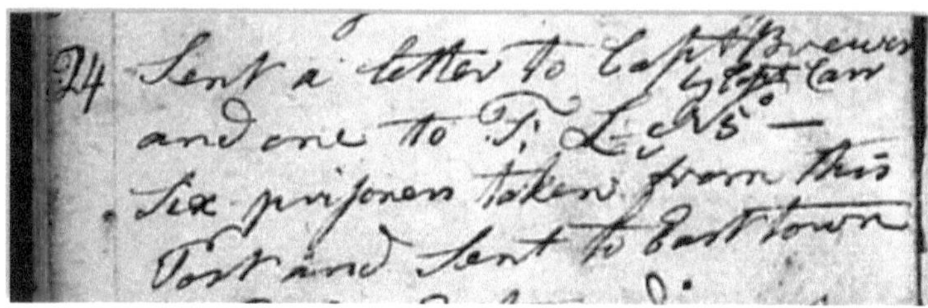

24 Sent a letter to Capt Brewer by Capt Carr
and one to T. L. No 5 —
Six prisoners taken from this
Post and sent to Easttown

Image from Lieutenant Samuel Benjamin's war diary

Samuel wrote letters to Tabitha and Elisha. He was trying to keep track of how many letters he'd sent to Tabitha since he was at Valley Forge. He wrote in his diary. "March 24 Sent a letter to Captain Brewer, and one to T. L., No. 5, by Captain Carr. Six prisoners were taken from this post and sent to Easttown."

March 24, 1781
West Point
Dear Tabitha,
I hope you received my last letter from December. I have not heard from you for a while. So, I'm never sure if my letters are making it through and the same of yours. I hope you are well. As for me, I am healthy and getting along mostly in good spirits But, I am eager for the days of winter to be over even if they are free of battles. We've already had to quell two mutinies this winter. The Pennsylvania and Jersey boys were tired of not being paid, clothed, and fed. Half of them went home. We need help from Congress. Politicians want victories without playing their part in this war. I hope we can gain some ground on the enemy when spring arrives. I don't think I can take another winter away from you. I am eager for us to marry and get on with

starting our own family. The British still hold New York and I believe His Excellency is planning on how to end them holding that ground. I shall continue my duties in the Light Infantry as soon as General Washington decides where we shall take our fight to the King's forces. My love for you is stronger than ever,

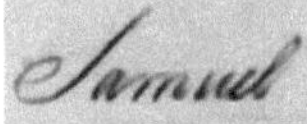

Samuel sealed the letter and found Captain Samuel Carr in his quarters. The Captain, a native of Newbury north of Boston, was in charge of getting the mail out.

"Hello, Captain," Samuel said.

"Greetings, Lieutenant. I see you've got a couple letters to send," replied the Captain.

"Yes sir. One for my girl back home. The other is for Captain Brewer," said Samuel.

"I miss having Elisha in camp. Didn't he marry your fiancée's sister?" asked the Captain.

"That's right. Married and two children so far," replied Samuel.

"Good for him. He was a good soldier. He's farming now, I think. I remember him saying he resigned to take care of his family and the farm," said Captain Carr.

"Yes. That's what I'll do when I finally leave the army," Samuel said.

"Farming is hard enough without having people steal your livestock. Delancey's Cowboys have been raiding more patriot farms across the river. I wish we could catch his thieves in the act and put them down," said Captain Carr.

"Me too," said Samuel.

"I'll make sure these letters get sent with the courier. Take care, Lieutenant," said the Captain and he turned to head back inside.

Samuel had heard there was growing concern about a force of roughly five hundred loyalist militia and dragoons named the Westchester Refugees. They attacked patriots on the east side of the

Hudson, stealing cattle and selling them to British troops in New York City.

Wealthy loyalist Colonel James DeLancey commanded the group, which most people called the Cowboys because of their raids to get cattle. DeLancey's group had the support of many loyalists who had been driven from their homes or had their property taken by patriots.

Samuel didn't have any sympathy for people who didn't have the courage to join the cause of liberty because they were comfortable serving King George.

A snowstorm blew into West Point on the second to the last day of March. The next day, word reached the garrison of a naval battle between the French and the British at the mouth of Chesapeake Bay. Samuel heard General Washington was in an uproar because the French fleet had the advantage and let the British ships retreat into Chesapeake Bay without challenge. His Excellency depended on the French ships sailing into Chesapeake Bay to carry General LaFayette's force south to Portsmouth, Virginia to capture Benedict Arnold. The French fleet failed to give General Washington his final chance at capturing the traitor. (139)

The patriots needed some good news. April arrived with little to celebrate. Samuel was put in charge of several men at Fort Putnam to assist Captain Smith. The ice would soon be off the river and the troops at Fort Putnam would be a crucial force in preventing the enemy from moving north.

On the eleventh, Samuel oversaw the soldiers tasked with moving the chain back across the river for the warm months ahead. Samuel was relieved from his duties and allowed to return to his main West Point duties of training recruits for the battles ahead.

Lieutenant Joseph Leland brought a group of new recruits on the sixteenth. Samuel liked Lieutenant Leland. He was another Massachusetts man, from Grafton. He had transferred to the 8th Regiment from the 9th. Like Samuel, he'd been in the fight since the Lexington Alarm serving as a Minuteman. He'd stayed committed to the army and was good at getting men to sign up. Lieutenant Leland arrived on the same day His Excellency visited West Point from his new winter quarters at the Hasbrouck House in Newburgh. The house was just two miles removed from where the bulk of the army was camped in New Windsor, about fourteen miles north of West Point. General Washington's visit seemed somewhat secretive. Samuel wondered if it had to do with John William being sentenced to hang for desertion. The soldier from the 6th

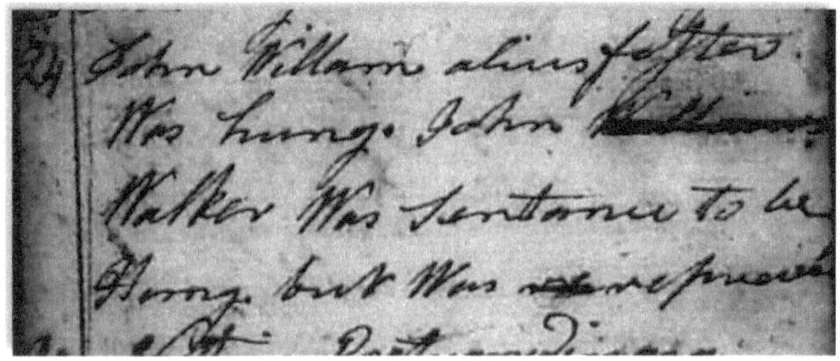
John William alias foster
Was hung. John
Walker Was Sentance to be
Hung but Was

Image of Lieutenant Samuel Benjamin's Diary

Massachusetts had been using the alias William Foster. And Samuel wondered why the soldier would use an alias unless he was also a spy?

Or perhaps he used the alias to collect two enlistment bounties and never had any intention of fulfilling his promise to serve the new nation.

Williams was not accused of being a spy at his court martial. He was hanged for desertion on Tuesday the twenty-fourth of April.

All the soldiers were ordered to attend his execution as a deterrent. Another soldier, John Walker, was spared when the new Provost Martial refused to carry out his execution.

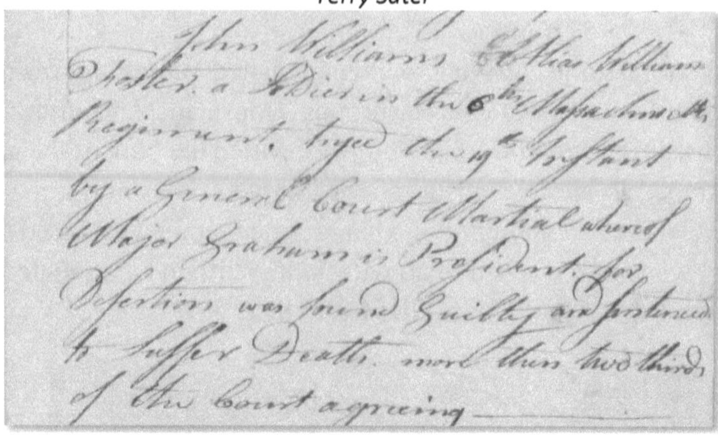
John Williams alias William
Shetter a Soldier in the 8th Massachusetts
Regiment, tryed the 19th Instant
by a General Court Martial whereof
Major Graham is President, for
Desertion was found Guilty and sentenced
to suffer Death. more than two thirds
of the Court agreeing —

Image from the Orderly book of the 8th Massachusetts Regiment, 1781, Mar. 12 to May 17, West Point, The Huntington Digital Library, p.52, https://hdl.huntington.org/digital/collection/p15150coll7/id/43066/rec/17

Samuel struggled with whether his faith allowed for death as a punishment for desertion. On the other hand, he knew that if desertion wasn't severely punished, desertions could destroy the army and any chance to win the war against the Crown. Perhaps if executing deserters was wrong, God was allowing for a chance to ask forgiveness. Congress called for a special day for people to set their hearts on the right path. And His Excellency wanted soldiers to take part. Samuel read the order with great relief.

> Extract from Genl Orders Headquarters New Windsor April 27th '81. Congress having been pleased to set apart, and appoint Thursday the 3rd of May next for fasting, humiliation, and prayer. The General enjoins a strict obedience to it in the Army and calls upon the Chaplain thence to prepare discourse
> suitable to the oration. All duties of fatigue are to ease on that day.

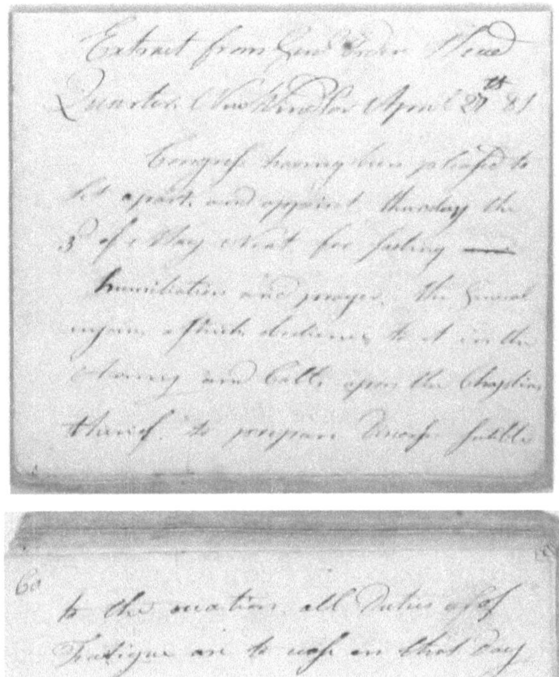

Extract from Genl Order Head
Quarters New Windsor April 27th 81

Congress having been pleased to
set apart and appoint thursday the
3d of May next for fasting —
humiliation and prayer, the General
enjoins a strict obedience to it in the
Army and Calls upon the Chaplains
thereof to prepare discourses suitable

60

to the occasion. all Duties of
Fatigue are to cease on that Day

Image from the Orderly book of the 8th Massachusetts Regiment, 1781, Mar. 12 to May 17, West Point, Huntington Digital Library, p. 59 to 60, https://hdl.huntington.org/digital/collection/p15150coll7/id/43073/rec/17

Samuel willingly followed the call to prayer and fasting and marked it in his diary. Three days later he got paid for four months' duty and was able to pay off his debts in camp.

Then another dozen men were caught deserting. This time the deserters were spared execution. And instead received a hundred lashes each on their bare backs. Then more awful news reached West Point. On the other side of the Hudson a Continental outpost had been ambushed by the Cowboys on the fourteenth of May.

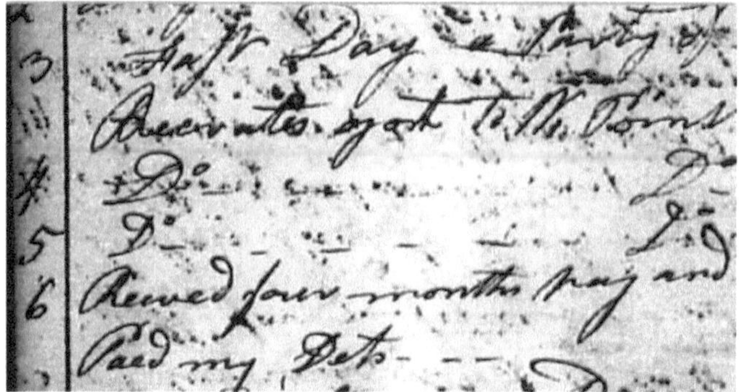

3 Half Day a Party of
Recruites got to the Point
4 Do ... Do
5 Do ... Do
6 Recevd four months pay and
Paid my Dets ---

Image of Lieutenant Samuel Benjamin's Diary

Samuel had served with some of the negroes and Indians of the First Rhode Island Regiment under the command of Colonel Christopher Greene at Pine's Bridge. There were also some soldiers from Massachusetts and New Hampshire. Some of those brave men were slaves who signed up to become free men.

The rich loyalist James DeLancey and hundreds of his men attacked overnight and killed some of the men in their beds, including Major Flagg. It appeared DeLancey tried to make an example of Colonel

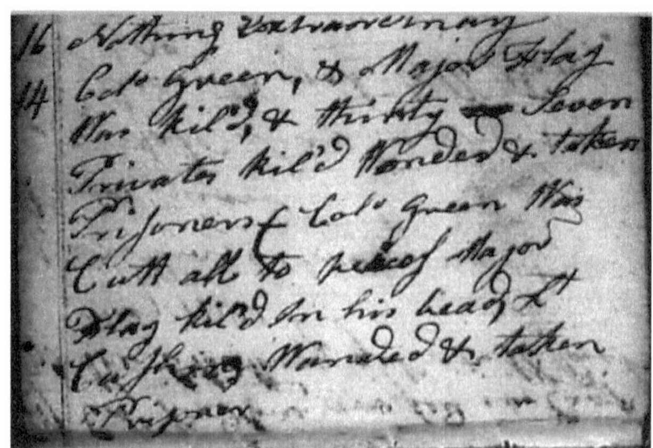

16 Nothing Extraordinary
14 Col. Green, & Major Flagg
Was Kil'd, & thirty Seven
Privates kil'd Wonded & taken
Prisoners Col. Green Was
Cutt all to peices Major
Flagg kil'd In his bed Lt
Cushing Wonded & taken
Prisoner

Image from Lieutenant Benjamin's War Diary

Greene for leading former slaves against the Crown. He was hacked to pieces with swords. Some of Greene's men apparently circled in defense of him and all died. DeLancey ordered his men to mutilate Greene's body. They rode off with his corpse. But his body fell on the ground in the woods, where he was discovered. The attack was a massacre. Samuel wrote of it in his diary. (140)

> 14th, Colonel Greene and Major Flagg was kil'd, & thirty-seven privates kil'd, wounded, & taken prisoners. Colonel Greene was cut all to pieces. Major Flagg kil'd in his bead, & Lieutenant Gushing wounded & taken prisoner.

Samuel couldn't believe the way DeLancey had dishonored Colonel Greene and Major Flagg as well as his men by killing some of them unarmed in their beds. But there wasn't time to ruminate on the awfulness of it.

Two days later the Light Infantry was ordered to march under the command of Colonel Alexander Scammell. Samuel readied for battle. (141) When some new officers walked into camp, Samuel saw a friend.

"Thomas!" Samuel yelled. Col. Scammell had apparently chosen Thomas as one his officers. Samuel and Thomas were separated again after Thomas was wounded at Stony Point.

"Samuel!" Thomas shouted back in surprise. They hurried to a handshake.

"It's great to see you've recovered from your wounds," said Samuel.

"Yes, although it took a few months, Samuel. I see you're now a lieutenant?" replied Captain Hunt.

"I was promoted after Stony Point," answered Samuel. "Let's try to keep you from being wounded again," he continued in a teasing manner.

"That's a good plan, Samuel. I'll try to keep my head down," laughed Thomas.

They parted ways and were glad to be serving again side by side.

General Washington told Colonel Scammell the redcoats were building some kind of fortress near Fort Lee, and they shouldn't be allowed to complete it. A fortification there could hamper future operations to challenge the British in New York. The journey would be more than forty miles. Colonel Scammell was also hunting for the Cowboys, so the daily marches were as much a scouting mission as anything else.

The Light Infantry arrived at Peekskill on June 1. All was quiet, so Samuel wrote a letter to Tabitha to have Lieutenant Armstrong carry it back to West Point.

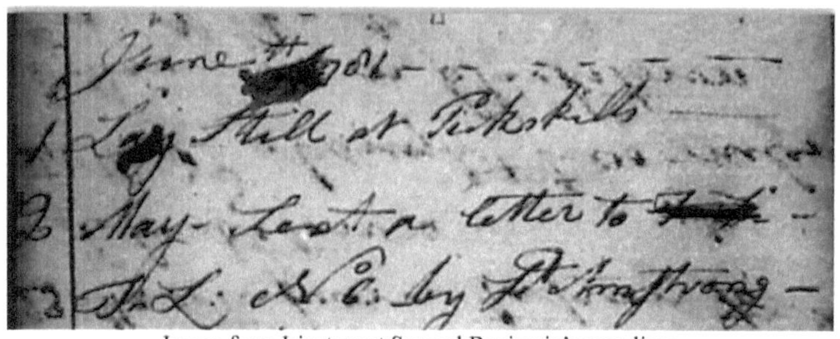

Image from Lieutenant Samuel Benjmain's war diary

"June I, 1781. Still at Peekskill; 12th May, sent a letter to T. L., No. 6, by Lieutenant Armstrong."

June 1, 1781

Peekskill, New York

Dear Tabitha,

I hope you are in good health. Now that winter is over it should be easier for letters to get through. I am happy to report I am in good health. I pray the same for you and all our loved ones back home. I'm back on patrol with the Light Infantry under Colonel Scammell. We've been on the lookout for a loyalist force that's been stealing cattle from patriot farmers. The cowboys butchered one of our Continental forces that had been protecting the farmers from loyalist raids. I know you will be horrified to learn the cowboys not only hacked to death a colonel and a

major but also slaughtered some of our freed slaves that were serving so they could be free men. The Rhode Island regiment also had a number of brave Indians who had joined in the fight for liberty. It was an awful affair. Please continue to pray for my safety and for all those who I serve with me. I miss you and can't wait to be with you.
In Christ – all my love –
Samuel

Tents arrived from West Point on some wagons on the fifth of June. Colonel Scammell and General Washington appeared to be planning a bigger attack. Samuel and the other soldiers set up and moved into the tents the sixth. The next day, Lieutenant Armstrong returned with mail from the garrison. There were letters from Tabitha and Elisha.

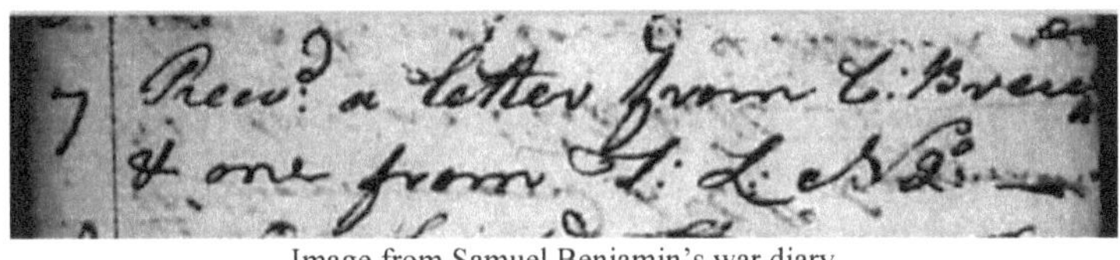
7 Recd. a letter from C. Brew[er]
& one from T. L. No 2.

Image from Samuel Benjamin's war diary

"June 7. Received a letter from C. Brewer, and one from T. L., No. 2."

Samuel could not open the letter from Tabitha fast enough. It was the second letter that made it to camp in the last year. The outside of the letter looked like it had been dropped in the snow. Some of the ink had smeared. Thankfully, the inside had stayed dry.

Dear Samuel,
I miss you so much today. I just had to write you. I never know if my letters are getting through. Some of yours arrive several weeks or months after you have written them.

Father has taken ill a few days ago with fever and dysentery. I am so worried about him. I wish you were here to hold me with your strength of spirit. I pray you are well. It doesn't seem like Christmas day with father being so ill and mother attending to him. I will do my best to help make it a special day for my brothers and sisters. They all send their best to you. Remember how much I love you and hold me dear in your heart. I continue to pray for you.
~ Love,

Tabitha

Samuel was sad to hear Nathaniel was so ill. He said a prayer for him, hoping that somehow his plea to God could reach back in time to restore his future father-in-law to good health. It would be too much for Tabitha to lose her father while Samuel was also in harm's way. Nathaniel was strong, and for now Samuel had to trust in God's providence.

A strong and unusually cold storm swept through the Light Infantry camp on the eighth and sent the men running for cover. A sentry had spotted the Cowboys nearby just before the storm hit. The howling wind must have chased them away. Samuel's tent was damaged by the wind, and he'd need to find another. Several trees were also felled. There was always the risk of a tree falling and killing you in severe weather. The soldiers had been spared that injustice this time. It took a few days to clear the timber and restore the camp. Samuel was sent back to West Point on the fifteenth to deliver a message from Colonel Scammell, who had taken a liking to Samuel and had placed his trust in him. Samuel was happy to make the journey. If for no other reason than to break the monotony of waiting for action. Once he arrived, he discovered two letters awaited him. One from Tabitha and the other from Elisha.

"June 16. Received a letter from Captain Brewer, and one from T. L., No. 3. Sent one home, No. 7."

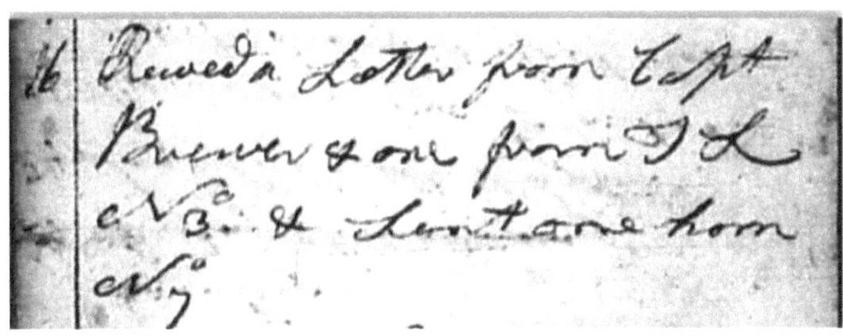
16 Receiv'd a Letter from Capt
Brewer & one from T L
No 3. & Sent one home
No 7

Image from Samuel Benjamin's war diary

Waltham
April 15th
My Dearest Samuel,
I just received your letters from December and March. I have read them several times each. I'm so glad the traitor Arnold's plot was foiled. I shudder to think of the consequences if he had not been found out. I fear you would have been killed along with so many of our brave patriot men. I hope they can capture him some day. We also read about the execution of John Andre in the Chronicle. I fear you had to witness the horrible ordeal. I was also saddened to read about the mutineers. I know you are not telling me about the dreadful conditions you have faced lest I worry. But it's so sad those Pennsylvania and Jersey boys were so desperate. We are all well here in Waltham. Spring planting went well and Father is looking forward to a good crop this summer. I have not seen your mother for several months. But when last I inquired about her I heard she was in good health and spirits. Oh, I pray you will be home for good soon. Is it too selfish of me that I want to get on with our lives? I am proud of your commitment to our new nation. Though I am concerned about what will happen to all of us if we should not succeed against the king. What will be our lot as patriots against the Crown? I yearn for your

return and I imagine myself in your arms. I plead with you to not be too brave.

My love forever,

Tabitha

Samuel was happy she spoke of her father planting and of the pending harvest. That meant he had survived the illness he suffered at Christmas. He hoped the weather would hold up and the ground would provide a bountiful harvest for Tabitha and her family.

And yes, he too hoped that Arnold would be caught. Samuel would not tell her he had witnessed the hanging of André.

He carried Tabitha's letters with him on his journey back to the camp in Peekskill. The Light Infantry was not there long before they received orders to head toward Dobbs Ferry, about ten miles north of Fort Independence.

The march took them to Pier's Bridge and on to Dobbs Ferry, where they camped with other Continental troops. General Washington wanted a closer look at British fortifications around New York City for a possible attack by Continental and French forces.

His Excellency and the Continental troops moved south on July 2 to get into position for a reconnaissance of the city. Hessian troops spotted the patriots on the third and opened fire. Their musket balls struck several soldiers near Samuel on the first volley.

General Washington stayed on his horse as the bullets continued to fly. Samuel thought His Excellency's courage might just get him killed this time. The general was more interested in what was beyond the Hessians—the British defenses on northern Manhattan. (142)

His Excellency was intent on attacking in New York and regaining the port. But more than a dozen of Washington's guards were wounded as well as some others. Ensign Amos Harden in Bailey's 2nd Massachusetts regiment was shot dead.

Samuel was reminded of how quickly a soldier's life could end after surviving so many battles. Harden was from Bridgewater, about thirty miles south of Boston. He had survived as a Minuteman at Lexington and six years later, he was killed during a routine reconnaissance mission. Samuel wondered how many more names of the dead he would enter in his diary.

July 1781...
2 Embarked & landed about one mile below Phillippy, & march to Fort Independence.
3 There we were attacked about sunrise the third day, Capt Allen Lieutenant Libby wounded, & Ensign Hardin killed & left on the ground. The number of men killed and wounded 1 captain wounded, 1 lieutenant wounded, 1 ensign killed, 1 seagt wounded, 30 rank & file wounded, & 5 killed. 1 volunteer wounded.

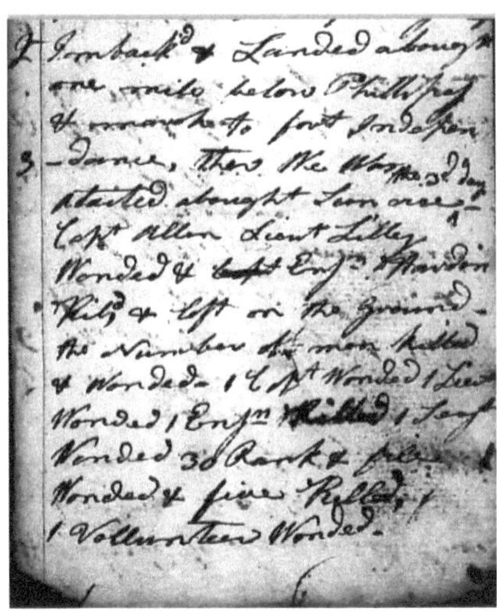

Image from Samuel Benjamin's war diary, Yale University Archives

The troops marched back to their camp. Within days the French forces arrived in the area and General Washington and General Ro-chambeau began planning another reconnaissance mission of the enemy's defenses. Washington and Rochambeau decided they needed another, more thorough assessment of attacking the King's forces in New York City.

By the night of the twenty-first, some 4,000 Continental and French troops marched south in the dark toward Manhattan. Washington and Rochambeau surveilled more thoroughly this time before ordering the Continental and French soldiers to retreat to Dobbs Ferry some twenty-four hours later. The American and French leaders decided attacking the British at New York City could lead to disaster.

Chapter 23
The Siege Of Yorktown

His Excellency and General Rochambeau began planning for a possible southern attack against Lord Cornwallis at Yorktown. Samuel knew from General Washington's hesitancy about attacking the British in New York that the southern campaign was the most likely next step. Especially since that's where the redcoats had shifted their efforts.

He decided he'd better write Tabitha a letter before he and the Light Infantry were ordered south. Who knew if he'd get another chance to tell her how much he loved her.

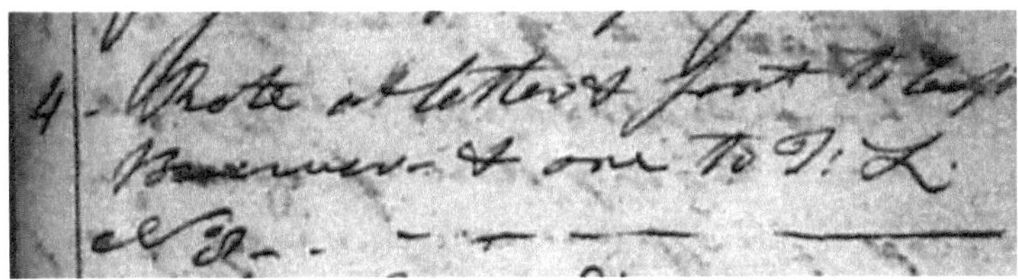

Image from Samuel Benjamin's war diary, Yale University Archives

"August 4. Wrote a letter & sent to Captain Brewer, and one to T. L., No. 8.- - - - -"

Dobbs Ferry

August 4 1781

Dear Tabitha,

I'm writing again to let you know I am still well. Thank you for your letter. It continues to be a great encouragement to me. It appears I may be heading father away from you for the remainder of the summer and into the fall. There is a major engagement being planned. I am not at liberty to tell you where it might take me and the rest of the army. But I hope if we are successful, I will be coming home for good. I have seen too many of my fellow patriots perish and I'm eager to be done with this war. I tell you again I love you beyond measure. I have been reading my bible near daily, and I place my life in the Lord's hands. Only he knows my path as I forge ahead. But know that my constant prayer is to be with you for the rest of my days after my service in the army and the cause of liberty end.

Eternally yours,

Samuel

Dobbs Ferry
August 4
Dear Elisha,
Your leedership is missed here in camp. I thank you for your recent letter. It sounds like married life with children suits you well. I am happy to hear you expect a good harvest. I am well. But we recently lost Ensign Hardin on a reconnisance mission. I know you remember him. He was a good man whose commitment to the cause of liberty never wavered. I wonder how many more we will have to sacrifice to rid ourselves of the redcoats. It appears we are preparing for a major campaign. We have the French on our side now which I think shall be of great help to His Excellency. I long to be home and to take Tabitha as my wife. I wish you well captain. Give my best to Martha and the little ones.
I shall keep all of you in my prayers and ask that you do the same for me.
Your brother in Christ –

On the fourteenth of August, General Washington received a letter informing him that the fleet of French Admiral François Joseph Paul de Grasse would sail to Yorktown.

The Continental Army began final preparations for a journey south. A few days later, Scammell's Light Infantry prepared to travel from Dobbs Ferry to King's Ferry, crossing toward New Jersey and on to Philadelphia with the eventual destination of Yorktown.

Samuel and his fellow soldiers began to march on August 19. But Samuel didn't get far before he got sick and was forced to stop. He tried to march again. But his illness made him too weak. To his great mortification, he was forced to stop again and the Light Infantry had to leave him behind.

In a few days he recovered and by the end of August, he'd reached Newark, then Brunswick, and overtook the regiment. He reached Philadelphia on the first of September.

They set sail and reached the Cristeen River (Christina

River). They reached land in Cristeen by noon on September 5 and began a march to Head of Elk. Samuel and about sixty of Scammell's Light Infantry boarded ships on the twelfth to sail toward Yorktown. Colonel Scammell placed Samuel in charge of protecting the Light Infantry surgeon and his mate on the schooner Glasco.

Dr. Thacher and Dr. Munson were handpicked by Colonel Scammell, who had also insisted on picking the officers of his Light Infantry regiment. Samuel was now twice honored and found Dr. Thacher and Dr. Munson to be pleasant fellows he was happy to protect.[38] The fleet of about seventy ships reached Chesapeake Bay on the twelfth. Samuel continued to write in his diary.

> September 12....From Chester to Annapolis is 15 miles, where we arrived about halfe an hour before sunset & came to anchor within about 2 miles of the town. Then Captain Frye, Doctor Thatcher, Doctor Munson & myself, went on shore to drink some punch that Dr. Thatcher had last. But to our great disappointment there was none to be found, but we charged ourselves with sangaree & about 9 o'clock, set out to go on board, but the storm & dark prevented our going. So we took up our lodgings at the coffeehouse.

Samuel was glad to be healthy and to be socializing with such fine, educated gentlemen. They returned to Annapolis again the next day.

---

[38] Selig, Robert, National Park Service, the Washington-Rochambeau Revolutionary Route Resource Study & Environmental Assessment, 2006, https://www.nps.gov/waro/learn/historyculture/washington-rochambeau-revolutionary-route.htm

Thatcher, Dr. Munson, & Esq. Smith, went on shore & reconnoitrered the sitte of Annapolis, the metropolis of Maryland, where we found a Court House. I suppose the most magnificent building in North America besides a number of other very fine buildings. A little before sunset, I and four other gentl went on shore and reconnoitered the back part of the town, where we found a number of the best buildings in the town, & a number of very fine ladies -
14 Nothing extraordinary, only went to the theatre in the evening, where there was a large collection of number of gentlemen & ladies, to see the play acted. To wind up this days work, went to the coffee-house and took a good drink of wine and a supper of coffee, & then retired to bed where I took repose.

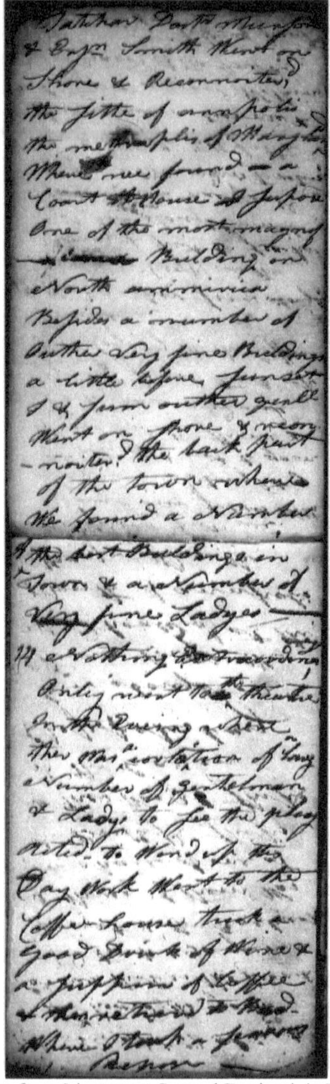

Saturday Doctr Munson
& Ensgn Smith Went on
Shore & Reconnoitred
the Sitte of Annapolis
the metropolis of Maryland
Where wee found — a
Court House I Suppose
One of the most magnificent
Building in
North America
Besides a number of
Other very fine Buildings
a little before Sunset
I & Some other gentln
Went on Shore & recon-
noitred the back part
of the town where
We found a Number
of the best Buildings in
Town & a Number of
Very fine Ladyes —
14 Nothing Extraordinary
Onley went to the theatre
In the Evening where
there was an invitation of Every
Number of Gentleman
& Ladys to See the play
Acted. To Wind up the
Day Work Went to the
Coffee house took a
Good Drink of Wine &
a Suppin of Coffee
& then returned to Board
Where I took a Sound
Repose —

Image from Lieutenant Samuel Benjamin's Diary

The next day, the fifteenth of September, the Continental fleet received a message that the French fleet had defeated the Royal Navy near the mouth of Chesapeake Bay on the fifth. It was glorious news that would save the Continental Army and their French allies from being challenged by the King's ships at Yorktown.

Samuel and Dr. Thacher had many enlightening conversations while sailing south. They discovered each was steadfastly against slavery.

"The labor of Virginia is performed by a species of the human race who have been stolen from their native land and doomed to bondage. Meantime, their masters are fighting for freedom and the rights of man," said Dr. Thacher.[39]

"It is cruel. And I say this quietly only for your ears, Doctor. I hope His Excellency and other slaveholders eventually see the error of their ways. Certainly, God does not approve!" replied Samuel.

"It's the inconsistency of human nature on full display. Perhaps, Lieutenant, we shall live to see the day when the African slave is slave no longer, and is allowed to live the blessings of the freedom we fight for. Until all men are free, are we slaves only to an ideal, and not to true liberty?" said Dr. Thacher.

"When we talk of this hypocrisy, I remember the negroes of the First Rhode Island who recently gave their lives trying to save that of Colonel Greene at Pine's Bridge. They laid down their lives for the cause of liberty and yet their liberty is not assured," said Samuel.

"Yes. And no doubt more negroes and Indians will die in this infernal war," said the doctor.

Samuel knew it was true. There were freed slaves and Indians who would be fighting with the Rhode Island regiments and others at Yorktown. And he was melancholy, at least for a moment, at the thought of it. On the twentieth of September, Samuel, the doctors, and all on board enjoyed "a distant view of the grand French fleet riding at anchor at the mouth of the Chesapeake, consisting of thirty-six ships of war, besides frigates and other armed vessels. This was the most noble and majestic spectacle any of them had ever witnessed." It appeared

---

[39] Thacher, James D., *A Military* Journal *during the American Revolutionary War, from 1775 to 1783* (Boston: Richardson and Lord, 1823), p. 269–270

Lord Cornwallis was trapped. But Samuel thought the British General would not go down without a fight.

Twelve days had passed on their 350-mile journey aboard the Glasco when they arrived at Williamsburg on the twenty-second of September and embarked. They camped near Jamestown. The remainder of the fleet arrived and dropped anchor over the following days. By the twenty-eighth, the whole army, including the French, had marched to within about one mile of Yorktown. Samuel had been writing in his diary each day now. Colonel Scammell saw Samuel writing and approached him.

"Lieutenant," the Colonel said as he walked up.

"Yes sir," replied Samuel as he placed his quill and diary aside, stood up, and tipped his Light Infantry helmet in salute.

"I see you can write, Lieutenant. My adjutant has taken ill, and I need you to replace him. Do you think you can fulfill the duty?" asked the Colonel.

"Yes sir, I would be honored, sir," answered Samuel.

"I will bring the regimental orderly book to you, Lieutenant, so that you can assume the duty of keeping the daily record for the Light Infantry," said Colonel Scammell.

"Yes sir," Samuel responded.

Samuel had recorded and signed muster rolls many times before for his regiment. He'd also helped Ensign Tufts in his role as adjutant. Samuel was experienced at keeping records. He knew he wasn't as meticulous as Tufts. But he would do his best to follow the standard Tufts had set.

Samuel had already sensed he was living in days before a battle unlike any other he had experienced. Now he was sure of it. The Lord had delivered him this far. But there was no guarantee that he would be delivered home alive.

So, he must write about what could be his last days or hours as well as keep records for the Light Infantry. September seemed to be ending with a hopeful sign. And he wrote in his diary.

"Last night, the enemy abandoned their outworks, & we moved & took possession of the above works. There was a small matter of cannonading. Genl. Mulenburgh's brigade & Hazen's were considered as the reserve picket. We lay upon our arms all night."

Samuel wondered why he hadn't seen Colonel Scammell since he'd given him the regimental orderly book. It was not like him to be absent in the trenches for the whole of an evening. Then Samuel and the rest of the Light Infantry received horrible news on the first day of October.

Colonel Scammel had been shot and taken prisoner. The Colonel was serving as officer of the day, leading the pickets as they probed at first light on September 30. He was on his horse and thought he recognized an officer at the front of a group of other soldiers on horseback. Two of the men rode up to the Colonel. One seized his bridle and pointed a pistol at him. Colonel Scammell asked who they were and surrendered. Then a third man rode up and shot him in the back. Another soldier tried to strike him with a sword. Colonel Scammell dodged the blow and fell to the ground. But he was badly wounded by a musket ball, taken prisoner, and hauled to the British camp in York. (143)

The British commanders decided they couldn't properly care for Scammell's wounds. The wounded colonel then reportedly asked to be transferred to the Continental Army hospital set up in a Williamsburg mansion. The British used one of their boats to carry the Colonel up the York River to the mouth of Queen's Creek. Dr. Munson then took over Scammell's care at the nearby hospital.

Samuel's treasured commander would not be leading them into battle. It was a devastating blow to the morale of the Light Infantry. Now they would fight for the honor of their beloved commander.

Samuel and the other soldiers knew the Colonel would want them to continue their work in the trenches without ceasing.

The men continued to shore up their redoubts as Samuel wrote in his diary.

> October 1, 1781. There was a smart cannonading last night on our people, who had been throwing up some work last night. About nine o'clock we retired to camp.
> October 2. Nothing extraordinary, only the enemy kept up a cannonading all day.
> October 3, Our brigade was on the covering party this night.

The enemy's cannon fire proved deadly. One cannonball killed three patriot soldiers near Samuel and mortally wounded another. Continental scouts also reported the redcoats killing hundreds of their horses because they lacked food for them. The carcasses were seen floating down river.

> October 4. As we were coming off of the covering party this morning, there was a cannon shot which struck within twenty yards of our battalion and hopped over it within about twenty feet of the ground.

The cannonball reminded Samuel again how quickly it could all end. A few inches here or there could be the difference between life or death. It wouldn't matter how experienced you were at soldiering or how alert you were on duty. He'd watched better soldiers than he die in front of his eyes. He knew it was God's providence, or as some less religious soldiers believed, just plain old bad luck.

Would he survive one more bayonet charge? Just as Samuel pondered that question, word reached the trenches that Colonel Scammell had died of his wounds. Samuel grieved his loss. Scammell had shown his trust in Samuel and treated him with great respect. Now the Colonel was gone. Who would take over leadership?

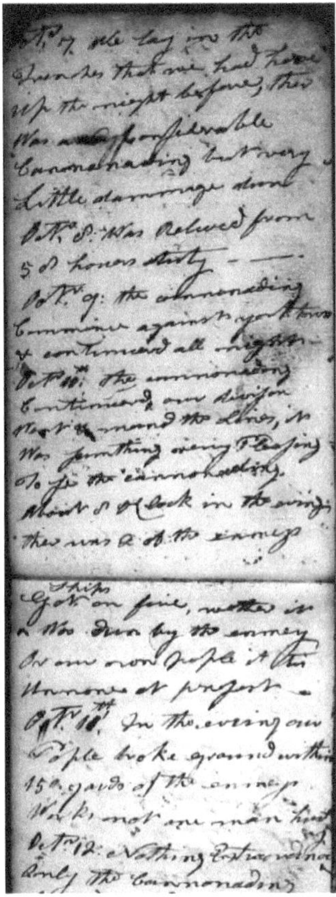

> "October 7. We lay in the trenches that we had hove up the night before. There was considerable cannonading, but very little damage done."

The next day, General Washington reorganized Scammell's Light Infantry companies into three new battalions with Lieutenant Colonel Alexander Hamilton having overall command.

Samuel's company would be led by Lieutenant Colonel John Laurens. The others were divided between Colonel Hamilton and Lieutenant Colonel Ebenezer Huntington.

The reorganization led to a delay in Samuel's company being relieved from their work in the trenches. But soon, the Continental and French cannons would open fire on Lord Cornwallis and his men.

> October 8. Was relieved from fifty-eight hours' duty. October 9. The cannonading commenced against Yorktown, and continued all night. October 10. The cannonading continued. Our division went and manned the lines. It was very pleasing to see the cannonading. About eight o'clock in the evening, two of the enemy's ships got on fire; whether it was done by the enemy or our people is not known at present.

Samuel learned the next day it was French artillery that had pummeled the British ships. The shells from each side crossed in the air as an incredible display of pending destruction. In the dark of night Samuel and Dr. Thacher had talked in the trenches about the cannonballs. They streaked across the sky like fiery meteors with blazing tails. Beautiful but deadly.

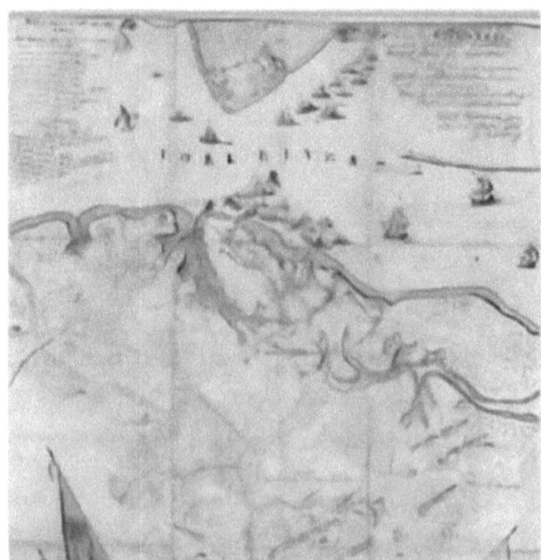

American map of the Siege of Yorktown. Courtesy of Geography and Map Division, Library of Congress.

> October 11. In the evening, our people broke ground within 150 yards of the enemy's works—not one man hurt. October 12. Nothing extraordinary, only the cannonading continued.

As Samuel wrote the entry on the twelfth, he knew an attack was imminent. The trenches they'd been digging and guarding were nearly complete. And yet the thirteenth came and the Light Infantry lay still. He wrote Tabitha a letter and hoped it would reach her with him still being alive.

Whenever they were ordered to attack, Samuel knew the Light Infantry would know first. They, as usual, would be the first to fight.

Samuel bowed his head and prayed for the success of the mission and for the souls of all those present. He had carried his small Bible in his haversack and now he read again in the book of Matthew.

"Matthew 5:44, But I say unto you, Love your enemies, bless them that curse you, do good to them that hate you, and pray for them which despitefully use you, and persecute you."

God said to pray for your enemies. How could he pray for men he was ordered to kill? His enemies were also ordered to kill him.

Samuel found it to be one of the most difficult verses to follow as a soldier. But he took it to heart.

The fourteenth arrived along with new orders. The Light Infantry soldiers were told to mount their bayonets and keep their muskets unloaded. Night fell with a moonless sky. Darker than most. It was a perfect time for a surprise attack on the British redoubts. Samuel spotted Colonel Laurens walking down the trench toward him.

"Lieutenant Benjamin," said Colonel Laurens.

"Yes sir," replied Samuel.

"I've already spoken with Captain Hunt and Captain Bets about this. But all of you officers are to make sure each man does not load his musket. We will be attacking with only bayonets. I know you are familiar with this method because of your experience at Stony Point," ordered Colonel Laurens.

"Yes sir. I will check with each man, sir, to make sure his musket is unloaded," replied Samuel.

"Your company of eighty men will remain as one unit," said Colonel Laurens.

"Yes sir," replied Samuel.

"We will begin to march at five. Tell your men to march in silence. Their lives depend on it. You will receive final orders as soon as the sun sets at half past the hour and we are in position for the assault. The signal to attack will be three shells fired quickly. Do you understand, Lieutenant?" asked Colonel Laurens.

"Yes sir," responded Samuel.

As soon as the Colonel walked away, Samuel began ordering each soldier to use their ramrod to make sure there was not a ball and powder in the barrel. He also told them to clear their pan of powder, and to make sure their bayonet was properly locked in place. Samuel only found one man who'd been careless and forgot he had loaded his gun. But the mistake was quickly corrected. They were ready for the march. Their march toward the British lines began within an hour.

"Quiet, men. No talking," ordered Samuel.

Samuel suspected the American and French soldiers would attack the two redoubts in front of the main British lines. That's where allied cannons had targeted their shells over the past few hours.

Samuel's company had staged in the second siege line they had dug. It was only 150 yards from the redcoats' number 10 redoubt near the river. And Samuel was right. That's where Colonel Laurens led his company.

They marched to a flanking position while Colonel Hamilton's men headed to the front. The French marched toward Redoubt 9, which was a quarter of a mile inland. More than a hundred British and German soldiers defended that little fort. The King's soldiers had heavily fortified the two redoubts by surrounding the works with rows of abatis.

The enemy added muddy ditches roughly twenty-five yards out. Colonel Laurens's company was told the password for the attack was Rochambeau and they were to wait for the signal shells firing before initiating the attack.

They were to assault the redoubt from behind so none of the British soldiers could escape. At half past six the allied commanders launched a diversionary attack on a redoubt further to the north of Yorktown. Then Samuel saw three shells fired one right after the other. Their fiery tails lit up the battlefield.

"Up, up, men," ordered Samuel. As the same order was heard down the line. The diversionary attack on the northern redoubt provided cover and gave the redcoats the impression the Continental and French soldiers would attack the town first.

The patriot soldiers rushed forward and began chopping at the wooden defenses, which quickly drew musket fire and grenades from the redcoats. The Light Infantry soldiers stopped chopping and began climbing over and around the sharply pointed logs used for defense.

Samuel climbed to the edge of the parapet, saw an enemy soldier about to fire, and thrust his bayonet forward finding the chest of the British soldier, who let out a pitiful groan and fell back.

Colonel Laurens's men and those of Colonel Hamilton reached the interior of the redoubt at the same time. Samuel grabbed his musket with his left hand and pulled his sword from his scabbard. He slashed at an enemy officer charging forward. Samuel had to duck the man's sword and dropped his musket as he stepped back and thrust his blade into the officer's belly.

Samuel could see large holes created by the Continental cannonballs, and a few of the soldiers were falling into them as they moved forward. Some of the redcoats continued to fire their muskets. But surrendered quickly when Colonel Laurens and his men captured their commander, Major Patrick Campbell of His Majesty's 44th Regiment.

The Continental force of some four hundred soldiers had quickly overwhelmed the redcoats. Samuel was still alive and unharmed. But then he spotted Captain Hunt. He was wounded again.

"Thomas. Are you badly hurt?" asked Samuel.

"I don't think so. A bayonet caught me in the side. But the pain is not my friend," replied Thomas.

"We'll get you to a man who is my friend. Dr. Thacher will patch you up at the hospital," Samuel assured him.

"That sounds good," said Thomas in a quiet groan.

Samuel helped get Captain Hunt loaded onto a wagon headed to the hospital. He would wait to update the regimental orderly book. The commanders often didn't want details of a battle written into the orderly book. Instead, Samuel wrote in his diary of the attack on redoubts 9 and 10.

> October 14. about 5 o'clock, the 2 brigades of infantry march, but it was unknown where. But before 7 o'clock we found ourselves storming the enemy's works, which we put in execution. Our loss was very inconsiderable. The Americans stormed one work, & the French stormed 2 Their loss was considerable, but the particulars not known. Col. Gimet was wounded; Maj. Barber, ditto; Col. Barber, ditto; Capt. Fitzpatrick, ditto. Our loss of killed and wounded did not exceed twenty.

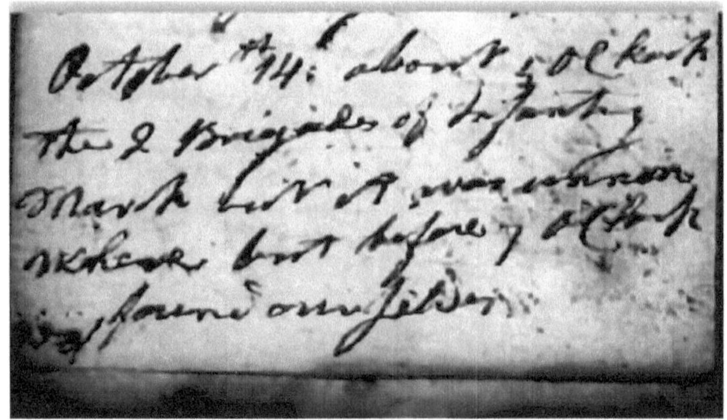

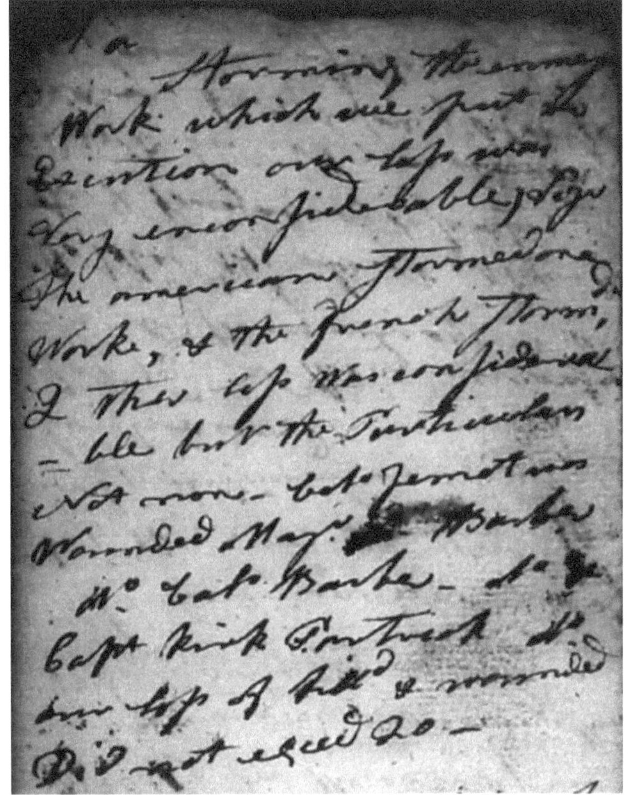

Image from Lieutenant Samuel Benjamin's war diary, Yale University Archives

Samuel received more accurate numbers of killed and wounded from Lieutenant Colonel Alexander Hamilton and entered it into the orderly book. Lieutenant Colonel Gimat received a musket ball in his foot. Captain Bets of Laurens's corps as well as Captain Hunt, Lieutenant Mansfield, and Captain Olney of Gimat's battalion suffered bayonet wounds. Captain Lieutenant Kirkpatrick of the corps of sappers and miners received a wound in the ditch. Colonel Barber was slightly wounded after being grazed by a musket ball. In all, the Continental Army had lost nine men killed and twenty-five men wounded.

The French losses were greater. Fifteen died and seventy-seven wounded. The British and Hessians lost eighteen men killed and fifty captured. (144)

The siege continued with Samuel and the rest of the Light Infantry taking turns manning the trenches. The patriot and French cannons continued their thunderous assault of the British lines.

Samuel was back in the trenches on the sixteenth when a ruckus arose from two unfinished French trenches. The redcoats made a futile attempt to take back their works. But the French fought back valiantly and repelled the British attack, leaving several soldiers dead on both sides.

Later that night Lord Cornwallis tried to make his escape by water. A violent storm blew in, scattering the British boats and foiling the attempt. On the seventeenth, Samuel witnessed a most glorious turn of events. He was overjoyed to record the event in his diary.

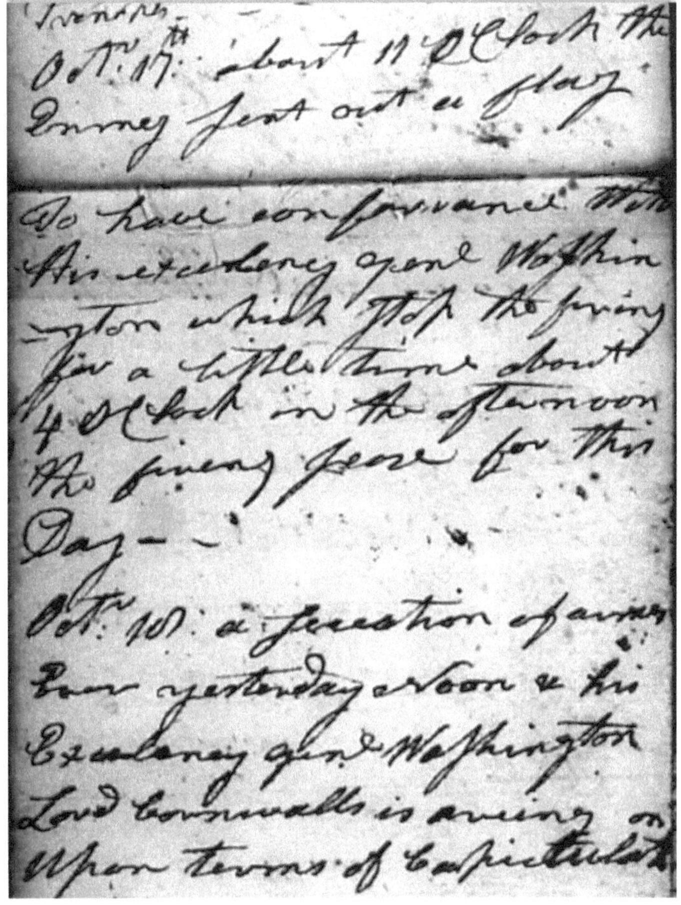

Image from Lieutenant Samuel Benjamin's war diary, Yale University Archives

> October 17. About 11 o'clock the enemy sent out a flag to have a conference with His Excellency General Washington which stop the firing for a little time. About four o'clock in the afternoon, the firing cease for this day - - October 18. A sessation of arms about yesterday noon, & His Excellency Genl Washington Lord Cornwallis is agreeing upon terms of capitulation.

The battle was over. Lord Cornwallis was surrendering. Samuel's direct commander, Colonel Laurens, was given the honor of dictating terms of surrender. Samuel knew the Colonel took some satisfaction in doing so, since his father, Henry Laurens, former president of the Continental Congress, and U.S. envoy to the Netherlands, was being held prisoner in the Tower of London after being captured at sea. (145)

The redcoats were upset that they would not be given customary honors of war to march out with their regimental flags flying and playing an enemy's tune in honor of the victor. Instead, they were treated as the American army was treated the year before when they were captured at Charlestown, South Carolina. The redcoats were directed to march out with "shouldered arms, colors cased, and drums beating a British or German march. They were then to ground their arms and return to their encampment, where they will remain until they are dispatched to the places of their destination..." They would be held as prisoners of war. (146) Once again, Samuel recorded the event.

> "October 19. The American and French army are paraded to receive the British army as prisoners. Our armies were drawn up in a line of battle, fronting each other, and the British march through them with three thousand troops."[40]

Claiming he was too sick to attend, Lord Cornwallis sent a replacement to greet General Washington on the field of surrender. The redcoats threw their muskets into a pile in a disrespectful manner.

On duty in Yorktown two days later, Samuel's brigade found the houses and other buildings nearly torn to pieces by the allied cannons. It became clear to Samuel how desperate the situation had become for Cornwallis before he finally surrendered.

The prideful British general had forced the situation on himself and thus had placed the town and its people into a horrible place. Yorktown became the target for more than seven years of patriot

[40] Transcript of Lieutenant Samuel Benjamin's war diary, Yale University Archives

frustration. When His Excellency, with the help of Rochambeau, finally had the upper hand over the British that had terrorized the south, the fury of the Continental and French armies rained down.

Images of Regimental Orderly Book as recorded by Lieutenant Samuel Benjamin, listed as adjutant, Samuel Benjamin Papers (MS 75). Manuscripts and Archives, Yale University Library, 1775 to 1782.

Sadly, as the new month arrived, there was an artillery accident that led to shells bursting. One man was killed immediately, and a corporal was mortally wounded.

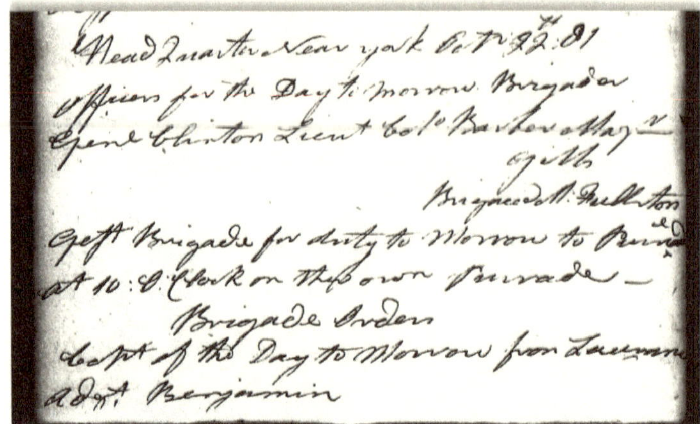

Head Quarters New york Oct 22: 81
officers for the Day to morrow Brigadier
Genl Clinton Lieut Col Barber & Majr [illegible]
[illegible]
Brigade [illegible]
[illegible] Brigade for duty to Morrow to [illegible]
at 10 O'Clock on the [illegible] Parade —
Brigade Orders
Capt of the Day to Morrow from [illegible]
Adjt Benjamin

Images of Regimental Orderly Book as recorded by Lieutenant Samuel Benjamin, listed as adjutant, Samuel Benjamin Papers (MS 75). Manuscripts and Archives, Yale University Library, 1775 to 1782.

Samuel boarded the French frigate La Diligente with twenty-six guns on the fourth of November, heading toward home as the air was turning cooler. [41] He was not out of danger yet.

Several days into the journey, a shell exploded and Samuel was hit by shrapnel. He spent the rest of the journey healing until they made landfall on the twenty-first at Head of Elk. Thankfully he recovered well enough to march back to New York.

Samuel had a lot of time to think and pray on his return. His time as a soldier was done. By December 8, Colonel Scammell's infantry was disbanded and the Light Infantry soldiers returned to their regiments. It would be one of the last entries Samuel would make in his diary.

"Col. Scammel's Regt. of Infantry was broak up, and the men joined the company of infantry. Myself crossed the North River. I got my furlough, and dined with Genl. Paterson. Prepared to set out for home."

---

[41] Miles, A.H. Cdr., U.S. Navy, U.S. Naval Institute, Sea Power and the Yorktown Campaign, https://www.usni.org/magazines/proceedings/1927/november/sea-power-and-yorktown-campaign

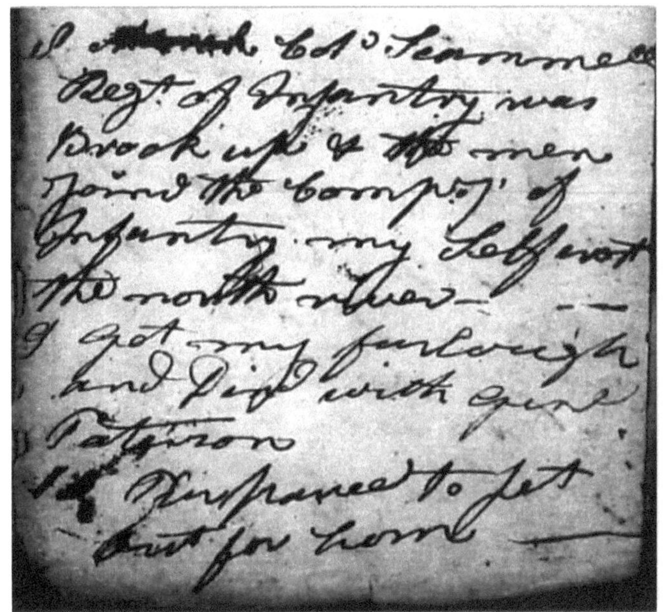
I Col° Seammel
Regt of Infantry was
Brook up & the men
Joind the Compy of
Infantry my Self went
the north river —
I got my furlough
and Dind with Genl
Paterson
10 Prepared to set
out for home —

Image from Lieutenant Samuel Benjamin's war diary, Yale University Archives

Samuel received his furlough on December 9, 1781, at West Point. One of his final actions as a soldier was to have dinner with General John Paterson.

He greatly admired General Paterson, and he noted the dinner in his diary. It was fitting. Samuel and General Paterson had traveled long parallel roads together from the creation of the Continental Army serving at Bunker Hill and the Siege of Boston to the Battles of Saratoga and Monmouth.

Their fathers had both served in the French and Indian War. Paterson had moved to Massachusetts from Connecticut before the war. And was quick to swear allegiance to the patriot cause, which quickly earned him Samuel's loyalty. Samuel revered Paterson for his Yale law degree and the time he had served in the Massachusetts legislature before the rebellion. The dinner with a well-known and well-regarded patriot general was a fitting honor to Samuel's more than seven years of military service to the new United States.

Samuel was more than ready to leave his life as a soldier behind and return to the gift God had given him—a future with Tabitha.

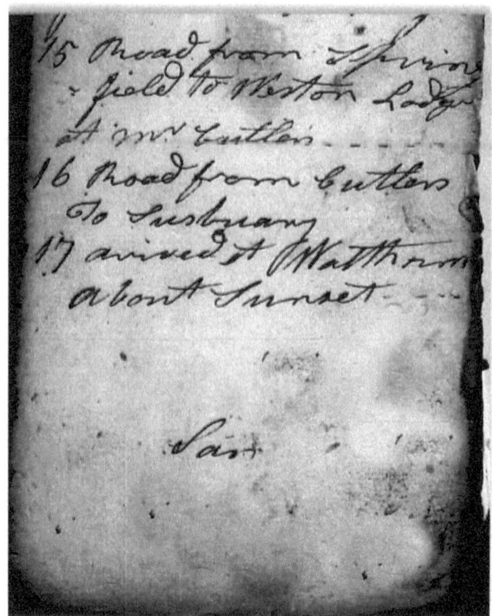
15 Road from Spring
field to Weston Lodged
at Mr Cutlers
16 Road from Cutlers
to Sudbury
17 arrived at Waltham
about Sunset

Image from Lieutenant Samuel Benjamin's war diary, Yale University Archives

He had served proudly under many great men. Some of those honored souls had not survived. His heart was still heavy from the death of Colonel Scammell. He had grown close to the Colonel while serving as his adjutant for the Light Infantry. Samuel couldn't get over such a distinguished military career ending with the horror of being shot in the back after Scammell had already surrendered. And he felt like he had already avenged his beloved colonel's death by bayoneting Brits in Redoubt 10.

So, bittersweet, Samuel left West Point for the final time on the eleventh of December and made the two-hundred-mile journey home on horseback two weeks before Christmas. He wrote in his diary on December 17.

"Arrived at Waltham about sunset."[42]

Tabitha heard the pounding of horse hooves outside. The sun was going down and she wondered who would be coming to their home in near darkness. She heard her mother's footsteps scurrying to the front hallway, the distinctive sound of the door opening, and her mother gasp. Then her mother called.

---

[42] From Lieutenant Samuel Benjamin's war diary, Yale University Archives

"Tabitha! Tabitha!" yelled her mother.

There was an urgency and excitement in her mother's voice she hadn't heard in a long time.

"I'm coming, Mother," replied Tabitha. She wondered who it could be.

She hurried into the front hall and there stood Samuel in his Light Infantry helmet and blue Massachusetts regimental coat with dried flowers in his hands. Tabitha let out a scream and burst into tears.

"I'm home for good, my dear Tabitha," said Samuel.

She rushed into his arms and let go of more than seven years of longing and worrying. Her body shook as tears of joy seemed to flow from the bottoms of her feet to the top of her head, pouring out of the eyes that Samuel cherished and missed so terribly.

"Oh, my precious Samuel! I have dreamed of this day and at the same time feared wishing for it should it never come true," she uttered into his shoulder.

"I have my furlough, dear. And I'm finished fighting," said Samuel.

"The war is behind us."

And now he too shed tears of joy. They embraced longer than they ever had before. There was no world around them. Just Tabitha and Samuel.

It was a moment they treasured now and would treasure for the rest of their lives. Liberty won for their new country, for their love, for their faith, for their families, together they'd helped create a nation.

Afterword

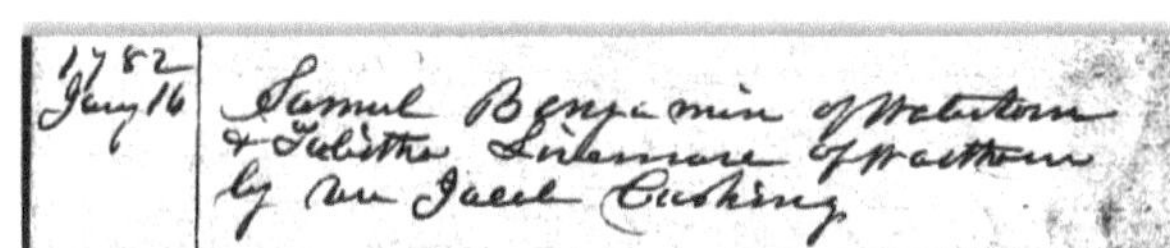

1782 Jany 16 Samuel Benjamin of Watertown & Tabitha Livermore of Waltham by Rev Jacob Cushing

Massachusetts, U.S., Town and Vital Records, 1620 to 1988 for Samuel Benjamin, Watertown, Births Marriages and Death, p. 30

Samuel and Tabitha were married in Waltham on January 16, 1782, shortly after he was furloughed. Reverend Jacob Cushing performed their vows.

Samuel was discharged from the Continental Army on August 6, 1782. He had served his beloved United States of America for seven years, three months, and seventeen days. In October, Samuel bought land for a farm from one of Tabitha's cousins in Livermore, Maine, which was still part of Massachusetts at the time. They moved to Livermore the next year.

Two years later Tabitha had their first child, Billy, who was born on March 13, 1785.

The image you see on the next page is from the back of one of Samuel's war diaries in the documents at Yale University's Archives.

It appears he spent a great deal of time studying his Bible during his service in the Continental Army. His faith journey, and Tabitha's, did not end with the war.

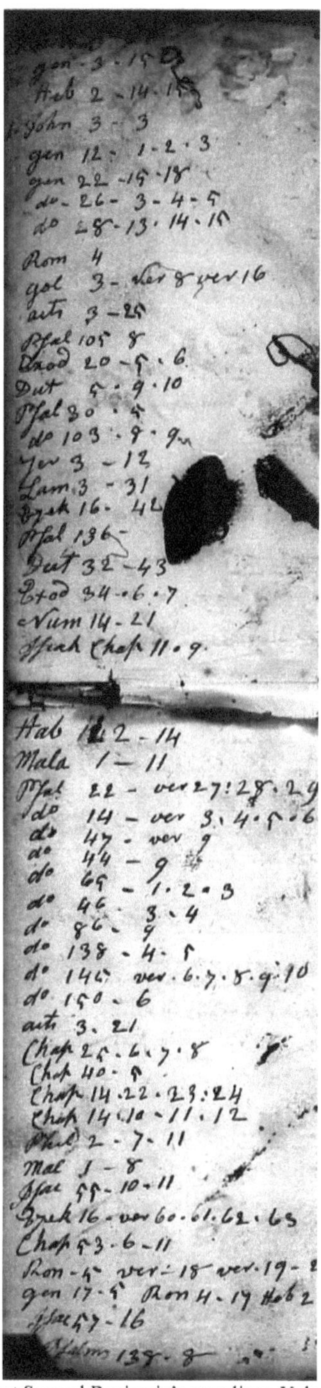

gen 3-15
Heb 2-14-15
John 3-3
gen 12-1-2-3
gen 22-15-18
do-26-3-4-5
do 28-13-14-15
Rom 4
gal 3-ver 8 ver 16
acts 3-25
Psal 105 8
Exod 20-5-6
Deut 5-9-10
Psal 30-5
do 103-8-9
Jer 3-12
Lam 3-31
Ezek 16-42
Psal 136
Deut 32-43
Exod 34-6-7
Num 14-21
Isiah Chap 11-9
Hab 2-14
Mala 1-11
Psal 22-ver 27:28-29
do 14-ver 3-4-5-6
do 47-ver 9
do 44-9
do 65-1-2-3
do 46-3-4
do 86-9
do 138-4-5
do 145 ver-6-7-8-9-10
do 150-6
acts 3-21
Chap 25-6-7-8
Chap 40-5
Chap 14-22-23-24
Chap 14-10-11-12
Phil 2-7-11
Mal 1-8
Isai 55-10-11
Ezek 16-ver 60-61-62-63
Chap 53-6-11
Rom-5 ver-18 ver-19
gen 17-5 Rom 4-17 Heb 2
Isai 57-16
Psalm 138-8

Image from Lieutenant Samuel Benjamin's war diary, Yale University Archives

For evidence of their continued reliance upon their faith in God, I turned to "A Genealogy of The Family of Lieut. Samuel Benjamin and Tabitha Livermore, His Wife, Early Settlers of Livermore, Maine."

Samuel descended from a Puritan family. But attended a Congregationalist Church in Waltham whose pastor, Jacob Cushing, embraced the view that the fight against the King's army was a just war.

Later, Samuel attended and helped fund a church in Livermore.

In addition to farming, Samuel was a businessman who owned a sawmill on the Androscoggin River as well as a blacksmith shop. He also manufactured potash. On the east side of the Androscoggin, he established a ferry near his home.

The genealogy book written by another of my ancestors, Mary Louise Benjamin, gives a description of Samuel in the prime of his life. "He was a man of dignified bearing, with a queue, and dressed in Continental fashion, in a blue, not dark, broadcloth, with buff broadcloth for collars and cuffs, knee breeches and silver buckles on his shoes, leaving in the mind the appearance of a very dignified and elegant gentleman."[43]

The genealogy book also includes a description of Tabitha as given by a grandchild.

> The remembrances of my grandmother are pleasant and abiding. To me she was a woman of great courage and fortitude, as evidenced in going to the then wilderness of Maine, a bride, when the long and cruel war was over. They were among the first families arriving in that section. There they lived, quite to themselves, with Indians all around them, who made frequent calls to their cabin, often finding my grandmother quite alone; but she met them without apparent fear, with courage and kindness. She was

---

[43] Benjamin, Mary Louise, A Genealogy of The Family of Lieut. Samuel Benjamin and Tabitha Livermore, His Wife, Early Settlers of Livermore, Maine,1900, p. 49

> a woman of strong and striking traits of character—a Christian in the true sense of the term. I remember her as of pleasing personality, of medium height, with nose slightly aquiline and eyes of very deep blue, very speaking or impressive. She was, I consider, a remarkable woman, and to me her memory is, and ever will be, a sacred remembrance.[44]

Samuel died at his Livermore home at age seventy-one. This inscription and a cross are on Benjamin's tombstone:
This monument is erected to the memory of Lieutenant SAMUEL BENJAMIN, who died April 14, 1824, in the seventy-first year of his age; an officer of the American Revolution, who fought in the sacred cause of his country and the rights of mankind, from the ever-memorable morning of the nineteenth of April, 1775, to the surrender of Lord Cornwallis, at Yorktown, on the nineteenth day of October, 1781, and from thence to the close of that sanguinary war, which established the freedom and independence of the United States, and gave to them a distinguished rank among the nations of the earth.
Tabitha was eighty-seven years old when she died.[45]

> Her funeral sermon was from the text: "Blessed are the dead who die in the Lord." She was laid to rest in the "Intervale" burying ground in Livermore between her husband and her son Charles, the only one of her ten children who did not survive her.

Samuel and Tabitha were the parents of ten children, all born in Livermore, Maine.

---

[44] Benjamin, Mary Louise, A Genealogy of The Family of Lieut. Samuel Benjamin and Tabitha Livermore, His Wife, Early Settlers of Livermore, Maine, 1900, p. 50

[45] Benjamin, Mary Louise, A Genealogy of The Family of Lieut. Samuel Benjamin and Tabitha Livermore, His Wife, Early Settlers of Livermore, Maine, 1900, p. 51

1. Billy, born March 13, 1785; died in Livermore, March 31, 1849.

2. Samuel, Jr., born Sept. 7, 1786; died in Winthrop, Maine, April 27, 1871.

3. Nathaniel, born May 16, 1788; died in Livermore, Dec. 19, 1867.

4. Betsey, born Dec. 29, 1790; died in Bangor, Maine, Dec. 12, 1860.

5. Polly, born Oct. 2, 1792; died in Bangor, Maine, March 6, 1865.

6. Martha (Patty), twin of Polly, born Oct. 4, 1792; died in Livermore, May 6, 1861.

7. David, born June 3, 1794; died in East Livermore, Oct. 3, 1883.

8. Charles, born Aug. 2, 1795; died in Winthrop, Maine, May 10, 1834.

9. Elisha, born Oct. 10, 1797; died in New Orleans, Louisiana, Dec, 1852.

10. Ruth, born May 20, 1799; died in Livermore, Feb. 3, 1869.

Their first child, Billy, served during the War of 1812. He was an ensign in Captain William Morison's Company and served in the defense of Portland in the fall of 1814. He served in every grade of the State Militia from Sergeant to Colonel, entering the service as early as 1808, and continuing until 1826, when he resigned.

Key Characters

Reverend Jacob Cushing: The pastor who married Samuel and Tabitha is still quoted for a sermon he preached during the Revolutionary War: "Divine Judgments Upon Tyrants: and compassion to the oppressed. A sermon, preached at Lexington, April 20, 1778, in commemoration of the murderous war and rapine, inhumanly perpetrated, by two brigades of British troops, in that town and neighborhood, on the nineteenth of April, 1775."

A Congregational minister, son of Reverend Job Cushing, of Shrewsbury, Massachusetts, graduated from Harvard College in 1748; was ordained pastor in Waltham, November 22, 1752; and died January 18, 1809, at the age of seventy-nine. See Sprague, Annals of the Amer. Pulpit, 1:514.

Colonel John Laurens: His brilliant and promising military career ended the year after the siege of Yorktown when he was fatally shot on August 27, 1782, during the Battle of the Combahee River or Chehaw Neck.

Captain Thomas Hunt: After the Revolution, he remained in the Army, transferring to the 3rd Massachusetts Regiment on January 1, 1783, and returned to Jackson's Continental Regiment in November of 1783. He became a Captain in the 3rd U.S. Infantry on March 4, 1791, and was promoted to Major on February 18, 1793. He was reassigned to the First U.S. Infantry on 1 November, 1796 and promoted to Lieutenant Colonel on April 1, 1802, and to Colonel on April 11, 1803. He died on August 16, 1808, and was buried at Fort Bellefontaine, Missouri. He was removed to Jefferson Barracks National Cemetery in St. Louis, Missouri, in April of 1904.

Elisha and Martha Brewer: Elisha died at age seventy-three on July 23, 1827. Martha died **on March 9, 1823**. They had three children. The first, Martha, born December 4, 1777, died at the age of eighty-four. Her sister, Fanny, was born October 4, 1779, and lived until the age of ninety-five. She died in Medford, Massachusetts. And son, Nathaniel, was born July 29, 1781.

Elizabeth Nutting Benjamin: Samuel's mother. Remarried Nehemiah Mills, after the death of Samuel's father. They lived in Needham, Massachusetts, and that was her home in 1770. She had six children by this marriage, all born before 1770, namely: Josiah, Joseph, Ephraim, Elizabeth, Sarah, and Jenny.

Of these children, half-brothers and sisters of Lieutenant Benjamin, little is known. Josiah Mills was in Livermore, Maine, as early as 1793, and left there before 1811. An "Obligation for the Support of our Mother," found among the papers of Lieutenant Benjamin, will be of interest.

> Livermore October 16, 1793,
> Know all men by these Presents that we whose Names are hereby Subscribed do each of us agree to Be their equal part towards the Support and maintenance of our mother as long as She lives. To be Dun in the following manner Viz—That She lives with each one of her Sons as long as She lives One year at a time unless otherwise agreed to by the whole.
> We also agree that the one She lives with Get her what Clothing She wants in that year and make a Charge of them and to be everidge at the end of every five years among the whole.
> We also agree to everidge all extraordinary Charges that Shall arise from her, among the whole.
> Josiah Mills has agreed to take her the first year which commences the twenty third day of October One Thousand Seven Hundred and Ninety three. Joseph Mills agrees to take her the next year John Benjamin Agrees to take her

the next year, Ephraim Mills is to take her the next year and Samuel Benjamin the next year. Our Mother agrees to the above obligation.
Josiah Mills
Samuel Benjamin
John Benjamin
Joseph Mills.[46]

Jonathan Benjamin: Samuel's second brother. Only one record found after he resigned from the army. A Jonathan Benjamin married Anna Cutter in 1811.
John Benjamin: After he resigned from the army he married Jemima Mills in Needham on February 15, 1781. He followed Samuel to Maine. They had four children. His first wife died in 1801 and he remarried Elizabeth Kenny. They had three children. John died in Whitefield, Maine in 1814.

A note to my readers. First of all, thank you. If you are so inclined please leave a review at terrysater.com

[46] Benjamin, Mary Louise, A Genealogy of The Family of Lieut. Samuel Benjamin and Tabitha Livermore, His Wife, Early Settlers of Livermore, Maine, 1900, p. 11

About the Author

Terry Sater is a three-time Emmy winning journalist with 40 years of experience in the world of television news and print media. He's a descendent of a Mayflower passenger and three Revolutionary War soldiers. He's a member of the National Society Sons of the American Revolution, The Society of the Cincinnati, and the General Society of Mayflower Descendents. Sater was born in Minneapolis, raised in Wisconsin, attended college in California, and earned his B.A. from the University of Minnesota, Twin Cities.

Acknowledgements

I would like to thank Copy Editor Brooks Becker for her thoughtful comments and her diligence in catching my typos. Brooks went beyond the call of duty in helping me connect with readers. Thanks also to Annemarie Lamprecht for her beautiful work formatting the manuscript.

A special thanks to my Massachusetts sweetheart, my wife Denise, for her encouragement and commitment to helping me tell Samuel and Tabitha's story. Thanks for putting up with my long hours of being hunched over my laptop.

I also want to thank my son-in-law Marco Pavoloni for his interest in this project and for his feedback on my writing along the way.

I couldn't have written this book without the help of the staff at the Beinecke Rare Book and Manuscript Library at Yale University including Jessica Dooling, Public Services Staff, Manuscripts and Archives, and other staff of Public Services at Yale University Library, special collections.

Thank you to Historian Michael J.F. Sheehan of the Stony Point Battlefield State Historic Site for sharing his expertise on the Battle of Stony Point and for preserving the legacy of an important place in Revolutionary War history.

I also thank Matthew Keagle, Ph.D., Curator Fort Ticonderoga for the incredible ongoing work at Fort Ticonderoga.

Elsa Gilbertson and Laura V. Trieschmann at the Vermont Division for Historic Preservation receive thanks for their help in discovering the history of Mount Independence.

Steve Zeoli of the Mt. Independence Coalition and Mike Barbieri and Ennis Duling also deserve thanks for their help and research on Bond's and Whitcomb's regiments at Fort Ticonderoga and Mount Independence.

The work of the Heritage Hunters of Saratoga County, the late Frank Goodway, and the Saratoga NYGenWeb Project deserve extraordinary recognition for their research on the soldiers who took part in the Battles of Saratoga.

I also thank Hilde Perrin, Library Assistant at the Massachusetts Historical Society and other staff for preserving precious documents of the Revolutionary War era.

Thank you Wayne T. McCarthy, President of the Waltham Historical Society, for allowing me to dig through your records and thanks to Joyce Kelly of the Historical Society of Watertown.

I also thank retired Livermore, Maine *Deputy Town Clerk Jean Tardif for her help as well as* the staff of the Norlands historical site in Livermore, April Payne, Assistant Director and Curator, Dan Pugh, Site Manager and School Age Programs Director, and Ashley Heyer, President & Director (volunteer), for preserving and allowing me to view the Samuel Benjamin artifacts that are part of Norlands collection.

And finally, I am very thankful for the staff at our National Parks and Revolutionary War historical sites who diligently maintain our nation's history.

Bibliography

1. Samuel Benjamin Papers (MS 75). Manuscripts and Archives, Yale University Library, 1775–1782

2. Watertown's Military History, By Watertown (Mass), "Published in 1907 under the direction of a committee representing the Sons of the American Revolution and Isaac B. Patten Post 81, Grand Army of the Republic": D. Clapp & Sons, Printers, Collection, Library of Congress, Americana, https://archive.org/details/watertownsmilita00water/mode/2up

3. Muster rolls of the participating companies of American militia and Minutemen in the Battle of April 19, 1775: mostly from the archives of Commonwealth of Massachusetts, but a few from other sources, Coburn, Frank Warren, 1855

4. https://www.ushistory.org/people/minutemen.htm?srsltid=AfmBOoprXF2Z0nvc4jlO80Av1GV7LG2S0s3G9xzNO0jSh6cA4AH0spq4, Andrew Ronemus, Copyright © 1999–2025 by the Independence Hall Association, a nonprofit organization in Philadelphia, Pennsylvania, founded in 1942. Publishing electronically as ushistory.org. On the Internet since July 4, 1995.

5. The Historical Society of Watertown, History of the Watertown Militia 1630–1919, Leonid E. Kondratiuk, Historical Services, The Adjutant General's Office, Concord, Massachusetts, April 2018

6. Ancestry.com, Massachusetts, U.S. Town and Vital Records, Watertown, births, marriages, and death, 1620–1988, 221 & p. 329

7. https://archive.org/details/benjaminfamilyin00bich/page/154/mode/2up, The Benjamin Family in America, Gloria Wall Bicha, Helen Benjamin Brown, 1977, Library of Congress Catalog Card Number: 76-56023

8. Project Gutenberg's The Loyalists of Massachusetts, by James H. Stark, The Loyalists of Massachusetts and the Other Side of the American Revolution, James H. Stark, W. B. CLARKE CO., 26 Tremont Street, Boston, 1907, March 31, 2012 [EBook #39316]

9. Library of Congress Blogs, British Spy Map of Lexington and Concord: A Detective Story, April 18, 2016, Ed Redmond, https://blogs.loc.gov/maps/2016/04britishspymapoflexingtonandconcord-a-detective-story/

10. How the weather helped to win an early Revolutionary War battle on April 19, John Roach, AccuWeather staff writer, April 19, 2020 4:00 AM CST, AccuWeather Chief Operating Officer Evan Myers, host of the This Date in Weather History podcast, https://www.accuweather.com/en/weather-news/how-the-weather-helped-to-win-an-early-revolutionary-war-battle-on-april-19/723026

11. Arlington Historical Society, The Battle of Menotomy, Sally Rogers, Battles of Lexington and Concord, Battles of Lexington and Concord (introduction)

12. "Foot of the Rocks." Freedom's Way. Retrieved October 25, 2024.

13. Thomas Fleming (March 6, 2019). "Battle of Menotomy—First Blood, 1775." HistoryNet. Retrieved April 16, 2019.

14. Arlington Historical Society. Retrieved April 16, 2019.

15. "Menotomy Minutemen Trail Guide" (PDF). Retrieved April 14, 2019.

16. "Menotomy, online exhibitions, April 19, 3:30 p.m. | 7:00 p.m.," Concord Museum, 2025 https://concordmuseum.org/online-exhibition/the-shot-heard-round-the-world-april-19-1775/menotomy-april-19-330-p-m-700-p-m/

17. "The Battle of Menotomy with A. Michael Ruderman," Freedom's Way National Heritage Area, April 25, 2023

18. "Jason Russell and His House in Menotomy," Old-Time New England, Volume LV, No. 2, Oct/Dec 1964 Serial No. 198, by Robert Harrington Nylander

19. "The Battle of April 19, 1775," by Frank Warren Coburn

20. "Paul Revere's Ride," by David Hackett Fischer

21. http://www.masshist.org/database/viewer.php?item_id=467&pid=2

22. http://britishredcoat.blogspot.com/2008/06/old-burial-ground-arlington-mass.html

23. "The nineteenth of April, 1775: exhibiting a fair and impartial account of the engagement fought on that day, chiefly in the towns of Concord, Lexington, and Menotomy, between a detachment of his Britannick Majesty's regular troops and the militia of the province of Massachusetts Bay; with candid remarks

upon certain relations of that sanguinary event set forth by other hands," by Murdock, Harold, 1862–1934, David Benjamin, pp. 1186–87

24. Heitman, Francis B., Historical register of officers of the Continental Army during the War of the Revolution, April to December, 1783. Washington, Rare Book Shop Pub. Co., 1914.

25. Memoirs of Major-General William Heath, By Himself, New Edition, with Illustrations and Notes, edited by William Abbatt, to which is added The Account of the Battle of Bunker Hill by Generals Dearborn, Lee and Wilkinson, New York, 281 Fourth Ave., 1901, Library University of California Davis, https://ia600903.us.archive.org/30/items/memoirsofmajorge00heatrich/memoirsofmajorge00heatrich.pdf

26. Mark, Harrison W. "Siege of Boston." World History Encyclopedia. Last modified January 03, 2024. https://www.worldhistory.org/article/2346/siege-of-boston/

27. Bunker Hill, Breeds Hill, Massachusetts, June 17, 1775, https://www.battlefields.org/learn/revolutionary-war/battles/bunker-hill

28. National Park Service, Boston National Historical Park, Dr. Joseph Warren, https://www.nps.gov/people/dr-joseph-warren.htm#:~:text=On%20the%20third%20and%20final,a%20ball%20between%20the%20eyes.

29. S. Swett, History Bunker Hill Battle (Munroe and Francis, 1826), pp. 41–42.

30. Boston Public Library, American Revolution in Massachusetts, An overview of Massachusetts' history during America's Revolutionary Era, https://guides.bpl.org/c.php?g=800717&p=10429131#:

~:text=On%20March%2017%2C%20after%20further%20de-
lays%20caused,way%20out%20of%20the%20harbor%20by%209AM.

31. Frothingham, Richard, Jr., A History of the Siege of Boston (Charles C. Little and James Brown, 1851)

32. Eric Jay Dolin, "The Enduring Boston Light," The Boston Globe, August 30, 2016, bostonglobe.com/opinion/2016/08/30/the-enduring-boston-light/aJO7478MtspJaDStoeHvkN/story.html, accessed Feb. 11, 2025.

33. Journal of HMS Lively, July 20, 1775, in Clark, Naval Documents, 1: 935.

34. Bender, Eric, https://ericbender.co/history-of-the-harbor/, (no publishing date listed) accessed Feb. 11, 2025.

35. Snow, Edward Rowe. The Islands of Boston Harbor. N.p.: Applewood Books, 2008.

36. Nissenbaum, Stephen W., Christmas in Early New England, 1620–1820: Puritanism, Popular Culture, and the Printed Word, American Antiquarian Society, 1996.

37. Jolicoeur, James R., Noble Train of Artillery, General Henry Knox (1750–1806), Shrewsbury Historical Society, accessed Feb. 18, 2025.

38. Portman, Evan, Henry Knox, Major General United States Army, July 25, 1750–October 25, 1806, National Museum United States Army, accessed Feb. 18, 2025.

39. Stockwell, Mary, Ph.D., Siege of Boston, https://www.mountvernon.org/library/digitalhistory/digital-encyclopedia/article/siege-of-boston, accessed Feb. 18, 2025.

40. American Revolution in Massachusetts, Boston Public Library, https://guides.bpl.org/c.php?g=800717&p=10429131, accessed Feb. 18, 2025.

41. NCC Staff, On this day, the Boston Massacre lights the fuse of revolution, National Constitution Center, https://constitutioncenter.org/blog/on-this-day-the-boston-massacre-lights-the-fuse-of-revolution, March 5, 2024, accessed Feb. 19, 2025.

42. Kiger, Patrick J., 8 Things We Know About Crispus Attucks, History.com, https://www.history.com/news/crispus-attucks-american-revolution-boston-massacre, August 9, 2023, accessed Feb. 19, 2025.

43. French, Allen, The Siege of Boston, Macmillan, 1911.

44. Gates, Horatio, 1776 March 15, William Bond Papers. MSS 80. Special Collections & Archives, UC San Diego.

45. Egleston, Thomas, The Life of John Paterson, Major-General in the Revolutionary Army, 1898, p. 75, G.P. Putnams Sons.

46. Garlick, Harriet Trubee, Daughters of the American Revolution Magazine, Vol. L. No. 6, June 1917.

47. Sparling, Reed, Sloops: the Special Boats That Transformed the Hudson, Hudson Valley Viewfinder Magazine, scenichudson.org, accessed March 12, 2025.

48. Meany Jr., Joseph F., "Batteaux and 'Battoe Men': An American Colonial Response to the Problem of Logistics in Mountain Warfare," New York State Museum, accessed March 12, 2025.

49. Kalm, Peter (edited by Thompson, George A. & Mayer, Carl), Hudson River Maritime Museum, 1749 Travels into North America. Vol. 2. Peter Kalm, excerpts, 2023

50. Cubbison, Douglas R. The American Northern Theater Army in 1776. The Ruin and Reconstruction of the Continental Force. 2010: McFarland Publishing, Jefferson, NC.

51. Schenawolf, Harry, Canada Lost: The American Retreat from Quebec January–June 1776, revolutionarywarjournal.com, September 20, 2018

52. Bond, Col. William, Letter to Lucy Bond, Crown Point, July 11, 1776, William Bond Papers. MSS 80. Special Collections & Archives, UC San Diego.

53. Niderost, Eric, Tarnished Hero's Victory, WarfareHistoryNetwork.com, 2005

54. Gruber, Kate Egner, The Daughters of Liberty, American Battlefield Trust, accessed January 28, 2025.

55. Keagle, Matthew, The Christmas Riot of 1776: Overlooked Moment of American Disunity, fortticonderoga.org, accessed Dec. 5, 2022.

56. Charles Henry, History of the Campaign For the Conquest of Canada, Philadelphia, Porter & Coates, 1882, p. 122

57. Frazer, Persifor, Some Extracts from the Papers of General Persifor Frazer, The Pennsylvania Magazine of History and Biography, Vol. 31, No. 2 1907, p. 134, https://www.jstor.org/stable/20085377

58. Mount Independence Research, Summary History of the Battle Involving Mount Independence, Agency of Commerce and Community Development,

State Historic Sites, historicsites.vermont.gov/mount-independence/research#, accessed April 10, 2025.

59. Starbuck, David R. and Murphy, William, Archaeology at Mount Independence: An Introduction, The Journal of Vermont Archaeology—Volume 1, 1994

60. Makos, Isaac, The Siege of Fort Ticonderoga, American Battlefield Trust, June 16, 2021

61. "To George Washington from Major General Benedict Arnold, 27 July 1777," Founders Online, National Archives, https://founders.archives.gov/documents/Washington/03-10-02-0427. [Original source: The Papers of George Washington, Revolutionary War Series, vol. 10, 11 June 1777–18 August 1777, ed. Frank E. Grizzard, Jr. Charlottesville: University Press of Virginia, 2000, pp. 433–435.]

62. Jane McCrae, National Park Service, https://www.nps.gov/sara/learn/historyculture/jane-mccrea.htm, accessed May 7, 2025.

63. McDonald, Robert M.S., Horatio Gates. "Generals Gates and Burgoyne on the Murder of Jane McCrea." Chronicle, September 06, 1777. From Teaching American History, https://teachingamericanhistory.org/document/generals-gates-and-burgoyne-on-the-murder-of-jane-mccrea/, accessed May 7, 2025.

64. Starbuck, David R., A Forensic Investigation of Jane McCrea's final resting place, The Mystery of the Second Body, Plymouth State Pulse, January 1, 2006

65. Trumbull, John, Oil on canvas, Architect of the Capitol, Surrender of General Burgoyne, https://www.aoc.gov/explore-capitol-campus/art/surrender-general-burgoyne, accessed May 12, 2025.

66. Hand, Tom, Arnold Leads Continentals to Relieve Fort Stanwix, American Corner, https://www.americanacorner.com/blog/fort-stanwix-saved?utm_campaign=shareaholic&utm_medium=email_this&utm_source=email, accessed May13, 2025.

67. Mellaci, Taylor, George Washington University, George Washington's Mount Vernon, https://www.mountvernon.org/library/digitalhistory/digital-encyclopedia/article/camp-followers, accessed May 15, 2025.

68. Schnitzer, Eric, Organization of the Army of the United States under the Command of Major General Horatio Gates at Bemis Heights, September 19 to October 7, 1777, Heritage Hunters, Saratoga County NYGenWeb Page, February 2009, updated July 2009.

69. Hopkins, Alfred F., Equipment of the Soldier During the American Revolution, National Park Service, Volume IV, No. 3, March, 1940, pp. 19–22

70. Jackson, Michael family, US Revolutionary War, US, Massachusetts, Soldiers and Sailors in the Revolutionary War, 1775–1801, Served For: United States of America, Volume 08, pp. 658, 661, 663, 680–681, 688

71. Maloy, Mark, The Battle of Freeman's Farm: September 19, 1777, American Battlefield Trust, accessed May 27, 2025.

72. Benjamin, Samuel, July 22, 1780, US, Revolutionary War Rolls, 1775–1783, M246, Nara catalog id: 602384, Revolutionary War Rolls, compiled 1894–1913, 1775–1783, NARA, Record group: 93, p. 5, Massachusetts, 8th Regiment, 1778–80, Folder: 11, US Revolutionary War, Roll: 0037

73. Demus, Joseph, US Revolutionary War, US, Massachusetts, Soldiers and Sailors in the

Revolutionary War, 1775–1801, https://www.fold3.com/sub-image/685565331/demus-joseph-us-massachusetts-soldiers-and-sailors-in-the-revolutionary-war-1775-1801, p. 670

74. Benjamin, Samuel, August/September 1780, US, Revolutionary War Rolls, 1775–1783, Publication number, M246, Nara catalog id: 602384, Revolutionary War Rolls, compiled 1894–1913, 1775–1783, Publisher NARA, Record group: 93, p. 144, State: Massachusetts, 8th Regiment, 1778–80, Folder: 11, US Revolutionary War, Roll Name: 0037

75. Maloy, Mark, The Battle of Bemis Heights, October 7, 1777, American Battlefield Trust,

76. National Park Service, The Decisive Moment, Breymann Redoubt (Continued...), Saratoga National Historical Park, https://www.nps.gov/places/the-decisive-moment-7-breymann-redoubt-continued.htm, accessed May 27, 2025.

77. Getchell, Abel, MA Berwick, Private, Capt. Silas Burbank's co., Col. Samuel Brewer's regt.; from 25 Feb 1777, killed 7 Oct 1777, https://saratoganygenweb.com/batlto.htm, and The National Park Service, https://www.nps.gov/people/abel-getchell.htm, accessed June 2, 2025.

78. US Revolutionary War, US, Massachusetts, Soldiers and Sailors in the Revolutionary War, 1775–1801, Company: Apt. Ebenezer Cleaveland's Co., Regiment: Colonel Sargent's Regiment, Reported killed Oct. 7, 1777, Served For: United States of America, Volume Number: Volume 17, pp. 38, 175, 360, 599, 949

79. https://saratoganygenweb.com/index.html, Saratoga NYGenWeb Project, Heritage Hunters of Saratoga County, NY, accessed May 30, 2025.

80. Craig, Joe, Park Ranger, Gone For a Soldier, https://friendsofthesaratogabattlefield.org/2023/10/07/gone-for-a-soldier/, accessed June 9, 2025.

81. Clay, Steven E., Staff Ride Handbook for the Saratoga Campaign, 13 June to 8 November 1777, p. 118, Combat Studies Institute Press, US Army Combined Arms Center, Fort Leavenworth, Kansas, https://www.armyupress.army.mil/portals/7/educational-services/staff-rides/staff-ride-handbook-saratoga-campaign.pdf, Army University Press, 2018

82. Armstrong, Lt. Samuel, 1777, Boyle, Joseph Lee (transcribed), Valley Forge National Historical Park, From Saratoga to Valley Forge: The Diary of Lt. Samuel Armstrong, Pennsylvania Magazine of History and Biography, vol.121, number 3, July 1997, https://journals.psu.edu/pmhb/article/view/45167

83. Armstrong, Samuel, 1777, Boyle, Joseph Lee (transcribed), Valley Forge National Historical Park, From Saratoga to Valley Forge: The Diary of Lt. Samuel Armstrong, Pennsylvania Magazine of History and Biography, vol.121, number 3, July 1997, p. 252

84. Brandywine, Brandywine Creek, American Battlefield Trust, Pennsylvania, Sep 11, 1777, https://www.battlefields.org/learn/revolutionary-war/battles/brandywine, accessed June 20, 2025.

85. Cole, Pamela McArthur, New England Weddings, The Journal of American Folklore, Vol. 6, No. 21, (Apr.–Jun., 1893), pp. 103–107, https://doi.org/10.2307/533295•https://www.jstor.org/stable/533295

86. WarMaps.com, Battles of the American Revolution, Battle of White Marsh, Dec. 5–8, 1777, Northern, https://war-maps.com/warmap/battles-of-the-

american-revolution/event/battle-of-white-marsh, accessed June 20, 2025.

87. George Washington, General Orders, 17 December 1777, in John C. Fitzpatrick, The Writings of George Washington (Washington: Government Printing Office, 1933), vol. 10, p. 168.

88. Armstrong, Lt. Samuel, 1777, Boyle, Joseph Lee (transcribed), Valley Forge National Historical Park, From Saratoga to Valley Forge: The Diary of Lt. Samuel Armstrong, Pennsylvania Magazine of History and Biography, vol.121, number 3, July 1997, p. 268, https://journals.psu.edu/pmhb/article/view/45167

89. “General Orders, 18 December 1777,” Founders Online, National Archives, https://founders.archives.gov/documents/Washington/03-12-02-0573. [Original source: The Papers of George Washington, Revolutionary War Series, vol. 12, 26 October 1777–25 December 1777, ed. Frank E. Grizzard, Jr. and David R. Hoth. Charlottesville: University Press of Virginia, 2002, pp. 626–628.]

90. “General Orders, 18 December 1777,” Founders Online, National Archives,

91. https://founders.archives.gov/documents/Washington/03-12-02-0573. [Original source: The Papers of George Washington, Revolutionary War Series, vol. 12, 26 October 1777–25 December 1777, ed. Frank E. Grizzard, Jr. and David R. Hoth. Charlottesville: University Press of Virginia, 2002, pp. 626–628.]

92. George Washington Papers, Series 3, Subseries 3G, Varick Transcripts, Letterbook 3, General Orders, Head Quarters, V. Forge, January 6, 1778, Library of Congress, http://www.loc.gov/resource/mgw3g.003

93. Buchanan, John, The Road to Valley Forge: How Washington Built the Army that Won the Revolution, Turner Publishing, 2004.

94. Chaie, Jane, & Homol, Lindley, The Forging of an Army, Pennsylvania Center for the Book, Spring 2009, Fall 2009, https://pabook.libraries.psu.edu/literary-cultural-heritage-map-pa/feature-articles/forging, accessed July 22, 2025

95. National Park Service, General von Steuben, https://www.nps.gov/vafo/learn/historyculture/vonsteuben.htm#:~:text=He%20inquired%20about%20serving%20in,paid%20by%20the%20French%20government, accessed July 23, 2025.

96. Armstrong, Lt. Samuel, 1777, Boyle, Joseph Lee (transcribed), Valley Forge National Historical Park, From Saratoga to Valley Forge: The Diary of Lt. Samuel Armstrong, Pennsylvania Magazine of History and Biography, vol.121, number 3, July 1997, p. 268

97. Ecelbarger, Gary, Critical Thinking, Permanent Losses and New Gains During the 1778 Valley Forge Encampment, Journal of the American Revolution, https://allthingsliberty.com/2024/02/permanent-losses-and-new-gains-during-the-1778-valley-forgeencampment/#:~:text=The%20hard%20data%20organized%20in,departed%20it%20late%20in%20, accessed May 15, 2024.

98. Camus, Raoul F., Military Music of the American Revolution, The University of North Carolina Press, Chapel Hill, 1976, p. 88

99. US, Massachusetts, Soldiers and Sailors in the Revolutionary War, 1775–1801, Vol. 2, p. 628

100. Lender, Mark; Stone, Gary, Fatal Sunday: George Washington, the Monmouth Campaign, and the Politics of Battle, 2017

101. Martin, Joseph Plumb, Narrative of some of the Adventures, Dangers, and Sufferings of a Revolutionary Soldier, 1830, Internet Archive, https://ia903208.us.archive.org/14/items/MartinTheAdventuresOfARevolutionarySoldier/Martin%20%20The%20Adventures%20of%20a%20Revolutionary%20Soldier%20%2B.pdf

102. Schenawolf, Harry, Firing Field Cannon in the American Revolution, September 3, 2014, https://revolutionarywarjournal.com/firing-field-cannon/

103. Wickersty, Jason R., In the Heat of the Moment at Monmouth, Hallowed Ground Magazine, American Battlefield Trust, https://www.battlefields.org/learn/articles/heat-moment-monmouth, updated February 16, 2023, June 5, 2019.

104. Revolutionarywar.us, The Battle of Monmouth Court House, the U.S. Army Center of Military History, https://revolutionarywar.us/year-1778/battle-monmouth-court-house/, accessed June 5, 2025

105. George Washington to William Livingston, 4 July 1778, Founders Online, National Archives, https://founders.archives.gov/documents/Washington/03-16-02-0024. [Original source: The Papers of George Washington, Revolutionary War Series, vol. 16, 1 July–14 September 1778, ed. David R. Hoth. Charlottesville: University of Virginia Press, 2006, p. 23]

106. Adelberg, Michael, Burying the Dead and Recovering the Wounded After the Battle of Monmouth, Monmouth County Historical Society, Monmouthhistory.org, accessed Aug. 14, 2025.

107. Tufts, Francis, Orderly book of the 8th Massachusetts Regiment, 1778, June 15–Aug. 4, Valley Forge to Monmouth to White Plains. July 2, 1778, p.

34, Huntington Digital Library, https://hdl.huntington.org/digital/collection/p15150coll7/id/43514

108. Harrington, Hugh T., Journal of the American Revolution, September 25, 2014, and Diamont, Lincoln, Chaining the Hudson, the Fight for the River in the American Revolution (New York: Carol Publishing Group, 1994), https://allthingsliberty.com/2014/09/the-great-west-point-chain, accessed June 11, 2025

109. Donck, Adriaen Van Der, and Jeremiah Johnson. Description of the New Netherlands. New York, 1841. Pdf. https://www.loc.gov/item/01015857/.

110. Tufts, Francis, Orderly book of the 8th Massachusetts Regiment, March 9, 1779, 1778, Aug. 5–1779, Apr. 21, West Point, p. 213, Washington, George, "George Washington to Major General John Sullivan, 31 May 1779," Founders Online, National Archives, https://founders.archives.gov/documents/Washington/03-20-02-0661. [Original source: The Papers of George Washington, Revolutionary War Series, vol. 20, 8 April–31 May 1779, ed. Edward G. Lengel. Charlottesville: University of Virginia Press, 2010, pp. 716–719.]

111. "General Orders, 12 June 1779," Founders Online, National Archives, https://founders.archives.gov/documents/Washington/03-21-02-0124. [Original source: The Papers of George Washington, Revolutionary War Series, vol. 21, 1 June–31 July 1779, ed. William M. Ferraro. Charlottesville: University of Virginia Press, 2012, pp. 138–141.]

112. John, Reese U., Brother Jonathan's Images, No. 13, Captain Judah Alden, 2nd Massachusetts Regiment (John Hannigan)

113. https://www.academia.edu/49128992/Brother_Jonathan_s_Images_No_13_Captain_Judah_Alden_2nd_Massachusetts_Regiment_John_Hannigan_, See the entry for July 25, 1779 in Citizen-Soldier in the American Revolution: The Diary of Benjamin Gilbert in Massachusetts and New York (New York State Historical Association, 1980); account of provisions supplied to eight Massachusetts Light Infantry companies, January 3–8, 1780, Box 1, Folder 3, Item 2 of the Rufus Putnam Papers, Marietta College; and the muster rolls of the light company, 2nd Massachusetts Regiment for January–June 1780 and July 1780, both in Revolutionary War Rolls, National Archives Publication M246, Reel 35, Folder 3-3.

114. Sheehan, Michael J.F., Battle of Stony Point, Washington Library Center for Digital History Encyclopedia, George Washington's Mount Vernon, https://www.mountvernon.org/library/digitalhistory/digital-encyclopedia/article/battle-of-stony-point, accessed Oct. 7, 2025.

115. Anderson, Eric, Our Officers and Men Behaved Like Men Determined To Be Free: The Battle of Stony Point, 15–16 July 1779, The Army Historical Society Foundation, https://armyhistory.org/our-officers-and-men-behaved-like-men-determined-to-be-free-the-battle-of-stony-point-15-16-july-1779/, accessed June 18, 2025

116. Post, Todd, July 16, 1779: Battle of Stony Point, The 2nd Virginia Regiment, https://secondvirginia.wordpress.com/2010/07/17/stony-point/#:~:text=Soldiers%20in%20these%20two%20attacking,the%20remainder%20were%20taken%20prisoners.

117. Kohmetscher, Max (USMA '23) & Bratten, Jonathan, (CPT, CHM) The Battle of Stony Point: A

Digital Staff Ride, "The Fort's our own!": The Daring Midnight Assault of the Corps of Light Infantry on July 16th, 1779, https://storymaps.arcgis.com/stories/0d69bf5dd4eb45939aa5c6cf4a000ed4, accessed June 9, 2022.

118. Anderson, Eric, Our Officers and Men Behaved Like Men Determined To Be Free: The Battle of Stony Point, 15–16 July 1779, The Army Historical Society Foundation, https://armyhistory.org/our-officers-and-men-behaved-like-men-determined-to-be-free-the-battle-of-stony-point-15-16-july-1779/

119. Washington, George, 21 July 1779, George Washington to John Jay, Founders Online, https://founders.archives.gov/documents/Washington/03-21-02-0492, accessed June 18, 2025

120. Troy, Michael, American Revolution Podcast, ARP231 Paulus Hook, December 26, 2021, https://blog.amrevpodcast.com/2021/12/arp231-paulus-hook.html

121. Ormande, Grace, The History of the Engagement Rings, Wedding Style, 2024, https://www.weddingstylemagazine.com/engagement/engagement-rings/history-of-engagement-rings#:~:text=The%20minimal%20interest%20in%20diamond,diamond%20rings'%20glamor%20and%20lure, accessed June 19, 2025

122. Auburn and the American Revolutionary War, The Thomas Drury Family, The Yankee Express, Auburn Historical Society & Museum, https://www.theyankeexpress.com/2025/05/27/533394/auburn-and-the-american-revolutionary-war-the-thomas-drury-family,

123. Steuben's Regulations Book, National Park Service, Valley Forge National Historical Park,

Pennsylvania, history, https://www.nps.gov/vafo/learn/historyculture/steuben_regulations_book.htm#:~:text=Once%20the%20troops%20were%20thoroughly,until%20the%20War%20of%201812.

124. The American Revolution Institute of the Society of the Cincinnati, Steuben's "Blue Book," Sequence and Procedure, https://www.americanrevolutioninstitute.org/steubens-blue-book manual/#:~:text=The%20final%20draft%20of%20the,hence%20the%20Blue%20Book%20nickname.

125. Whittlesey, Derwent Stainthorpe, The Springfield Armory: A Study in Institutional Development, A Dissertation Submitted to the Faculty of the Graduate Schools of Arts and Literature in Candidacy for the Degree of Doctor of Philosophy, The University of Chicago Department of History, 1920 Transcribed and edited 2006 by John McCabe, Objects Curator and Richard Colton, Historian Springfield Armory NHS One Armory Sq., Suite 2 Springfield, MA 01105-1299

126. Caitlyn Dantzman and Jennifer Dorsey. "The Van Wyck Homestead: Headquarters For Washington's Fishkill Supply Depot." Clio: Your Guide to History. December 16, 2024, https://theclio.com/entry/187929, accessed November 14, 2025.

127. Schenkman, A.J., General Washington and His Walnuts, Hudson Valley Table, July 11, 2016

128. Ryan, Evelyne H., The Burning of Bedford Village, History re-examined, the Record Review, Beford Historical Society, July 9, 2004

129. Pfister, Jude (2009), The Jacob Ford Jr. Mansion, Charleston, South Carolina: The History Press, p. 58

130. Adams, Samuel Dr., Diary of Doctor Samuel Adams, Unpublished Papers of Dr. Samuel Adams on microfilm in the Manuscript Room at the NY Public Library, ZL-307, 3 Reels.

131. Maloy, Mark, "The Hard Winter" of 1779–1780, (2016), https://emergingrevolutionarywar.org/2016/01/23/the-hard-winter-of-1779-1780/

132. "George Washington to Major General Robert Howe, 30 March 1780," Founders Online, National Archives, https://founders.archives.gov/documents/Washington/03-25-02-0156. [Original source: The Papers of George Washington, Revolutionary War Series, vol. 25, 10 March–12 May 1780, ed. William M. Ferraro. Charlottesville: University of Virginia Press, 2017, pp. 231–233.]

133. Charleston, Siege of Charleston, South Carolina, American Battlefield Trust, Feb. 11–May 12, 1780

134. Frazza, Al, Revolutionary War New Jersey, The Ultimate Field Guide New Jersey's Revolutionary War History, https://www.revolutionarywarnewjersey.com/new_jersey_revolutionary_war_sites/towns/teaneck_nj_revolutionary_war_sites.htm

135. The Death of John André, John André Letter to Henry Clinton, September 29, 1780. Henry Clinton Papers, William L. Clements Library, University of Michigan, https://clements.umich.edu/exhibit/spy-letters-of-the-american-revolution/stories-of-spies/death-of-john-andre/

136. Thacher, James D., A Military Journal during the American Revolutionary War, from 1775 to

1783 (Boston: Richardson and Lord, 1823), pp. 223–226

137. Yordy, Charles S. III, The Pennsylvania Line Mutiny, its Origins and Patriotism, Penn State University Libraries, https://libraries.psu.edu/about/collections/unearthing-past-student-research-pennsylvania-history/pennsylvania-line-mutiny-0

138. The mutiny of the New Jersey troops, Orderly book of the 8th Massachusetts Regiment, 1781, Jan. 1–Mar. 12, West Point, pp. 52–58, https://hdl.huntington.org/digital/collection/p15150coll7/id/44456/rec/14

139. Schellhammer, Michael, Mutiny of the New Jersey Line, Journal of The American Revolution, https://allthingsliberty.com/2014/03/mutiny-of-the-new-jersey line/#:~:text=On%20the%20evening%20of%20January,to%20the%20Army%20itself.%E2%80%9D%5B

140. Schenawolf, Henry, Battle of Cape Henry, Revolutionary War Journal, https://revolutionarywarjournal.com/battle-of-cape-henry/

141. Schenawolf, Harry, First Cowboys Were Not from the West But Cattle Rustlers of the American Revolution, Revolutionary War Journal, July 1, 2019, https://revolutionarywarjournal.com/first-cowboys-were-not-of-western-lore-but-from-new-york-loyalist-partisan-groups-terrorized-farmers-during-the-american-revolution/#:~:text=On%20May%2014%2C%201781%2C%20he,Greene's%20body%20to%20be%20mutilated

142. "George Washington to Colonel Alexander Scammell, 17 May 1781," Founders Online, National Archives, https://founders.archives.gov/documents/Washington/03-32-02-0129. [Original source: The Papers of George Washington,

Revolutionary War Series, vol. 32, 6 May–4 July 1781, ed. William M. Ferraro. Charlottesville: University of Virginia Press, 2023, p. 180.]

143. Stoltz, Joseph F. III, Le Plus Détaillée: The July Reconnaissance of New York, the Journal of the American Revolution, https://allthingsliberty.com/2017/06/le-plusdetaillee-july-1781-reconnaissance-newyork/

144. Reynolds, William W., A Yorktown Footnote: the Last Days of Col. Alexander Scammell, Journal of the American Revolution, Letter of October 4, 1781 published in Freeman's Journal (Philadelphia) October 24, 1781 Issue XXVII, 2–3, found on the website GenealogyBank.com. This letter was "written by a gentleman in Williamsburg" who also stated "I have seen his wound, and think he may recover." https://allthingsliberty.com/2015/05/a-yorktown-footnote-the-last-days-of-col-alexander-scammell/#_edn5

145. "October 1781," Founders Online, National Archives, https://founders.archives.gov/documents/Washington/01-03-02-0007-0006. [Original source: The Diaries of George Washington, vol. 3, 1 January 1771–5 November 1781, ed. Donald Jackson. Charlottesville: University Press of Virginia, 1978, pp. 424–436.] 781

146. Yorktown Battlefield, Lieutenant Colonel John Laurens, National Park Service, https://www.nps.gov/york/learn/historyculture/laurens-bio.htm#:~:text=Perhaps%20if%20the%20British%20commissioners,time%20arguing%20with%20the%20son

147. Yorktown Battlefield, The Moore House and Articles of Capitulation, National Park Service, https://www.nps.gov/york/learn/historyculture/mooore-houseandarticle.htm

www.ingramcontent.com/pod-product-compliance
Lightning Source LLC
Chambersburg PA
CBHW050032110726
47973CB00033B/293/J
* 9 7 9 8 9 9 5 2 0 6 0 2 6 *